entury

SERIES

riswold, and Larry Griffin

the best current scholarship to today's
authored by leaders of a new generation
addresses its subject from a comparative,
ve, and, in doing so, connects social science
ents seeking to make sense of our dramatically

Ethnicity and Race

Making Identities in a Changing World

Stephen Cornell
University of California, San Diego

Douglas Hartmann
University of Minnesota

PINE FORGE PRESS
Thousand Oaks • London • New Delhi

For information, address:

Pine Forge Press
A Sage Publications Company
2455 Teller Road
Thousand Oaks, California 91320
(805) 499-4224
Internet: sdr@pfp.sagepub.com

Sage Publications Ltd.
6 Bonhill Street
London EC2A 4PU
United Kingdom

Sage Publications India Pvt. Ltd.
M-32 Market
Greater Kailash I
New Delhi 110 048 India

Production Editor: Sanford Robinson
Designer: Lisa S. Mirski
Typesetter: Rebecca Evans
Cover: Lisa S. Mirski
Print Buyer: Anna Chin

Printed in the United States of America

99 00 01 02 10 9 8 7 6 5 4 3 2

Library of Congress Cataloging-in-Publication Data

Cornell, Stephen E. (Stephen Ellicott), 1948-
    Ethnicity and race : making identities in a changing world / by
Stephen Cornell and Douglas Hartmann.
        p.   cm. — (Sociology for a new century)
    Includes bibliographical references and index.
    ISBN 0-7619-8501-8 (pbk. : acid-free paper)
    1. Race. 2. Ethnicity. 3. Minorities. 4. Group identity.
I. Hartmann, Douglas. II. Title. III. Series.
HT1521.C64   1997
305.8—dc21   97-4892

 This book is printed on acid-free paper that meets
Environmental Protection Agency standards for recycled paper.

For Maura,
Teresa,
and Ben—who laughed

Contents

ABOUT THE AUTHORS

Stephen Cornell teaches sociology at the University of California, San Diego. His Ph.D. is from the University of Chicago. He is the author of *The Return of the Native: American Indian Political Resurgence*, coeditor of *What Can Tribes Do? Strategies and Institutions in American Indian Economic Development*, and author of numerous academic articles on collective identity, intergroup relations, and related topics. He also co-directs the Harvard Project on American Indian Economic Development, an ongoing research project on poverty, development, and political culture on American Indian reservations.

Douglas Hartmann is Assistant Professor of Sociology at the University of Minnesota. He received his B.A. and M.A. degrees from the University of Chicago and his Ph.D. from the University of California, San Diego. Most of his work is on the intersections of politics and culture, including popular culture. He is completing a book titled *Golden Ghettoes: The Cultural Politics of Race, Sport, and Civil Rights in the United States Since 1968.*

ABOUT THE PUBLISHER

Pine Forge Press is a new educational publisher, dedicated to publishing innovative books and software throughout the social sciences. On this and any other of our publications, we welcome your comments, ideas, and suggestions. Please call or write to us at:

Pine Forge Press
A Sage Publications Company
2455 Teller Road
Thousand Oaks, California 91320
(805) 499-4224
E-mail: sales@pfp.sagepub.com

Visit our new World Wide Web site, your direct link to a multitude of online resources:

http://www.sagepub.com/pineforge

Foreword

Sociology for a New Century offers the best of current sociological thinking to today's students. The goal of the series is to prepare students, and—in the long run—the informed public, for a world that has changed dramatically in the last three decades and one that continues to astonish.

This goal reflects important changes that have taken place in sociology. The discipline has become broader in orientation, with an ever growing interest in research that is comparative, historical, or transnational in orientation. Sociologists are less focused on "American" society as the pinnacle of human achievement and more sensitive to global processes and trends. They also have become less insulated from surrounding social forces. In the 1970s and 1980s sociologists were so obsessed with constructing a science of society that they saw impenetrability as a sign of success. Today, there is a greater effort to connect sociology to the ongoing concerns and experiences of the informed public.

Each book in this series offers a comparative, historical, transnational, or global perspective in some way, to help broaden students' vision. Students need to be sensitized to diversity in today's world and to the sources of diversity. Knowledge of diversity challenges the limitations of conventional ways of thinking about social life. At the same time, students need to be sensitized to the fact that issues that may seem specifically "American" (for example, the women's movement, an aging population bringing a strained social security and health care system, racial conflict, national chauvinism, and so on) are shared by many other countries. Awareness of commonalities undercuts the tendency to view social issues and questions in narrowly American terms and encourages students to seek out the experiences of others for the lessons they offer. Finally, students also need to be sensitized to phenomena that transcend national boundaries, economics, and politics.

One such phenomenon that is both common, in that it occurs everywhere, and global, in that it crosses and often denies national boundaries, is the construction of identity. While there are many such constructions—

gender, religion, class—this book deals with two of the most significant and vexing in the contemporary world: ethnicity and race. Cornell and Hartmann clearly demonstrate that ethnicity and race are social constructions. Political opportunities, economic constraints, cultural assumptions all draw and redraw ethnic and racial boundaries and infuse them with meaning. Globalization, moreover, picks up the pace of such reformations of personhood and peoplehood.

At the same time, the fact that ethnicity and race are social constructions does not render them insignificant or epiphenomenal. Far from it. Ethnic and racial catagorizations are powerful in their consequences for objective hierarchies of advantage and for subjective feelings of membership or exclusion. Cornell and Hartmann have written an evenhanded and provocative exploration that shows how these characterizations can both be imagined and at the same time be absolutely fundamental to social life and to one's deepest sense of the self. Readers of their book will see everything from ethnic conflict in Eastern European cities to multiculturalism in American schools with a fresh understanding and a sociological eye.

Preface

Weeks after this book was substantially out of our hands, making its way from editor to editor and then to press, we found ourselves still combing the newspapers, the magazines, and the Internet, to say nothing of the social scientific literature, for news from the ethnic and racial frontiers of the world. This impulse to keep gathering material reflects in part a continuing search for ammunition for argument, for new mysteries or old puzzles, for information or ideas that might help in the quest for understanding, a quest that seldom ends with the completion of such a project. But part of it is simply habit. When you begin to pay focused attention to a topic, trying to think it through, your radar tends to expand in both sensitivity and reach. You become a compulsive reader, and it takes a while to wind back down again, to return the system to the less focused and more casual sweeping of the horizon that constitutes the everyday observational life of most members of society.

Among the gleanings from the first few months of 1997: reports of ethnic insurgency in western China; a piece on the likelihood that Whites will become a minority in California; an item on army efforts to subdue ethnic rebellion in urban areas of Indonesia; a report on the outrage expressed by Russian Americans over ethnic slurs in the wake of the arrest of a Russian immigrant for the murder of entertainer Bill Cosby's son; an item on the successful effort of an English-descent Australian to pass off her own art as the work of an Aborigine, one of Australia's indigenous people, angrily described as "culture theft"; news of recurrent ethnic violence in northeastern India; a passionate, at times furious discussion of the pros and cons of interracial adoption; a piece on the disputed ethnicity of Russia's Cossacks and their efforts to gain recognition as a distinct people; numerous reports on the near-fatal beating of a Black boy by three White teenagers in Chicago; and so on.

It is sobering to undertake a book about topics that arouse as much passion as is evident in these stories and others like them. Ethnicity and race touch deep feelings in many people around the globe and occupy much of the world's attention. One of our purposes is to understand why, but we would be the first to admit that in the process of writing this book, we have sometimes found ourselves with questions for which we have no answers.

Be that as it may, we want to point out four features of what we offer here. First, the book is *global* in scope. As the gleanings from our media radar suggest, ethnic and racial frontiers—by which we mean the places where ethnicity and race are making waves and, in turn, are themselves being made and remade —today can be found virtually everywhere. This book consciously acknowledges that fact. One of the goals of the **Sociology for a New Century** series is to present sociological thinking that is focused less exclusively on the United States and is more attentive to the diversities and continuities in social life around the world. In the field of ethnicity and race, we believe such a perspective is particularly important. Despite the global distribution of ethnic and racial phenomena, much theorizing about ethnicity and race has been based on the U.S. experience. This is understandable. One reviewer of some of our work even argued that ethnicity is a useless concept outside the United States and that the only ethnic groups in the United States are those of European descent. Our disagreement with this view should be amply apparent throughout this book—see Chapter 2 in particular—but it remains the case that the concept of ethnicity was taken up by social science in an attempt to understand American situations and gained much of its currency in an American context. Furthermore, the legacy of conquest, slavery, and large-scale immigration has required Americans of all backgrounds to confront race, racism, and intergroup relations in forms and with an urgency that many western nations, whose racial "others" for a long time were largely in colonies thousands of miles away, have only recently experienced.

But the making of ethnic and racial identities is a process apparent around the globe. This invites social science to adopt a broad perspective on these topics and to do the kind of comparative work that will help us to distinguish among localized patterns and the factors that produce them. This book is not systematically comparative, but it does attempt that broad perspective. Although the experience of the United States looms large here—each of us has done research largely on American topics—our intention has been to bring in as much of the rest of the world as possible, and thereby, through cases and illustration, to enrich our understanding of ethnicity and race everywhere. Indeed, we believe that the study of U.S. cases can be advanced partly by looking elsewhere, avoiding the parochialism that often limits the American vision of these phenomena.

Our approach is global in another way as well. It pays particular attention to the fact that the dynamics of ethnicity and race are inextricably linked with macro-historical forces that are global in their reach. These forces—rationalization, industrialization, urbanization, and other developments; in short, the project of modernity—have shaped the context in which contemporary ethnic and racial identities are made and remade, and have provided much of the social and cultural foundations on which those identities are formed.

Second, we have a particular understanding of *the relationship between ethnicity and race*. Some scholars have seen these as referring to very different phenomena. Some have seen race as a subset of ethnicity. Some have seen them as virtually the same. Our own approach, detailed in Chapter 2, sees ethnicity and race as referring to distinct but often overlapping bases of identification. They also potentially involve two different processes of identity construction. Either one may be rooted in assignment by others, but when groups assert their own identities, filling them with their own content, they are acting in classically ethnic ways. Thus, a race may be, but is not necessarily, at the same time an ethnic group, and an ethnic group may be, but is not necessarily, at the same time a race.

This approach departs from some that distinguish between ethnicity and race in terms of power. Such approaches generally argue that race typically is a product of differential power relations and that most ethnic identities are more likely to be matters of choice and convenience. One of the drawbacks of focusing on the American experience is that it can be seen to support this distinction, which fails to hold up in much of the rest of the world. The contrast between ethnicity and race, which sometimes seems unambiguous in the American context, begins to break down or become inverted elsewhere. In Rwanda, for example—a case we discuss in more detail in Chapter 3—it is ethnic rather than racial ties that are directly linked with privilege and power and have become lethally consequential in people's lives. The qualities and consequences associated with race in one context may be associated with ethnicity in another.

Third, our focus is on ethnic and racial *identities*. Although we discuss the dynamics of intergroup relations and ethnic and racial stratification in various parts of the book, our primary concern is with processes of group formation and identity construction: the ways that people come to conceptualize themselves and others—and to act—in ethnic and racial terms. By adopting this focus, we do not mean to minimize or dismiss the important role that these phenomena play in organizing intergroup social life. The concrete consequences of ethnicity and race, the purposes they serve, and their implications in systems of power are crucial elements in much of our discussion. What is more, our own explanation of why these phenomena are powerful features of the contemporary global landscape is predicated directly on our understanding of the crucial functions that they serve. But our emphasis is not so much on what ethnicity and race do in societies as on how ethnic and racial identities come into being in the first place, and on the social processes by which they are reproduced and transformed. Our purpose is to bring out the bases on which ethnic and racial groups form and act as groups.

This directs our attention to the collective forms of these identities. Although the acquisition of an ethnic or racial identity by individuals is a critical part of collective identity, we pay little attention here to the social psychology of individual identity formation. Our concern is with the processes by which ethnic and racial designations come to be asserted by or assigned to particular groups: the construction of "we" and "they."

Of course, individual and collective aspects of identity and identity construction are often closely linked and mutually supporting. Much of what we have to say in this book about collective identity may resonate with many readers' individual experiences; certainly we hope so. However, in some circumstances the two levels may not fit together at all or may even be in conflict. For example, in a rapidly changing, multiethnic, multiracial society such as the United States, many individuals are not automatically channeled into one ethnic or racial identity. Some may be assigned to different identities at different times; others may have choices to make or options to exercise. But again, although these processes of individual assertion or assignment are interesting and important, our focus is on the making of the larger identities that are asserted or assigned.

Finally, our approach is *constructionist*. It treats ethnicity and race—both as general categories and as specific identities—not as natural phenomena but as human creations, as produced by groups of human beings trying to solve problems, defend or enhance their positions, justify their actions, establish meanings, achieve understanding, or otherwise negotiate their way through the world in which they live. This constructionist view of ethnicity and race is one of the chief advances in the social scientific understanding of these phenomena in recent years, and we consciously adopt and build on it. But we also depart from it in certain ways. Many constructionist accounts end up being reductionist, seeing ethnicity and race as by-products of more fundamental economic, political, or social forces. As those forces change, so do their ethnic and racial products. Ethnicity and race thus become epiphenomenal, with little independent influence on social life. We see this view as incomplete. Ethnic and racial identities, once established, have impacts of their own; furthermore, for many people they carry an emotional charge that cannot be accounted for by appeals to interests alone. Our effort in what follows is to show how ethnicity and race are not only products but also producers of social relations and collective action.

Acknowledgments

This book has been a genuinely joint effort. The original conception was Cornell's, but that conception changed significantly once Hartmann came on board, well before the writing began. Together we extensively rethought both the argument and how to present it. In the process, the scope of the project grew substantially. We then divided up first-draft duties, largely by chapter. In every case, each of us revised the other's work in a back-and-forth process that continued right down to the wire. Cornell took responsibility for giving the final version a single voice.

We have been the beneficiaries of generous and intelligent assistance at several stages. Pine Forge Press sent an incomplete first draft of the manuscript to several anonymous reviewers. Their early feedback showed us some major gaps and sent us back to the drawing board on several chapters and some central ideas. Joane Nagel read most of the manuscript twice. Her often critical comments were not only helpful, detailed, and right, but were leavened with enthusiasm and encouragement, and we are deeply grateful to her. We should all have such friends. There are others we need to thank as well. Ana Devic, Ivan Evans, Rod Ferguson, and Jeanne Powers each cast a critical eye over portions of the manuscript, with beneficial results. Students in Cornell's graduate seminar on Ethnicity in the spring of 1996 provided a valuable testing site for some of our ideas and improved a number of them. Michael Gonzalez gave us some early research assistance. Teresa Swartz tracked down a lot of facts and references and put up with a lot of tense times, while Patricia Stewart did far more than duty required and was there just when we needed her. Maura Grogan repeatedly cracked the whip, which helped. Rebecca Smith raised important questions, rearranged some things, streamlined some of the prose, and made all of it better. We are grateful to Wendy Griswold, Charles Ragin, and Larry Griffin for proposing the book and then being more patient than we had any right to expect, and to Wendy for her substantive comments and her encouragement. Finally, Steve Rutter of Pine Forge Press has done it all, from making crucial suggestions on content, to keeping the door open up to the last possible moment, to being encouraging when the chips were down. We should all have such editors.

Despite all this help, we know gaps remain—and surely errors, too. We accept responsibility for them. If only there were world enough, and time. . . .

1

The Puzzle of Ethnicity and Race

Despite predictions to the contrary, the 20th century has turned out to be an ethnic century. The conflicts and claims organized at least partly in ethnic or racial terms are legion, but consider a few examples:

- During World War II, Germany's Nazi regime undertook the systematic extermination of Europe's Jewish population, along with Gypsies and other "undesirables." Six million people died as a direct result of this "holocaust," which gave to the world indelible images of brutality and evil and became one of the defining events of the modern era.

- In 1960, the African state of Nigeria won its independence from Great Britain, but conflicts over the distribution of power among ethnic groups and regions erupted soon afterward. In 1967, in the most dramatic and costly of these, the Igbo people of the southeastern part of the country declared their area the independent Republic of Biafra, precipitating nearly 3 years of open warfare with the Nigerian government. Biafra eventually lost the war, but not before hundreds of thousands of Igbos and other Nigerians had been killed.

- In the United States in the 1960s and 1970s, ethnic political mobilization seemed to be happening everywhere as an array of ethnic and racial groups not only loudly proclaimed their distinctive identities but also struggled for recognition, rights, and resources. Ethnic and racial boundaries surfaced both as primary sources of identity and as major fault lines within U.S. society, from the civil rights sit-ins and riots in Black ghettoes to the legal efforts of the Mexican-American Legal Defense Fund to the confrontations led by the American Indian Movement to the angry protests of an assortment of European-ancestry groups. At century's end, those fault lines remain, and many racial and ethnic identities seem as important in American life as they ever did.

- In 1971, the government of Malaysia amended that country's constitution, adopted at independence from Great Britain in 1957, to secure the preferential treatment of Malays in education, business, and government, against the objections of the sizable Chinese and other ethnic populations. Among other things, the changes made it an act of sedition to even question such entitlements.

- In the late 1970s, on the Gulf coast of Texas, competition over scarce fishing resources led to violence between Euro-Americans and immigrant Vietnamese. A White fisherman was killed, Vietnamese fishing boats were burned, and eventually the Ku Klux Klan joined the fray. Many Vietnamese immigrants finally fled the region.

- In the 1980s and 1990s, minority Tamils launched a violent insurgency against the majority Sinhalese in Sri Lanka, an island nation off the southeastern coast of India, crippling its economy and killing thousands. As we approach the 21st century, Sri Lanka's seemingly insoluble "ethnic fratricide" (Tambiah 1986) continues.

- The 1991 disintegration of the Soviet Union—one of the world's most ethnically diverse states—pried open the lid of what was supposedly a socialist melting pot, to reveal a boiling stew of ethnic sentiments and political movements. Ethnic conflicts followed in several regions of the former Soviet Union. Among them are the following: Ukrainian and Russian minorities in Moldova battled against majority Romanians, Abkhazians and southern Ossetians struggled for their own independence in newly independent Georgia, Armenians and Azerbaijanis fought over territorial rights and occupancy, and Chechens envisioned independence from Russia and entered a devastating war in their efforts to achieve it.

- The decade of the 1990s has seen a flurry of attacks by German skinheads and other right-wing groups directed against Turks, Greeks, Spaniards, North Africans of various ethnicities, and other immigrant groups who came to Germany over the preceding three decades in search of jobs. Arsonists torched immigrant-occupied apartment houses; men, women, and children have been beaten on the street; and dozens of foreigners have been killed.

- In the fall of 1993, in a special issue devoted to multiculturalism in America, *Time* magazine published a story titled "The Politics of

Separation." The subject was the impact of growing ethnic diversity on U.S. campuses. The magazine reported a perception among some students that "to study anyone's culture but one's own . . . is to commit an act of identity suicide" (W. Henry 1993:75).

- In October of 1995, French Canadians in the province of Quebec came within a few votes of deciding that the province should separate from the rest of Canada, in all likelihood eventually becoming an independent country. "We were defeated by money and the ethnic vote," said the province's premier, a leading separatist, referring to the non-French-speaking voters of various ethnicities who narrowly defeated the separatist effort (Farnsworth 1995:1). Before the vote, the Crees, an indigenous people living within the province, took out a full-page advertisement in newspapers across the country announcing their own overwhelming vote against Quebec's separation. The Crees promised that if Quebec were to separate, they and the vast lands under their control in turn would separate from Quebec, remaining part of Canada.

- In the early and mid-1990s, the term *ethnic cleansing* emerged from the chaos of warfare that followed the breakup of the former Yugoslav federation in southern Europe and engulfed the nascent country of Bosnia. The term, coined by Serbian nationalists, referred to the forced removal of non-Serbs from territory claimed or sought by Serbs. It was accompanied in the Bosnian case by wholesale human slaughter, starvation, and rampages of sexual violence directed against Bosnian Muslims by Serbian and Croatian soldiers and civilians. As one commentator pointed out, "ethnic cleansing" had now joined "the euphemistic lexicon of zealotry," along with Nazi descriptions of the Jewish Holocaust as "the final solution" (Williams 1993:H-3).

These examples admittedly focus on conflict and division, which are not the whole of the ethnic story. Ethnic and racial diversity and identity have been sources of pride, unity, and achievement. When the U.S. women's gymnastics team won a gold medal at the 1996 Olympic Games in Atlanta, the ethnic composition of the team—"an Asian American, an African American, and white girls with names like Miller and Moceanu" (Lexington 1996)—was itself viewed as an American accomplishment, something the entire nation should look upon with pride. Ethnic bonds brought Germans together in a reunified country in 1990, after decades of division into East and West. Mexico proudly proclaims its multiracial heritage, which mixes Indian and Spanish blood and cultures. Ethnic festivals, foods, and customs continue to enrich the life of numerous U.S. and Canadian cities and the lives of group members themselves. The Kwanzaa festival, for example, has become an annual African American celebration, a time for family, reflection, and rededication. In Nigeria, long troubled by ethnic tensions and conflict, novelist Wole Soyinka (1996) argues that Nigeria's viability as a state depends on learning to reconcile and even celebrate its ethnic diversity. On U.S. college campuses, in corporations, and in major cities, leaders dealing with ethnic and racial issues argue that diversity should be a strength, not a weakness.

Whether ethnicity is a division or a bond, the point is the same: As these and a hundred other examples from around the world illustrate, at century's end ethnic and racial identities have emerged as among the most potent forces in contemporary societies. They have become sources of pride, vehicles of political assertion, foundations of unity, and reservoirs of destructive power. (The map of the world in Figure 1.1 shows the locations of all the countries mentioned in the examples used in this book.)

An Unexpected Persistence and Power

It was not supposed to be this way. Ethnicity was expected to disappear as a force to be reckoned with in the 20th century. The latter half of the century, by numerous accounts, was supposed to see the end—or certainly a dramatic attenuation—of ethnic and racial ties. As the century wore on, these and other seemingly parochial and even premodern attachments were expected to decline as bases of human consciousness and action, being replaced by other, more comprehensive identities linked to the vast changes shaping the modern world.

Certainly a good many sociologists expected as much. As early as 1926, Robert Park, a professor at the University of Chicago and perhaps the most influential American sociologist of his day, observed that certain forces at work in the world were bound to dismantle the prejudices and boundaries that separated races and peoples. Powerful global factors, argued Park—trade, migration, new communication technologies, even the cinema—were bringing about a vast "interpenetration of peoples." These factors, he claimed, "enforce new contacts and result in new forms of competition and of conflict. But out of this confusion and ferment, new and more intimate forms of association arise." Indeed, wrote Park, "In the relations of races there is a cycle of events which tends everywhere to

FIGURE 1.1

Approximate Locations of Countries or Regions Mentioned in the Book

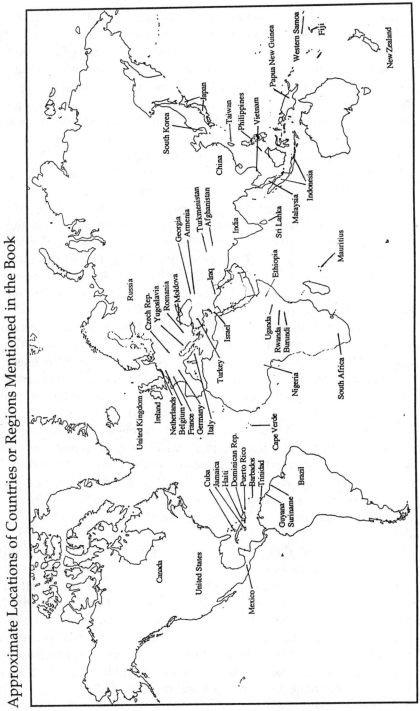

repeat itself. . . . The race relations cycle which takes the form, to state it abstractly, of contacts, competition, accommodation and eventual assimilation, is apparently progressive and irreversible" (Park 1926/1950:150).

Park wrote at a time when the term *race* had a broader meaning than it does now. Park's conception of "races" treated separately, for example, the Slavic peoples, Jews, Chinese, Japanese, Puerto Ricans, Portuguese, and others (Park 1934, 1939; see also Banton 1983, chap. 3). Today, if we were to encounter these peoples in communities outside their countries of origin, we would consider them ethnic groups or would combine them into more inclusive racial categories: Japanese and Chinese as Asians, for example, and Slavic peoples and Portuguese as Whites.

Embedded in Park's ideas is a clear sense of transformation. The forces of history already were transforming the world's peoples, and the rest of the 20th century would only accelerate the process. The impact would integrate peoples with one another, leading ultimately to universal participation in a common life and culture. "If America was once in any exclusive sense the melting pot of races," wrote Park in 1926, "it is no longer. The melting pot is the world" (1926/1950:149).

Not everyone saw things quite this way. More skeptical voices could be heard in the sociological chorus in the early decades of the 20th century (see Berry 1965:129-35). Park, however, articulated an increasingly widespread view about the future of the world and in particular about the future of industrial, multiethnic societies such as the United States. Over time, they would become less "multi" and less ethnic. The melting pot—both global and local—would work its magic, and the peoples of the world would be integrated into a broad stream of shared culture and social relations. "Everywhere there is competition and conflict; but everywhere the intimacies which participation in a common life enforces have created new accommodation, and relations which once were merely formal or utilitarian have become personal and human" (Park 1926/1950:149).

Park was much influenced in his thinking by studies of the immigrant experience in North America. He and his fellow social scientists at the University of Chicago paid great attention to the stream of migrants from the various countries of Europe who, late in the 19th and early in the 20th centuries, poured into the growing cities and insatiable labor markets of the industrializing United States. They found that gradually, over time and through generations, these immigrants learned English, sent their children to school, struggled for economic and political success, spread across the continent, replaced customs from the old country with customs from the new, and began even to marry across the ethnic boundaries that originally separated them. These early students of European immigration frequently found evidence of Park's proposed sequence: contact with other groups; competition and conflict among them over territory and opportunities; eventual accommodation to one another's presence, character, and interests; and gradual assimilation as newcomers began to participate more and more in the dominant society and its institutions and all came to share in "a common culture and a common historical life" (Park 1926/1950:149).

The idea that ethnic attachments and identities would decline in significance emerged from other contexts as well. In the aftermath of World War II, a good deal of scholarly attention turned to the developing societies of the so-called Third World, many of them struggling for independence from colonial powers and most of them experiencing rapid social change under the massive impacts of industrialization and urbanization (see, for example, Deutsch 1961). Many of these states had been carved out originally through negotiation and conflict among the European colonial powers. Often they were composites of diverse peoples, carriers of distinct cultures and political histories who were brought together by the circumstances of forced colonial appropriation and administrative convenience. Nigeria, for example, which was consolidated as a British colony in 1914, drew under a single administrative umbrella a broad collection of peoples and previously independent kingdoms: Fulani, Igbo, Tiv, Ijaw, Oyo, and many others (Young 1976).

A common assumption from the late 1940s to at least the early 1960s was that the ethnic identities of these peoples would disappear gradually as the colonies or newly independent countries they were now part of continued to develop. Urbanization would bring members of these various groups together in cities where they would mingle, intermarry, and exchange ideas, losing touch with their regions of origin. Growing markets for industrial labor would be indifferent to the origins of the workers they attracted, treating group members indiscriminately as individuals and mixing them in the workplace, leveling their differences. The new technologies of mass communication would leap across the parochialisms of tribal connection and local experience, linking people to people and idea to idea on a scale never before seen in these countries. Expanded and modernized educational systems would teach them a common language, a common body of knowledge, and a common culture, fostering a shared and broadened consciousness of self and society. The political processes of nation-building would bind their loyalties to rising new states, institutionalizing a comprehensive new identity and undermining older ties to kinship, local community, and traditional cultures (for example, see Black 1966; Deutsch 1966; McCall 1955; Pye 1966). All of this might take time—after all, some groups surely would resist these changes (Eisenstadt and Rokkan 1973)—but the modernizing dynamic would prevail. In Nigeria, for example, the Tiv and the Ijaw and all the others would become Nigerians before long, not only by virtue of the formalities of independence and citizenship, but also through a newly comprehensive political and cultural consciousness. In this view, ethnicity was merely part of "the unfinished business for political modernizers" (Burgess 1978:272), certain to be finished before long.

Finally, the expectation that ethnic and racial attachments would decline found support in some of the classical sources of sociological thought. Karl Marx's radical historical vision saw capitalism as the hammer that eventually would pulverize ties of nationality or tribe, fashioning in their stead the iron bonds of class, linking people to each other on the basis of their positions in the process of economic production. By the 1960s, a growing body of work in the social sciences, influenced in part by Marxist analyses, was displaying this "radical expectancy" (Glazer and Moynihan 1975:7), the belief that class interests would emerge as the bedrock of collective identity and political consciousness, displacing alternative bases of action. As capitalism developed around the world, other sources of group ties—language, religion, national origin, and the like—would disappear or at least become far less significant. Persons and groups would discover that their "true" interests were defined by their positions in productive processes or markets, and they would reconceptualize and reorganize themselves along class lines.[1]

Another European social thinker, Max Weber, agreed that ethnicity would decline in importance but envisioned a different mechanism at work. For Weber, the rationalization of human action and organization was the hallmark of modernity. Ethnicity, in contrast, was a communal relationship. It was based not on the rational calculation of interest but on subjective feelings among group members "that they belong together" (Weber 1968:40). As modernity and hence rationalization progressed, thought Weber, communal relationships would be displaced. Only where "rationally-regulated action is not widespread"—that is, where modernization had yet to take root—would such relationships remain compelling (p. 389). In the Weberian scheme, "ethnicity could hardly be expected to survive the great tidal wave of bureaucratic rationality sweeping over the western world" (Parkin 1979:32). Weber's and Marx's ideas, although very different, had similar implications: Over time, ethnicity and race would decline as significant social forces in the modern world. This line of thinking was by no means entirely wrong. Immigrants often did adopt the practices and ideas of the societies they entered; political and economic development in the Third World did transform social relations, daily experience, and even identities; and as capitalism developed, class-based interests, cutting across ethnic, racial, and other boundaries, often did become mobilized into political conflict. Somehow, however, the decline of ethnic and racial attachments failed to follow, at least on a large scale. Indeed, the last third of the 20th century made a shambles of these projections. In recent decades, far from disappearing, ethnicity has been resurgent around the world—often, as the preceding examples make clear, with lethal consequences. As Donald Horowitz wrote in 1985, "Ethnicity is at the center of politics in country after country, a potent source of challenges to the cohesion of states and of international tension. . . . [It] has fought and bled and burned its way into public and scholarly consciousness" (p. xi).

In short, modernity—that gradual and eventually global process by which industrialization, urbanization, mass communications, and other institutional changes transformed human life and society—was supposed to bring an end to ethnicity. The phenomenon was supposed to go away. But the predictions did not come true. It turned out to be an ethnic century after all.

This book is an attempt to understand why. Why have ethnicity and race, defying predictions, remained such persistent and powerful forces in the modern world?

The Challenge of Diversity

The unexpected persistence of ethnicity is not the only puzzle here. Equally as puzzling and as intellectually challenging is its diversity. The diversity to which we refer has to do not with the variety of peoples in the world or with their interactions; it is not the diversity of a college campus or a developing nation that we have in mind. That the world contains many ethnic groups and a number of races and that these sometimes have difficulty getting along is not particularly astonishing. What is remarkable is the diversity of forms that ethnicity and race seem to take, the variety of functions they apparently serve, and the quite different kinds of attachments that claim the ethnic label.

For example, consider the diverse form that Armenian identity has taken. In 1894, the sultan of the Ottoman Empire, Abd al-Hamid, caught up in the chaos of a crumbling empire, launched a massacre of the Armenian population in the eastern part of what is now Turkey. The extermination effort continued for more than two decades. Hundreds of thousands of Armenians died, and thousands more fled the country.

A significant number of those Armenians who fled ended up in the United States. By 1900, 12,000 Armenians had taken refuge on American soil; by World War I, there were 60,000. They continued to come, for a variety of reasons and from various parts of the Middle East, up to the present time (Arlen 1975; Bakalian 1992). Somewhere between half a million and a million Armenian Americans live in the United States today, descendants of these immigrants. Many of them are now members of the third or fourth generation on American soil. Anny Bakalian (1992), in her study of Armenian Americans, traces the reconstruction of Armenian identity in these later generations. She describes it as a passage from "being" to "feeling" Armenian. "Being" Armenian referred to sharing a distinct language, living a similar and distinct style of life, carrying a common and identifiably Armenian culture, and living one's life within predominantly Armenian sets of social relations, from marriage to friendship. "Feeling" Armenian is quite different. For American-born generations of Armenians,

> the Armenian language is no longer used as a means of everyday communication. The secular culture, even cuisine, is relegated to special occasions and acquires symbolic connotations. Frequency of attendance at Armenian religious services is gradually reduced, as is participation in communal life and activities sponsored by Armenian voluntary associations. Social ties, even intimate relations and conjugal bonds, with non-Armenians become increasingly the norm. (Bakalian 1993:5-6)

Despite this change, however, Bakalian argues that "the majority of Armenian-Americans, even the great-grandchildren of the immigrant generation, continue to maintain high levels of Armenian identity, fierce pride in their ancestral heritage, and a strong sense of we-ness or peoplehood" (Bakalian 1993:6). They have not lost their identity. They have held onto it, but they also have transformed it.

Joane Nagel (1996:25) invites us to compare this experience of Armenianness with the experience of Armenianness "in Turkey during World War I when Armenians were the targets of pogroms, or in post-Soviet Azerbaijan, where Christian Armenians and Muslim Azerbaijanis fight for control of borders and minority enclaves." Obviously, what it means to be Armenian in each of these times and places is very different, yet all these persons lay claim to an Armenian identity. Do they actually have much in common, other than the label they attach to their identities? What is the ultimate meaning of Armenianness, embracing as it does such a diverse set of experiences and persons?

So it is with ethnicity more generally. The examples with which we opened this chapter capture ethnic and racial identities at their most dramatic and compelling. The identities in those examples, for the most part, are surrounded by passion and conflict. Not all ethnic and racial identities are experienced this way. Some are quietly assumed or unconsciously left behind. Some are used to mobilize people or register claims; others seem to have no uses at all. For some groups, ethnic or racial background reliably predicts life chances, organizes social relations and daily experience, and plays a prominent role in individual self-concepts. For others, it may do only one or two of these things or none. Some people are reminded of their ethnic or racial identity—proudly, angrily, sadly, or indifferently—every day. Others for the most part ignore it or trot it out on holidays or at family reunions where the old ethnic stories are told for the umpteenth time and the traditional foods get their once-yearly airing. What is more, all these different manifestations of ethnic or racial identity may be apparent within a single group all at once, as some group members build their lives around such an identity and others turn their backs on it, building their lives around another identity altogether. Nor is identity—particularly in the case of race—always a matter of choice. Some can pay their ethnic or racial identity little mind, but others are never allowed to forget it.

Such diversity begs an explanation. Why is ethnicity one thing here, another there, and both things somewhere else? If ethnicity can be so many things, has it any distinctive core at all? As John Comaroff (1991:663) put it, "If the Gods—or social scientists, it makes little difference—do know the answer, maybe they could explain: Why is ethnicity sometimes the basis of bitter conflict, even genocide, while, at other times, it is no more than the stuff of gastronomic totemism?"

Thus, the puzzle of power and persistence is accompanied by the puzzle of variation and change. That second puzzle, too, drives the argument in this book. How are we to account for the rise and fall of ethnic and racial identities and conflicts and for their myriad variations? And what about the future? Will ethnicity and race continue to wield their peculiar power in the 21st century? Powerful or not, what forms will they take, and what consequences will they have for human beings and for society?

Ethnicity and Race as Sociological Topics

In recent decades, it has become apparent that ethnicity and race are among the most common categories that contemporary human beings use to organize their ideas about who they are, to evaluate their experiences and behavior, and to understand the world around them. In some societies, of course, ethnic and racial categories and ties are more salient than in others. It is increasingly evident nevertheless that ethnicity and race are among the fundamental organizing concepts of the contemporary world. That fact alone would make them central topics within sociology.

Ethnicity and race also appear to have striking potency as bases of collective identity and action. The unanticipated and often dramatic staying power of ethnic and racial identities demonstrates as much. Groups organized around ethnicity and race are reshaping societies, upsetting old assumptions, and challenging established systems of power. In essence, they are remaking significant parts of the modern world.

The distinctive contribution of sociology as a discipline has been the study of just such processes: of variously defined groups within society, of intergroup relations, of collective action, and of the multitudinous forces and factors that impinge on these. The study of ethnicity and race, in other words, is a fundamentally sociological enterprise.

One of the great strengths of sociology has been its insistence on placing social phenomena within broad social and historical contexts. From its beginnings in the classical works of 19th- and early 20th-century thinkers, sociology has been preoccupied with social change on a grand scale, in particular with the onset of modernity and industrialism and with their diverse effects on human relationships and on the human search for meaning, community, order, and understanding.

Ethnicity and race are arenas in which those relationships and that search are continually in flux. They have to do with fundamental group processes: how human beings come to see themselves and others in particular ways, how they come to act on those perceptions, and how their understandings and actions are shaped by social and historical forces. Two very different—if typically related—sets of factors are at work in those processes. One set consists of the attributes, resources, and ideas of groups themselves; the other consists of the environment that those groups encounter. To understand ethnicity and race, therefore, we have to study both composition and context. We have to look both at what groups bring with them to their encounters with other people and with the world around them, and what the world that they encounter consists of. We need to understand both how people interpret and negotiate their lives in ethnic or racial ways, and how larger historical and social forces organize the arenas and terms in which those people act, encouraging or discouraging the interpretations they make, facilitating some forms of organization and action and hindering others.

These issues and concerns also shape the inquiry in this book, most of which has do in one way or another with the following questions.

- What is it that makes ethnicity and race such powerful bases of identity and action, and how do we explain their striking diversity?

- How are ethnic and racial identities constructed, maintained, and transformed?

- Under what conditions are ethnic or racial forms of identification and action likely to arise?

- What will happen to ethnicity and race in the future? Will they survive as prominent organizational themes in the modern world? Or will the 21st century finally realize the misplaced predictions of the 20th century and see the demise of ethnicity and race as bases of identity and action?

An Outline of What Follows

We begin our approach to these questions with definitions. Chapter 2 maps the confusing terrain of ethnicity, race, and nationalism; discusses the ways these terms are commonly used (and confused); and provides the definitions that are used throughout this book.

Chapter 3 then examines the two models of ethnic and racial identities that have organized a great deal of social scientific thinking in recent years, commonly known as the primordialist and circumstantialist accounts. We situate these schools of thought in the context of global change, discuss their strengths and weaknesses, and suggest that they may be less diametrically opposed to each other than is generally assumed.

Chapter 4 lays out the key elements of a constructionist conception of ethnicity. It uses pieces of both primordialist and circumstantialist perspectives to account for the power of ethnic and racial identities and for their persistence and variation but adds to those perspectives a central concern with the ways that groups participate in the construction of their own (and others') identities.

In Chapter 5, we illustrate some constructions of ethnic and racial identities through a series of case studies, both historical and contemporary. The emphasis in these narratives is on the interplay between group characteristics and ideas, on one hand, and contextual factors, on the other, in the making and remaking of identity.

Chapters 6 and 7 take up the elements involved in the construction of ethnicity and race more systematically and in more detail. Chapter 6 examines the arenas of social life—the construction sites—where ethnic and racial identities are built and transformed and the ways that contextual factors shape those constructions. Chapter 7 examines the materials that groups bring to those sites and the ways group factors are used in the construction process.

Finally, Chapter 8 looks ahead, considering two apparently contradictory trends—mixing and multiplicity on one hand, separation and consolidation on the other—that give to ethnicity and race two very different faces as we enter the 21st century.

NOTE

1. Robert Park, although hardly a Marxist, shared the general view that economic relations were the ones that would endure. "Race conflicts in the modern world," he wrote, "will be more and more in the future confused with, and eventually superseded by, the conflicts of classes" (Park 1939:45).

2

Mapping the Terrain: Definitions

Before exploring ethnicity and race in detail, we need to clarify what it is we are talking about. We have made no attempt thus far to distinguish between ethnicity and race and have written as if the two were more or less interchangeable terms. They are not. They refer to distinct sets of phenomena that at times overlap. Some of the groups we think of as races are at the same time ethnic groups, and some of those we think of as ethnic groups may be or may at some point have been races, but the two are not the same.

Distinguishing between race and ethnicity, on the other hand, is not easy, but the task is worth spending some time on. We also need to map the sometimes confusing terrain that includes both ethnicity and nationalism, which again sometimes overlap but are not the same thing.

We take up ethnicity in the first section of this chapter and race in the following section. The next section explores both the differences between ethnicity and race and their commonalities. Finally, we consider nationalism and its relationship to ethnicity.

The Definition of Ethnicity

In the last 30 years, words such as *ethnic group, ethnic identity*, and *ethnicity* have become commonplace. We increasingly encounter them not only in academic analyses of social phenomena but also in the mass media. *The Los Angeles Times,* for example, published a story in 1992 on tribal conflict in Ethiopia under the headline "Ethnic Pride Gets a Test in Africa" (Hiltzik 1992). A 1995 *New York Times* article on disputes among groups within some Middle Eastern states was headlined "Arabs, Too, Play the Ethnic Card" (Hedges 1995). Another story a week later in the same paper, discussing recent Irish immigrants' dissatisfaction with St. Patrick's Day celebrations in the United States, announced that "Ethnic Clichés Put Anger in Irish Eyes" (Clines 1995). Although most people who encounter such references probably believe that they know, at least approximately, what the words mean, terms such as *ethnic, ethnic group,* and *ethnicity* are in fact slippery and difficult to define. The confusion has not been limited to readers of mass media; they are slippery terms in the academic lexicon as well.

The word *ethnic* has a long history. It is a derivative of the Greek word *ethnos,* meaning nation. The reference, however, is not to a political unity but to the unity of persons of common blood or descent: a people. The adjectival form, *ethnikos,* eventually entered Latin as *ethnicus,* referring to heathens, those "others" who did not share the dominant faith. This is more or less the meaning that the word carried when it first found English usage around the 15th century. In English, "ethnic" referred to someone who was neither Christian nor Jew—in other words, a pagan or heathen. The matter of belief is less important in this usage than the drawing of a boundary. "Ethnic" clearly referred to others, to those who were not "us" (Just 1989; Oxford University Press 1993; Petersen 1981).

By the 20th century, the meaning of the word had changed again but had reasserted some of the original Greek conception. Gone, for the most part, was the specific reference to religion and with it the idea that only "others"—certainly not "us"—could be ethnics. Increasingly, ethnicity referred to a particular way of defining not only others but also ourselves, and this is how it entered sociology.

Sociological Definitions

The shift toward the subjective in the meaning of ethnicity is most readily apparent in a discussion of ethnic groups by the German sociologist Max Weber, the only one of the classical sociological theorists to offer an explicit definition. Weber (1968) devoted a chapter to the topic in his great work *Economy and Society,* written early in this century, in which he says, "We shall call 'ethnic groups' those human groups that entertain a subjective belief in their common descent because of similarities of physical type or of customs or both, or because of memories of colonization and migration" (p. 389). He goes on to say, "It does not matter whether or not an objective blood relationship exists." Several things are worth noting about Weber's definition.

- At the foundation of ethnic attachments lies real or assumed common descent. Ethnic ties are blood ties.

- The fact of common descent is less important than belief in common descent. What matters is not whether a blood relationship actually exists, but whether it is believed to exist, "not *what is* but *what people perceive*" (Connor 1993:377). Ethnicity is a subjective matter; the crucial issue is how we see ourselves.

- The potential bases of this belief in common descent are multiple, varying from physical resemblance to shared cultural practices to a shared historical experience of intergroup interaction. Any of these, or some combination, might be the basis or justification of our assumption of common descent.

- An ethnic group exists wherever this distinctive connection—this belief in common descent—is part of the foundation of community, wherever it binds us to one another to some degree.

Weber's emphasis on common descent is central to a number of subsequent definitions of ethnicity (for example, Alba 1990; Connor 1978, 1993; Horowitz 1985; Schermerhorn 1978; Shibutani and Kwan 1965). Much of sociology, however, particularly in the classroom, eventually abandoned Weber's definition and came to equate ethnicity with shared culture. The core of the definition shifted from Weber's concern with putative origins and shared history—for the most part, that is, with how the past shapes present self-concepts—to currently shared culture, to what group members now do. An ethnic group became a group of persons distinguished largely by common culture, typically including language, religion, or other patterns of behavior and belief. For example, one recent edition of a widely used textbook defines an ethnic group as "a group of people who are generally recognized by themselves and/or by others as a distinct group, with such recognition based on social or cultural characteristics" (Farley 1995:6). Another accepts either culture or national origin as the basis of ethnicity, defining an ethnic group as "a group socially distinguished or set apart, by others or by itself, primarily on the basis of cultural or national-origin characteristics" (Feagin and Feagin 1996:11). Combining shared history and shared present practices, a third argues that "when a subpopulation of individuals reveals, or is perceived to reveal, shared historical experiences as well as unique organizational, behavioral, and cultural characteristics, it exhibits its ethnicity" (Aguirre and Turner 1995:2-3).

A moment's reflection will reveal the ambiguities that such specifications of ethnicity create. If all that is required to distinguish an ethnic group is some level of shared "social or cultural characteristics" or "historical experiences," then lawyers, military families, university students, Deadheads, the citizens of Switzerland, prison inmates, and numerous other groups potentially join Polish Americans, the Chinese minority in

Malaysia, and the Kurds of Iraq, among others, in the pantheon of ethnic groups. Analytic precision and utility suffer as the concept of ethnicity slips away into the enormously diverse mosaic of self-conscious collectivities—sharing varying degrees of history and culture—that any society generates. This definition nevertheless has become common. Even the massive and hugely informative *Harvard Encyclopedia of American Ethnic Groups* (Thernstrom, Orlov, and Handlin 1981:vi) defines an ethnic group in effect as a group sharing cultural attributes. It then leaves out of its survey all sorts of groups that ought, by that loose definition, to qualify: the working class, physicists, inner-city African Americans (as distinct from other African Americans), and even Amway representatives.

Our concern about such definitions goes beyond their imprecision. One of the striking things about ethnicity in recent decades has been its survival, in some cases, despite rapidly declining cultural distinctions. This development has been especially apparent in the United States. In Chapter 1, we mentioned Anny Bakalian's (1993) discussion of the path Armenian Americans have followed "from being to feeling Armenian." Distinctive cultural practices have declined over time, but the identity— that sense of ethnic distinctiveness—has not. Similar processes are apparent among other European-descent Americans as well, many of whom display few culturally distinct practices but proudly proclaim their ethnic identities (see, for example, Alba 1990; Gans 1979; Waters 1990). In what way are such groups ethnic? Once the supposedly primary definitional element—shared cultural characteristics—disappears, of what does their ethnicity consist?

The colloquial American understanding seems closer in some ways to the Weberian one than to some of the more recent academic usages. Although most Americans may consider various ethnic groups culturally distinct to one degree or another, they generally seem to view the origins of these groups as what sets them most clearly apart and accounts for whatever distinctive cultural characteristics remain. The classic case is immigrant groups. To say that you are Irish or Italian in the United States is to say, most importantly, that your people came originally from Ireland or Italy. To many Americans, it is the fact that group members came originally from "there, not here," or at least not from where "we" came from, that ultimately is the source of their distinctiveness, with homeland approximating Weber's concept of shared ancestry.

Ethnicity as a Distinctive Set of Claims

It is most unlikely that any one definition of *ethnic group* or *ethnicity* will satisfy all the specialists or fully escape the ambiguities that seem an in-

evitable part of the study of ethnicity. We nevertheless join those sociologists who have remained close to the Weberian tradition, and we follow
Richard A. Schermerhorn's (1978) definition, which describes an ethnic
group as "a collectivity within a larger society having real or putative
common ancestry, memories of a shared historical past, and a cultural
focus on one or more symbolic elements defined as the epitome of their
peoplehood" (p. 12). Among the examples Schermerhorn offers of such
symbolic elements that may be viewed as emblematic of peoplehood are
kinship patterns, geographical concentration, religious affiliation, language, and physical differences. The common history a group claims may
be viewed the same way. For example, the historical experience of slavery
plays a powerful symbolic role in many Black Americans' conceptions of
themselves.

Schermerhorn adds to this definition the criterion of self-consciousness.
Ethnic groups are self-conscious populations; they see themselves as distinct.

Again, there are several points to be made about this definition.

- It involves three kinds of claims: a claim to kinship, broadly defined; a claim to a common history of some sort; and a claim that
  certain symbols capture the core of the group's identity.

- As in Weber's conception, these claims need not be founded in
  fact. The kinship claim, for example, has to do with either real or
  putative common ancestry.

- The extent of actual cultural distinctiveness is irrelevant. Contrary to many common definitions, not all ethnic groups are culture groups (and not all culture groups are ethnic groups). Although group members may draw attention to certain cultural
  features as "the epitome of their peoplehood," they are not necessarily practitioners of distinct cultures, and such features frequently have more symbolic power than practical effect on group
  behavior. In fact, the cultural practices of an ethnic group may
  vary little from those prevalent in the society of which it is a part.

- An ethnic group is a subpopulation within a larger society.

- An ethnic group is self-consciously ethnic.

We should point out that, in practice, descent from a common homeland often serves as a broad assertion of common ancestry. It is doubtful,
for example, that all those who came to the United States from Cuba actually claim to be descended from a common ancestor, but they do claim
descent from a common homeland, which serves as a metaphor for kinship. Such metaphors often are explicit: We may speak, for example, of

the fatherland, or of Mother Russia, or of the "children" of Africa. Ethnicity is family writ very large indeed. It typically involves the assertion of some ineffable bond among group members, a bond we think of as rooted ultimately in shared, distinctive origins (see Horowitz 1985, chap. 2).

This definition still casts the net fairly widely—variation in claim and assertion can be substantial—but it gives us a more distinctive universe of groups, and it classifies those groups according to the particular kinds of claims they make or the particular claims made about them. This last point is crucial. Although an ethnic group is self-consciously ethnic, its self-consciousness often has its source in outsiders. The identity that others assign to us can be a powerful force in shaping our own self-concepts. To say that ethnicity is subjective is not to say that it is unaffected by what others say or do. Indeed, outsiders' conceptions of us may be a major influence leading to our own self-consciousness as an ethnic population. Others may assign to us an ethnic identity, but what they establish by doing so is an ethnic category. It is our own claim to that identity that makes us an ethnic group. The ethnic category is externally defined, but the ethnic group is internally defined (Jenkins 1994).

It also should be apparent from this definition that what is ethnic about an ethnic group is the fact that it identifies itself in a particular way. Members of some ethnic groups may share a great deal more than that particular way of identifying themselves, including extensive cultural practices; others may share little more than the identity claim that they make. Groups that share a great deal and groups that share very little clearly are different but are equally ethnic. The mode or idiom of identification makes them so.

Finally, ethnicity is a matter of contrast. To claim an ethnic identity (or to attempt to assign one to someone else) is to distinguish ourselves from others; it is to draw a boundary between "us" and "them" on the basis of the claims we make about ourselves and them, that "we" share something that "they" do not. An ethnic group cannot exist in isolation. It has meaning only in a context that involves others—ultimately, in a collection of peoples of which it is only a part. An ethnic population, however, is not necessarily a minority population. An ethnic group may be politically or numerically dominant within a single state; it may dominate one state and at the same time be a minority in others. It is never conceptually an isolate.

Ethnicity, then, is identification in ethnic terms—that is, in the terms outlined above. An ethnic identity is an identity conceived in such terms. A population or social collectivity may be simply an ethnic category, assigned an ethnic identity by outsiders. Once that identity becomes subjective—that is, once that population sees itself in ethnic terms, perhaps in response to the identity outsiders assign to it—it becomes an ethnic group.

The Definition of Race

What about race? Are races ethnic groups? Consider Black Americans. Certainly many people consider them a race or at least a part of one. How so? If they are a race, are they not an ethnic group? Could they be both?

Before we can answer these questions, we have to wrestle with the definition of a race. As with ethnicity, it is common in contemporary society to talk about races, race relations, and racial conflict as if we had a clear idea about what constitutes a race and where the boundary falls between one race and another. Race, however, is as slippery a concept as ethnic group, and its slipperiness has a long history.

Race as Biology

In technical terms, a race can be thought of as a genetically distinct subpopulation of a given species. This statement is of little use in thinking about human races, however, for the genetic differences among human groups that we commonly view as races are inconsistent and typically insignificant. This has made it difficult to figure out what a race, conceived in terms of human biology, actually is. In fact, biologists, physical anthropologists, and other students of human physiology and genetics have long disagreed about which, if any, genetic differences mark the boundaries between races and about how many human races there are. For several centuries, scholars of one stripe or another from various countries tried to specify the number of races in the world.

> Linnaeus had found four human races; Blumenbach had five; Cuvier
> had three; John Hunter had seven; Burke had sixty-three; Pickering had
> eleven; Virey had two "species," each containing three races; Haeckel had
> thirty-six; Huxley had four; Topinard had nineteen under three headings;
> Desmoulins had sixteen "species"; Deniker had seventeen races and thirty
> types. (Gossett 1963:82)

Clearly, consensus regarding the nature and number of human races has been elusive.

The federal government of the United States has been anything but consistent in its own classifications. In 1870, according to historian Paul

Spickard (1992:18), the U.S. Bureau of the Census listed five races in the United States: "White, Colored (Blacks), Colored (Mulattoes), Chinese, and Indian. . . . In 1950, the census categories reflected a different social understanding: White, Black, and Other." By the 1990s, federal programs, responding more to the demands of various groups than to any biological theory, required various public and private entities to report racial data using, once again, five categories, but they were different from the 1870 ones: White, Black, Asian, Hispanic, and Indian.

Other societies have made other choices. For a long time, the South African government recognized four races: White, African, Colored, and Asian. In many parts of Brazil, the history of which includes widespread mixing among Europeans, Africans, and the indigenous Indians, people more or less gave up on the notion of distinct races and instead established a set of sometimes overlapping categories that recognize varying degrees of racial mixture, usually determined by an individual's appearance and ranging from the lightest complexions to the darkest.

If biologically distinct human races do exist, it seems odd that there is so little agreement on what they are. Indeed, the persistence of the idea of biologically distinct human races owes more to popular culture and pseudoscience than to science, and the idea's pedigree is not scientific but historical. It emerged originally in the extended encounter between European and non-European peoples that began in the late 15th and early 16th centuries. Discovering human beings in Asia, Africa, and the Americas who looked—and often acted—very different from themselves, Europeans concluded that these superficial differences were surely indicators of much more fundamental differences as well. This conclusion helped them justify their efforts to colonize, enslave, and even exterminate certain of those peoples. Europeans came to believe that races are in fact distinct and identifiable human (and some of them, in the extreme version, nonhuman) groups; that there are systematic, inherited, biological differences among races; and that the non-White races are innately inferior to Whites—that is, to Europeans (Jordan 1968).

Systematic physiological differences among many human groups are obvious. Skin color is only one example. Deciding which of these physiological differences should serve as a racial marker is a complicated process. Racial boundaries turn out to be messy. For one thing, the distribution of human physical characteristics, aided by millennia of mixing among human communities, is persistently irregular. Blood types, hair textures, skin colors, and body forms all vary, sometimes dramatically, not only between populations we often think of as racially distinct but within them as well. In fact, the extent of genetic variation among individuals within supposed racial groups typically exceeds the variation between the groups. We can speak of a group of persons as having, on average, a greater frequency of some set of genes than some other group has, but those genes seldom will be limited to that group; the differences in frequency will be differences of degree.

It would be easier to know how to mark racial boundaries if the supposed physical differences among races were consistently apparent, but they seldom are. It would be easier likewise if some set of characteristic physical distinctions were correlated consistently with some set of characteristic abilities or behaviors, but science has been unable to link such physical differences persuasively to differences in ability or intelligence or very much else. In other words, the scientific arguments for any particular way of dividing up and identifying races of human beings are at best modest. As geneticist Richard Lewontin and his colleagues point out (Lewontin, Rose, and Kamin 1984:126-27),

> In practice, "racial" categories are established that correspond to major skin color groups, and all the borderline cases are distributed among these or made into new races according to the whim of the scientist. But . . . the differences between major "racial" categories, no matter how defined, turn out to be small. Human "racial" differentiation is, indeed, only skin deep.

As a result, most contemporary scholars dismiss the entire idea of race as a meaningful biological category that can be applied to separate groups of human beings (Gould 1981, 1994; King 1981; Lewontin et al. 1984; Smedley 1993).

The Social Construction of Race

Despite the lack of a biological basis for the conception of distinct human races, race still wields monumental power as a social category. In many societies, the idea of biologically distinct races remains a fixture in the popular mind, a basis of social action, a foundation of government policy, and often a justification for distinctive treatment of one group by another. Despite the paucity of scientific support, human beings tend to assume racial categories and to take them seriously. They do so for social, not biological, reasons.

Races, like ethnic groups, are not established by some set of natural forces but are products of human perception and classification. They are social constructs. As geneticist James King remarks (1981:156), "Both what constitutes a race and how one recognizes a racial difference are culturally determined." We decide that certain physical characteristics—

usually skin color, but perhaps also hair type, stature, or other bodily features—will be primary markers of group boundaries. We invent categories of persons marked by those characteristics. The categories become socially significant to the extent that we use them to organize and interpret experience, to form social relations, and to organize individual and collective action. In other words, the categories become important only when we decide they have particular meanings and act on those meanings. The characteristics that are the basis of the categories, however, have no inherent significance. We give them meaning, and in the process we create races.

We can define a race, then, as a human group defined by itself or others as distinct by virtue of perceived common physical characteristics that are held to be inherent. A race is a group of human beings socially defined on the basis of physical characteristics. Determining which characteristics constitute the race—the selection of markers and therefore the construction of the racial category itself—is a choice human beings make. Neither markers nor categories are predetermined by any biological factors.

These processes of selection and construction are seldom the work of a moment. Racial categories are historical products and are often contested. In one famous case from the early 1980s, a Louisiana woman went to court to dispute the state's conclusion that she was Black, claiming a White racial identity. The state's argument was that her ancestry was at least 1/32nd "Negro" which, according to state law, meant she was Black (Dominguez 1986). The law had roots in the long history of Black-White relations in Louisiana and in the American South more generally, in slavery and its legacy and in the enduring White effort to maintain the supposed "purity" of their race. It was a legal manifestation of what is known as hypodescent, or the "one-drop" rule, which in the United States holds that any degree of African ancestry at all is sufficient to classify a person as Black (see Davis 1991). This rule has a history. People have fought over it, and as the Louisiana case shows, it has been tested in the courts. It has been reserved largely for Blacks. Americans do not generally consider a person who is 1/32 Japanese or Dutch to be Japanese or Dutch, but "one drop" of Black blood has long been considered sufficient for racial categorization.

The woman in Louisiana lost her case (although the law eventually was changed), but her story underlines the point made by Michael Omi and Howard Winant (1994) in their path-breaking study of race in the United States: Racial categories are not natural categories that human beings discover; on the contrary, they are "created, inhabited, transformed, and destroyed" by human action and are, therefore, preeminently social products (p. 55). They change over time as people struggle to establish them, overcome them, assign other people to them, escape them, interpret them, and so on. The outcomes of those struggles often have enormous consequences for the individuals involved, but it is not biology that determines who will suffer and why. People determine what the categories will be, fill them up with human beings, and attach consequences to membership in those categories.

Ethnicity and Race

To pose again the question we raised some pages ago: Are races ethnic groups? The answer, which may not yet be obvious, is sometimes yes, sometimes no. Ethnicity and race are not the same, but they are not mutually exclusive categories either. They sometimes overlap. In short, races may be but are not necessarily ethnic groups. In the following two subsections, we first explore the ways that ethnicity and race are different and then the things they have in common.

Differences Between Ethnicity and Race

Most societies have treated races very differently from ethnic groups, and the differences have been crucial. In the United States, for example, although some ethnic groups have been privileged over others at various times in history, Whiteness—a racial category—consistently has been privileged over non-Whiteness, with persons of color consigned to the margins of American society and culture. In different ways at different times, race has been institutionalized in the organization of the society and ideologized in its culture.

Race has been the most powerful and persistent group boundary in American history, distinguishing, to varying degrees, the experiences of those classified as non-White from those classified as White, with often devastating consequences. The racial boundary that White society historically has drawn around itself has excluded different groups at different times. Along with Black, Asian, Latino, and Native Americans, both Jews and the Irish, among others, have been perceived as non-Whites at one time or another in the United States (Ignatiev 1995; Sacks 1994). Both struggled to alter the perception, knowing all too well the costs of being non-White in the eyes of Whites.

Designating a group of people as a distinct race has been sufficient in the United States to mark them off as more profoundly and distinctively "other"—more radically different from "us"—than those ethnic groups who have not had to carry the burden of racial distinction. Where racial designations have been used, ethnic distinctions within racial categories have tended to be overshadowed by the racial designation. All of the commonly designated racial groups in American life are multiethnic: Mexicans, Puerto Ricans, Cubans and others among Latinos, for example; West Indians and American-born Blacks, whose ethnicities operate at a less comprehensive level than the African American ethnicity they more generally share; various groups among Asian Americans; a multitude of tribal identities among American Indians; and various European-descent ethnicities among Whites. With the important exception of Whites, however, the society at large generally has either ignored or minimized these identities throughout much of its history, emphasizing more comprehensive racial distinctions.[1] Furthermore, it has been far more reluctant to allow movement across racial boundaries than across ethnic ones. For example, "a Cambodian American does not have to remain Cambodian, as far as non-Asian Americans are concerned, but only with great difficulty can this Cambodian American cease to be Asian American" (Hollinger 1995:28). This does not mean these ethnicities are unimportant. They are of great importance to the groups involved and a key to understanding much of what goes on among and within those groups. It does illustrate, however, the particular power of race, which has been a foundational feature of American life in a way that ethnicity has not: the ultimate boundary between "us" and "them." This pattern of racial categorization also illustrates the tendency in American life to recognize diversity among Whites but to ignore it among others.

Not all societies have experienced race in this same way. Relative to ethnicity, race has played an even greater and more obvious role in the organization of society and culture in South Africa, for example, than it has in the United States. Race was a fundamental organizing principle in most colonial societies around the world, remains a significant dimension of social organization in various societies of the Middle East and Latin America, and is of rapidly growing significance in much of contemporary Europe. In Canada, on the other hand, as the case of French-speaking Quebec indicates, ethnicity has been fully as important a fault line as race. In Belgium, ethnicity has considerably overshadowed race as a dimension of social organization and politics.

Despite the varying prominence of racial categories across societies, race everywhere has taken on a distinctive set of meanings and uses. Some of these are apparent in remarks made by a British gold and tin miner in colonial Malaya, in Southeast Asia, in the early part of the 1900s. Malaya was a British colony, populated by an ethnically diverse indigenous population known to the British as Malays, along with significant numbers of Chinese and Asian Indians (Tamils), brought in both before and during British colonial rule to meet growing labor needs. Writing of the situation in Malaya, the miner remarked,

> From a labour point of view, there are practically three races, the Malays (including the Javanese), the Chinese, and the Tamils (who are generally known as Klings). By nature the Malay is an idler, the Chinaman is a thief, and the Kling is a drunkard, yet each in his own class of work is both cheap and efficient, when properly supervised." (quoted in Hirschman 1986:356-57)

A good deal of importance about race is apparent or hinted at in these remarks, and we can use them to further elaborate the differences between race and ethnicity. First, race typically has its origins in assignment, in the classifications that outsiders make. Ethnicity often has similar origins, but it frequently originates in the assertions of group members themselves. The ethnically diverse Malays did not see themselves originally as a single people, much less as a distinctive "race"; this conception seems to have been largely a European inspiration (Nagata 1981). There are exceptions to the rule of racial assignment. For example, some groups in the United States, Germany, and elsewhere have more and more forcefully asserted Whiteness as a self-conscious racial identity in recent years. Most racial categories, however, have been constructed first by those who wished to assign them to someone else; race has been first and foremost a way of describing "others," of making clear that "they" are not "us."

Second, race first took on its distinctive contemporary meanings and uses as part of a monumental historical meeting of peoples. It is a product of the global era, with roots in European colonialism in places such as Malaya and elsewhere in Asia, Africa, and the Americas. Beginning late in the 15th century, in an enduring burst of expansive energy, certain European nations—in particular Spain, Portugal, England, France, and the Netherlands—sent explorers, exploiters, missionaries, and settlers across the world, most of which was previously unknown to them. Human beings have long noted the physical differences among themselves, but the magnitude of the differences that Europeans encountered over the next two centuries was unprecedented in their experience. Entire continents entered European consciousness for the first time, with populations that differed dramatically both physically and culturally from the peoples of Europe. These differences prompted classifications that were unprecedented in their comprehensiveness, a grand division of the world into Europeans, on one hand, and racially distinct others.

Third, this meeting of peoples and the ideas that came out of it were aspects of power relations. The designation of race is, in and of itself, an assertion of the power to define the "other" and in doing so to create it as a specific object. Europe exerted such power in its racial classification of the world's peoples, inventing the contemporary idea of race in the process. Racial designation also has been linked to power in more material ways. It was not idle curiosity that drove Europe's captains and missionaries across the globe, but a massive quest for wealth, political clout, and souls. They found justification for their activities in part in the idea of race, in the belief that human groups are inherently different and that those differences constitute "natural" physical and moral hierarchies that are replicated in social organization, with Caucasians in dominant social positions and various "others" ranging downward from there (Spickard 1992). "From a labour point of view," wrote the miner in Malaya—the only point of view that mattered to colonialists—"there are practically three races," and each of those three, "in its own class of work," is cheap and efficient "when properly supervised" (quoted in Hirschman 1986: 356-57). The place these races occupied in the European conception is clear in these remarks: They are a resource to be exploited. Such beliefs both nourished and were nourished by colonialism, but they have been among the more durable products of human intellectual ingenuity, and not only in the hands of Europeans. From the slaughter of indigenous peoples in the Americas to the racial exclusionism of Japan, from Europe's exploitation of colonial labor to the extermination campaigns that Hutus and Tutsis have repeatedly waged against each other in Rwanda and Burundi, the domination of one group by another has turned repeatedly to race for its dubious legitimacy. Thus, race and power, historically and today, have been tightly intertwined.

Fourth, as this history suggests, racial designation typically implies inferiority. Sometimes it is physical or biological inferiority, as in the notions—prevalent at certain times in various societies—that some races are inherently less intelligent than others or have attained only a lower stage of evolution. It also is, most importantly and almost invariably, an inferiority in moral worth. "By nature the Malay is an idler, the Chinaman is a thief, and the Kling is a drunkard" (Hirschman 1986:357). The history of race is a history of moral judgments, a division of the world into more or less worthy categories of persons. The ways in which some persons fail to meet the standard of worthiness may vary, but the idea of failure usually is implicit in the racial designation. The primary exception is the designation White. This designation commonly occurs as the unspoken flip side of the assignment of some other group to a racial category. In assigning another group to a racial category, Whites inevitably—if only implicitly—assign themselves to a different racial category. Historically, the category White has been the moral opposite of non-White categories. There is nothing inherent in Whiteness that produces such a difference; other groups may make racial assignments that simultaneously define and positively value their own race. The simple fact is that in much of the world's recent history, Whites have been more likely than others to have the power to make racial assignments, to organize social life in racial terms, and to define and value the categories as they saw fit.

Finally, there is a further implication: The unworthiness attached to race is inherent. The miner's characterization of Malaya's races claimed they were so "by nature."

Thus, in the European conception, Whites represented the norm, and others were just that—Other. The norm was taken for granted; "the white Western self as a racial being has for the most part remained unexamined and unnamed" (Frankenberg 1993:17). Its normality has been assumed. Otherness, thanks to the power that Europeans exercised, was racially marked and defined, which is characteristic of racial classification systems. Others are uncivilized or pagan or incapable; perhaps more physical and less intellectual or less cultured; and closer to nature, less fully realized in their humanness than those more fortunate in their racial makeup. Of course, in defining others we implicitly define ourselves, if only through unspoken contrast. If "they" are evil, "we" must be good; if "they" are notable for their laziness or dim-wittedness or violence, it goes without saying that "we" are notable for the opposites. At the heart of racial identification lie the claims we wish to make about "them," and about how different "they" are from "us."

Ethnicity usually escapes these burdens, although it is by no means immune to them. Like race, ethnicity may be an assigned identity. That is, it may have its origins in the claims others make about us or we make about them. For example, Italian immigrants to the United States came not, in their own minds, as Italians but as carriers of narrower regional identities: Neapolitans or Sicilians or Lucanians or something else. U.S. immigration officials and the larger public, however, saw them as Italians and so classified them. Over time, Italian immigrants came to see themselves the same way and subsequently as Italian Americans (Alba 1985). At that point, they moved from an ethnic category (assigned an identity as Italian) to an ethnic group (asserting an identity as Italian American).

Assignment thus may sow the seed of ethnicity by creating an ethnic category, but an ethnic group emerges only when that identity becomes part of the group's own self-concept.

Assignment, however, is not necessary to ethnicity, which often has its origins in assertion, in the claims groups make about themselves instead of the claims others make about them. The people known for a long time as Eskimos in Alaska and northern Canada have joined hands with others of the northernmost peoples around the globe and call themselves Inuit. They assert their own commonality, rooted in history, culture, and kinship, transcending national borders. As this case suggests, ethnicity's primary concern is as often identifying ourselves as identifying and classifying others.

In fact, this process of self-construction—"self" in this case referring to the collective or group—not only is a common characteristic of ethnicity but also is part of what makes some races at one and the same time ethnic groups. Ethnic and racial categories may be delineated first by others, but when groups begin to fill those categories with their own content, telling their own histories in their own ways and putting forth their own claims to what their identities signify, then they are engaged in a classical process of constructing ethnicity. When a racial group sets out to construct its own version of its identity, it makes itself both race and ethnic group at once.

Such typically ethnic activities are usually bound up in power relations. Ethnicity, like race, often is linked to power. Subsequent chapters will show that the origins of both ethnic and racial identities frequently are to be found in conflicts of various kinds, in struggles over scarce resources such as land or jobs or status or power. Ethnic identities also emerge or become important sometimes in an effort—unattached to concrete material interests or assertions of power—simply to make sense of the differences among persons in complex situations. They also may emerge during people's search for identities that can provide them with meaning, that can make them feel a part of some manageable community of sentiment and cultural heritage. The links between ethnicity and power, therefore, are more context dependent than are those between power and race. Power is almost invariably an aspect of race; it may or may not be an aspect of ethnicity.

As for moral worth, ethnicity certainly makes such claims often enough. Ethnocentrism—a belief in the normality and superiority of one's own people and their ways of doing things—is a common aspect of ethnic identity, but ethnocentrism is generally less virulent than is the assumption of inherent, biologically based inferiority and superiority typically attached to race. This difference may be one reason why the older and broader usage of the term *race* in the social sciences—as in Robert Park's use of the term to refer to Slavs or Portuguese or Jews or Puerto Ricans as well as Africans or Asians—gradually was displaced by *ethnic group*, which carries less implication than race does of some essential, unchangeable difference.

Commonalities of Ethnicity and Race

If these two forms of collective identity—race and ethnicity—are so different, why do we link them in this book? In fact, they share a great deal. For one thing, common usage—both among scholars and in the society at large—tends to link them and often to confuse them. They are indeed linked, but they should not be confused.

Second, both ethnicity and race are products of interaction between diverse populations. Such situations pose certain questions for the populations involved, questions that typically include the conceptual (What are the important differences between us and them, and what is the significance of this interaction?), the material (What are the implications of this encounter for the welfare of the group, and how can it be turned to our material advantage?), and the political (How can we control the situation in which we find ourselves?). Ethnicity and race both are products of the efforts groups make to effectively answer these questions.

Third, both ethnicity and race are commonly held to be "natural" categories—based on common descent or origin, on one hand, and on systematic physical differences, on the other. In fact, both are elastic. Both depend far more on the claims people make about one another or themselves than on any physical or genealogical difference. We say "held to be" natural because, although characteristics such as kinship or physiology appear to be natural or inherent, their uses in defining groups are fundamentally arbitrary. How many generations back must we go to find a connection before descent ceases to be "common"? To what does "common origin" refer—the same county or province? The same country? The same region of the world? How much physical diversity can one race contain before the category ceases to make any sense at all?

The answers people make to these questions in any particular situation are social conventions, driven by culture and social circumstance, not by any inherent attribute of the groups involved. They may refer to classes of "natural" characteristics—blood ties or biology or place of origin—but the specific identities they describe—Kurd or Afrikaner or Croat or Mexican American or Black—are not in any meaningful sense "natural," for the boundaries that mark them are arbitrarily chosen. Both ethnicity and race, in other words, are social constructions.

Fourth and most important, race and ethnicity often overlap. Ethnicity refers to perceived common ancestry, the perception of a shared history of some sort, and shared symbols of peoplehood. Race refers to a group of human beings socially defined on the basis of physical characteristics. A human group might well meet both sets of criteria at once. The identification of common physical characteristics often also involves a claim to some form of shared ancestry; groups making such a claim typically claim a distinctive history as well and may signify their peoplehood in culturally distinctive ways. Likewise, numerous ethnic groups have been described at times as physically distinct and explicitly as races: as short, dark, swarthy, stupid-looking, primitive, noble, animal-like, and so on. At such times, they fit the definition of racial groups. Definitionally, in other words, there is nothing that says that a race cannot be an ethnic group, or vice versa.

What is more, a group may move from one category to another over time. To the English of the 18th and much of the 19th centuries, the Irish, although the same color as the English, were a distinctly inferior race. A Cambridge University historian of the period (quoted in Hechter 1975) captured the assigned racial inferiority of the Irish perfectly, writing of his visit to Ireland:

> I am haunted by the human chimpanzees I saw along that hundred miles of horrible country. . . . I believe there are not only many more of them than of old, but they are happier, better, more comfortably fed and lodged under our rule than they ever were. But to see white chimpanzees is dreadful; if they were black, one would not feel it so much, but their skins except where tanned by exposure, are as white as ours. (p. xvi)

The racial status of early Irish immigrants to the United States was a matter of debate. "In the early years, Irish were frequently referred to as 'niggers turned inside out'; the Negroes, for their part, were sometimes called 'smoked Irish,' an appellation they must have found no more flattering than it was intended to be" (Ignatiev 1995:41). In the United States today, the Irish are no longer assigned a distinct racial identity but are clustered with other European Americans in the racial category "White." At the same time, in standard ethnic fashion, they have laid claim to an Irish American identity that fits easily within the definition of ethnicity.

The Irish were not the only group whose racial status changed over time. Different portions of U.S. society have viewed Jews, Italians, and Latinos as both White and non-White at different times (Frankenberg

1993; Sacks 1994). Certainly Jewish and Italian Americans are generally viewed today as ethnic groups; Latinos straddle the divide, being both a race, in some common understandings, and an ethnic group.

American Blacks also fit both definitions. They are held by others and often by themselves to be members of a distinct race, identified primarily by skin color and other bodily features. At the same time, they also have become an ethnic group, a self-conscious population that defines itself in part in terms of common descent (Africa as homeland), a distinctive history (slavery in particular), and a broad set of cultural symbols (from language to expressive culture) that are held to capture much of the essence of their peoplehood. When they lay claim to an identity of their own making and meaning, and when they act on the basis of that identity, they are acting as an ethnic group.

The case of African Americans draws attention to two different but similar processes: racialization and ethnicization. Racialization is the process by which groups of persons come to be classified as races. Put more precisely, it is the process by which certain bodily features or assumed biological characteristics are used systematically to mark certain persons for differential status or treatment. U.S. society has racialized Blacks, American Indians, Asians, and Latinos to one degree or another; South African society has racialized Blacks, Coloureds, and Asian Indians. Each case has a history that traces the establishment of the category, the assignment of certain persons to it, the development of codes of behavior for dealing with those persons, and a set of statuses assigned to them. Throughout much of the history of the American South since slavery, for example, Blacks continued to be assigned low status in the social order and were systematically disadvantaged in jobs, social resources, and politics. A code of racial etiquette directed Whites to treat Blacks as inferiors and directed Blacks to act deferentially toward Whites. All of these are aspects of racialization.

Less obvious is the less explicit racialization of Whites. In establishing the category non-White, U.S. society also established the category White, assigned certain persons to it, and assigned a distinct set of statuses to that category and its occupants. At first, prior to the founding of the United States, the English, Dutch, and a few others were virtually alone in the category, but as other peoples came to America, the dominant society included many of them in the category White. Some European groups, such as the Irish, Italians, and some Jews, were not classified as Whites at first, but that changed. Even some Hispanics were classified as Whites for a time.

Ethnicization is the making of an ethnic group. It is the process by which a group of persons comes to see itself as a distinct group linked by bonds of kinship or their equivalents, by a shared history, and by cultural symbols that represent, in Schermerhorn's terms, the "epitome" of their peoplehood. It is a coming to consciousness of particular kinds of bonds: the making of a people.

Racialization and ethnicization yield different products, but they are similar in that they both organize society into distinctive kinds of groups. They also are at times related. It is in part the racialization of Blacks in the United States that led to their ethnicization: By categorizing them as different and treating them as such, U.S. society laid the foundations for a sense of peoplehood that cut across the diverse origins of the African American population and led eventually to Black assertions of a distinct identity. Not all cases of racialization lead to ethnicization, and not all ethnic groups originate in racialization, but the two processes are often linked, and the products they yield may overlap.

Figure 2.1 depicts this overlap. It indicates that some groups may be ethnic groups, best described by the list on the left; others may be races, best described by the list on the right. Some may fit both descriptions, being races and ethnic groups at once.

Nationalism and Ethnicity

Nationalism refers to the expressed desire of a people to establish and maintain a self-governing political entity. It has proven to be one of the most powerful forces in the contemporary world, both a creator and a destroyer of modern states and a source of both pride and anguish. Consider, for example, the experience of Yugoslavia.

At the end of World War I, a number of independent Slavic states emerged from the ruins of the Habsburg Empire and other portions of southern Europe. Among them was the Kingdom of Serbs, Croats, and Slovenes, which in 1929 became the state of Yugoslavia. That state united a number of regionally concentrated groups—not only Serbs, Croats, and Slovenes, but also Macedonians, Bosnian Muslims, and others—who shared a language and a great deal of cultural practice but also carried distinct national and sometimes religious histories. These groups, nevertheless, "were much more different from any of the nations neighboring Yugoslavia than from each other. The idea of Yugoslav unity was strong" (Djilas 1991:E3).

Sixty years later, in the late 1980s, with rapid changes under way in the Soviet Union and much of Eastern Europe on the verge of dramatic change, simmering nationalist movements began to raise their voices in

FIGURE 2.1

Ethnic Groups and Races

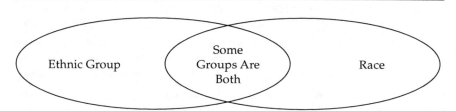

- Identity is based on putative common descent, claims of shared history, and symbols of peoplehood

- Identity may originate in either assignment by others or assertion by selves

- Identity may or may not reflect power relations

- Identity may or may not imply inherent differences in worth

- Identity usually constructed by both selves and others

- Identity is based on perceived physical differences

- Identity typically originates in assignment by others

- Identity typically reflects power relations

- Identity implies inherent differences in worth

- Identity is constructed by others (at point of self-construction, group becomes ethnic group as well as race)

Yugoslavia. By the start of 1990, Croatians and Slovenes were planning formal secession from the country; Serbs were pushing for a new state, a "Greater Serbia," embracing all the Serbian people of the region; and in Bosnia, Croatia, and elsewhere—all regions of Yugoslavia—various groups were preparing for war. Macedonia, Croatia, and Slovenia eventually seceded from Yugoslavia, and by June of 1991, war had come to Croatia as Serbs resisted the establishment of the new Croatian state. When Bosnia seceded in 1992, the Bosnian Serbs, with assistance from neighboring Serbia, went to war against the Bosnian Croats and Muslims. The term *ethnic cleansing* subsequently entered the vocabulary of modern warfare, and the world watched the ethnic mosaic of former Yugoslavia disintegrate in nationalism, hatred, and violence.

Nationalism commonly is based on ethnic ties, but nationalism and ethnicity are not the same. At the core of nationalism lie three themes:

autonomy, unity, and identity (Hutchinson and Smith 1994:4-5). Nationalism involves the effort by a people to determine their own destiny and free themselves from external constraint, to end internal divisions and unite, and to find and express their authentic cultural heritage and identity.

The first of these themes—autonomy—most clearly distinguishes nationalism from ethnicity. "A crucial difference between ethnicities and nations," writes Craig Calhoun (1993:229), "is that the latter are envisioned as intrinsically political communities, as sources of sovereignty, while this is not central to the definition of ethnicities." Nationalism is most importantly a political sentiment and movement. Ethnic groups that seek distinct corporate rights for the group as a whole within an encompassing state, or who seek a substantial degree of political autonomy (which may or may not include independent statehood) are claiming status as nations, and their efforts can be described rightly as nationalist (Brass 1991). These claims typically are based on assertions of peoplehood and common cultural heritage and on an appeal to the past, to blood ties, and to shared understandings and practices that set the group apart from other groups. This apartness justifies, in the nationalist vision, the claim to self-determination. The separatist movement in the Canadian province of Quebec, for example, which seeks to establish Quebec as a separate state, sees itself as the protector of a society and people with a very different heritage from that of English-speaking Canadians and therefore with the right to determine their own future.

Not all nationalism, however, is based on preexisting ethnic ties. Some nationalist movements try to create or enhance common identities where they did not exist before or were of little prominence in people's lives. Yugoslavia itself was such an effort, although ultimately a failed one. France, whose identity as a nation we today take for granted, is the product of a long historical effort to build a sense of common fate and common culture among people who had little sense of being part of a French nation, and whose identities were more likely to be tied to villages or other localities (Weber 1979). Perhaps the most striking example is the United States, which has engaged in more than two centuries of effort to construct a common sense of peoplehood within an ethnically and racially diverse population. This complex effort qualifies as nationalist less by its roots than by its ambitions. Nationalism claims that there are certain similarities—cultural and otherwise—within a population that should form the basis of its political unity (Calhoun 1993). Sometimes those similarities are more assumed than real. The nationalist effort of the United States has achieved a remarkable degree of success, especially in view of the diverse groups it has had to bring together, but that effort is by no means fully accomplished. It has stumbled repeatedly over its reluctance to include some non-White populations in the peoplehood it imagines and over its insistence that they accept a European heritage as their own. Thus, some nationalisms assert unity even as they seek to create it.

Nationalism and ethnicity are related, then, but they are not the same. What most clearly distinguishes nationalism from ethnicity is its political agenda. Ethnicity may become nationalist, and nationalism typically is based on real or assumed ethnic ties. It is the goal of sovereignty and self-determination that sets nationalism apart.

Conclusion

Ethnicity and race are the main subjects of this book; however, our interest in race is largely, although not entirely, in races as ethnic groups—that is, as self-conscious collective actors in social life and social relations. The reason for this focus is embedded in our own perspective on these topics, which is laid out in detail in Chapter 4. We are concerned generally with the ways that historical events, social relationships, and human action come together to create or construct identities, and with how those identities are reproduced, maintained, and transformed. Our primary concern, in other words, is with transformations in consciousness and with how those transformations occur.

This central preoccupation points us toward ethnicity. Stuart Hall, who has offered some of the most interesting recent scholarly analyses of race and ethnicity, argues that collective identity and experience are not givens but "are constructed historically, culturally, politically—and the concept which refers to this is 'ethnicity.' The term ethnicity acknowledges the place of history, language and culture in the construction of subjectivity and identity" (1992:257). Race, in its colloquial usage at least, implies a naturalness that is difficult to overcome. Ethnicity, on the other hand, conveys both this constructed quality—something made by history and culture and therefore variable and changing—and, in its emphasis on self-consciousness, the participation of groups themselves in the construction, reproduction, and transformation of their own identities. We will be discussing race, but our interest in how groups make themselves, typically in dialogue with how other groups perceive them, places ethnicity at the center of our inquiry.[2]

NOTES

1. There are exceptions to this. For example, some employers in New York City pay significant attention to ethnic differences within the Black population of the United States, distinguishing between West Indian immigrant Blacks and their descendants, on one hand, and American Blacks, on the other. See Gladwell (1996) and Kasinitz (1992).

2. Readers familiar with Michael Omi and Howard Winant's *Racial Formation in the United States* (1994) will have noted that we depart significantly from their conception of ethnicity, which they limit theoretically and empirically to a concern with assimilation and to the experience of the United States. Although we have learned a great deal from their powerful treatment of race, we find their discussion of ethnicity narrow and parochial, leaving out as it does a vast sociological and anthropological literature that considers ethnic phenomena not only in the United States but around the world, pursues very different theoretical agendas including concerns with collective identity and action, and makes no assumption that assimilation is a necessary or even common aspect of ethnic processes.

3

Fixed or Fluid? Alternative Views of Ethnicity and Race

On April 6, 1994, an airplane carrying the president of the small central African country of Rwanda was shot down by unknown persons as it attempted to land at the airport in Kigali, Rwanda's capital. The president, who was a Hutu, a member of the majority ethnic population of the country, died. That night, within hours of the crash, Hutus across the country commenced the systematic killing of members of Rwanda's Tutsi minority. Early reports were sketchy, but over the next few days the extraordinary magnitude of the continuing massacre became clear as news bulletins trickled out. Television film showed tens of thousands of Tutsis fleeing across the Kagera River into Tanzania, mounds of dead bodies—many decapitated—in the streets of Kigali and elsewhere, and the stunned horror in the faces of the survivors. In the 100 days following April 6, half a million people—some estimates say twice that number—"were hacked, shot, clubbed and burned to death" (Keane 1995:29). It was as concentrated a paroxysm of genocidal violence as the world has ever seen.

The massacres of 1994 were not the first time interethnic warfare had ravaged Rwanda. A German colony late in the 19th century and then a Belgian one after World War I, Rwanda had gained its independence in 1961 after 2 years of ethnic violence. In 1959, the Tutsi monarch who had reigned under Belgian governance died, and the Hutu majority rose in rebellion against the dominant Tutsis, killing tens and perhaps hundreds of thousands of them. Belgian support shifted from the Tutsis to the Hutus; following independence a republic replaced the monarchy, with a Hutu as the country's first president. Pogroms and more large-scale killings followed in the 1960s and 1970s as the Hutus consolidated their own domination of the country's institutions, but nothing matched the ferocity or extent of the 1994 slaughter.

That slaughter also may not be the last. The systematic murders slowed in mid-1994 as a Tutsi insurgency, under way since 1990, began to reclaim significant portions of Rwanda from the Hutu-dominated government. In 1995, the Tutsi rebels took over the country, and hundreds of thousands of Hutus fled to refugee camps in neighboring Zaire. The intensity of the conflict declined, although fighting continued in parts of the countryside. Meanwhile, in Burundi, which borders Rwanda to the south and has an almost identical ethnic mix, casualties were rapidly mounting as Hutu rebels fought the largely Tutsi army. By the middle of 1996, more than 150,000 lives had been lost in Burundi (Buckley 1996:16).

Much of the journalistic analysis of the most recent Rwandan calamity focused on deep and long-standing ethnic hatreds between the Hutus and the Tutsis, the country's two major ethnic groups, who respectively made up about 85% and 15% of the country's population. Many saw the massacres as Hutu revenge after generations of subordination to the Tutsis, who despite their smaller numbers had long had the upper hand in political and economic life. Such accounts tended to see the ethnic groups of Rwanda as static and unchanging entities. Scholars tended to agree, focusing on relations between two populations whose identities were long established and rigid and whose relations of dominance and subordination were likewise durable and of long standing (see Maquet 1961 and the discussion in Newbury 1988).

Even some Hutus and Tutsis seemed to hold this view. At mid-century, two stereotypes appeared to dominate both Hutu and Tutsi conceptions. These stereotypes included both physical components—Tutsis were held to be taller, more fine featured, and lighter skinned; the Hutus were considered short, stocky, and dark—and moral qualities. "Tutsi were said to be intelligent . . ., capable of command, refined, courageous, and cruel; Hutu, hardworking, not very clever, extrovert, irascible, unmannerly, obedient" (Maquet 1961:146-47, 164). Furthermore, these qualities were held to be fixed and unchanging. "When asked if a Hutu brought up with Tutsis, and as a Tutsi boy, could not develop the Tutsi qualities, Hutu and Tutsi informants answer that such a training could change the boy to some extent, but not completely; the differences pertain to nature" (Maquet 1961:164). It is not surprising that the language of race became increasingly common in Rwanda. In a discussion with a journalist, one Hutu invoked Tutsi intransigence to justify the slaughter: "The Tutsis don't want to share this country with another race"—that is, with the Hutus (Keane 1995:165).

History, however, finds no such clear divide (see Destexhe 1995; Gourevitch 1995; Newbury 1988). The dominance of Tutsi herdsmen over Hutu cultivators was established by at least the early 19th century and solidified well before the beginning of German colonialism in 1897. Certainly the German and later Belgian support for the dominant Tutsis so-lidified the importance of the boundary between the two groups, but it is not clear how well established these two identities were in common con-sciousness or just what they meant. In fact, the line between the two groups often was fuzzy, and understandably so. The groups occupied much the same territory and were culturally similar, speaking the same language and sharing most customs and traditions. As one observer wrote, "It would be extremely difficult to find any kind of cultural or folkloric custom that was specifically Hutu or Tutsi" (Destexhe 1995:36). Hutus and Tutsis intermarried, although not often. Hutus could become hereditary Tutsis, and vice versa. Although many Rwandans themselves have believed the physical stereotypes in recent decades, some outside observers have found these stereotypes difficult to confirm. As one jour-nalist wrote, "I never saw any evidence in Rwanda or Burundi to support the proposition that Tutsis were lighter skinned than Hutus. Like much else that has been written about the two groups, it appears to be fanciful nonsense" (Keane 1995:15).

Nonsense or not, in 100 days, half a million people died. For the pur-poses of this book, that is just the point: The Rwandan tragedy captures both the power and some of the puzzle of ethnicity. The power seems clear enough in the events themselves, but what is the source of it? Is ethnicity indeed fixed and unchanging, as both Hutus and Tutsis some-times seem to believe? Are contemporary Hutus and Tutsis separate races, rooted in nature, and therefore forever at odds? Or are these two identities, as history seems to suggest, contemporary rigidifications of previously fluid, or at least more malleable, collective conceptions? If so, how did they get that way?

We will return to the Rwandan case at the end of this chapter and offer an answer to the questions raised here about Tutsi and Hutu ethnicities. First, we want to consider the more general issue embedded in the Rwan-dan case. Is ethnicity fixed and unchanging, or is it fluid and contingent?

These two alternatives—the fixed and the fluid—are in fact poles around which much of the sociological debate about ethnicity and race has revolved. Those two poles have carried a number of different names but have come to be known most commonly as the primordialist and the circumstantialist perspectives. In this chapter, we explore their origins, their strengths, and their weaknesses in an effort to come to grips with the puzzle of ethnicity. We begin with what preceded them: a model of interethnic relations that could never have accounted for the extended Rwandan tragedy.

The Assimilationist Assumption

In the latter half of the 19th century and the early part of the 20th, when sociology was just beginning to establish itself as a scholarly discipline, a good deal of social science tended to explain racial and ethnic differences (making little distinction between the two) largely in biological terms. The prevalent social Darwinism of the period saw human behavior as deeply rooted in biology. Accordingly, it conceived ethnic and racial groups as biologically distinct entities and gave to biology the larger part of the responsibility for differences in the cultures and the political and economic fortunes of these groups. Those who prevailed in the struggle for wealth and power and those who spread their cultures across the world did so thanks in large measure to their genetic superiority. Such differences in fortunes, therefore, were viewed as in some sense "natural," a working out of the inherent capacities of groups. Racial and ethnic groups were not alone in this bondage to biology. A good deal of social science, such as it was at the time, tended to see most differences between men and women; most variations in temperament, intelligence, and sexuality; and even differences between classes in such terms as well (see Altschuler 1982; Banton 1977; Gossett 1963; and Stanton 1960). Beginning in the first decades of the 20th century, however, social scientists began a serious and systematic reconsideration of these biological and genetic theories.

The Rise of the Assimilationist Model

One of the key figures in the reconsideration of biological models of ethnicity and race was an anthropologist at Columbia University named Franz Boas. Boas had the temerity to apply scientific research techniques to the supposedly scientific conclusions of the social Darwinists and effectively demolished them. In showing that there was no systematic correlation between the physiological inheritance of individuals and their intelligence or temperament, he poked a very large hole in the idea that differences in the fortunes of racial or ethnic groups could be explained by biology.

There was more to Boas's agenda, however. His own statistical and ethnographic studies of immigrants in the United States, various Native American groups, and others convinced Boas that culture was far more involved than biology in explaining how different peoples behaved and why some did better than others economically (Gossett 1963, chap. 16; Stocking 1968). In effect, Boas cleared the way for a series of social scientific works suggesting that differences between ethnic and racial groups were rooted in culture, not biology, and redefining ethnic and racial relations in terms of cultural contacts.

These reconceptualizations opened up a number of possibilities. Biology was largely static, at least in the short run, but culture was mutable. If ethnic groups were most importantly cultural groups, not biological groups, then they were mutable as well. Both they and their fortunes might change over time. What had been thought of as rooted in biology and therefore permanent was now seen as rooted in culture and therefore changeable.

The ideas derived from work by Boas and his students had an influence not only in anthropology but in sociology as well. They were particularly influential in the emerging Chicago School of sociology, a body of ideas and thematic concerns taking shape in the 1910s and 1920s under Robert Park, W. I. Thomas, and others at the University of Chicago. Among the interests of the Chicago sociologists, and in particular Park, were the massive influxes of immigrants to the United States. What happened to these immigrant populations? What sorts of adjustments did they make to the society they had entered? What happened to the identities they brought with them? How did the larger society adjust to them? Out of these kinds of inquiries, Park developed his famous race relations cycle: the notion that immigrant groups—and, by implication at least, ethnic or racial populations more generally—typically went through a series of phases as they gradually melted into the larger society. These phases were contact, competition and conflict, accommodation, and ultimately assimilation. In this final phase, group members "acquire the memories, sentiments, and attitudes of other persons or groups [in the society], and, by sharing their experience and history, are incorporated with them in a common cultural life" (Park and Burgess 1921:735). The assimilated person "can participate, without encountering prejudice, in the common life, economic and political" (Park 1930:281). The assimilationist model of ethnicity, discussed briefly in Chapter 1, was thus heavily influenced by Park and his colleagues.

There are several key points to be made about these developments. First, they resulted in a view of ethnicity as most fundamentally a cultural phenomenon. Second, against the notion of a biologically rooted ethnic stasis, they posed a socially and culturally rooted ethnic dynamic. Ethnicity, in the new account, was variable and contingent; it could change. Third, they projected a general process of assimilation, a process in which minority identities eventually would disappear. Ethnic and, in the more ambitious versions, even racial groups would be integrated into the majority society's institutions and culture. The world itself would move away from ethnic and racial particularism and toward a universalistic model in which the fortunes of individuals were tied to their merits and to markets (in the liberal democratic vision) or to their place in the system of production (in the socialist one).

This, in highly condensed and summary form, was the model of ethnicity that got into such trouble at mid-century. A series of events made the limits of assimilationism painfully clear.

The Collapse of Assimilationism

As we suggested in Chapter 1, the source of the trouble lay in two major world developments. The first was the postindependence experience of the so-called "new nations," the former European colonies in Asia and Africa, newly granted their freedom in the great retreat of colonialism in the extended aftermath of World War II. Both for the retreating European powers and for the indigenous, educated, elite groups who dominated the first governments in these new nations, a major objective was to build modern states, overlaid on the boundaries that the colonial powers had established. This effort typically found both its inspiration and its political and civil institutions not in indigenous African or Asian models but in European-derived ones, either the liberal democracies of Europe and North America or, in some cases, the socialist models of the Soviet Union and China. These imported institutions, however, often were at odds with the political and civil traditions of the former colonial societies that now tried to put them to work.

Furthermore, the boundaries of the new states were themselves artifacts of the colonial era. As the European powers had taken control of vast territories around the world, in many cases they had combined in single administrative units peoples with very different histories, cultures, and languages. Until the period of European domination, many of those peoples had been completely independent of one another and had no tradition of common political action. When colonialism came to an end, the colonial powers treated these former colonies as new states. Colonialism had created the states they now recognized. As Basil Davidson (1992) argues, writing about Africa, the liberation of these colonies "was not a restoration of Africa to Africa's own history, but the onset of a new period of indirect subjection to the history of Europe" (p. 10). Liberation placed Africans and others in the former colonies in control of states and institutions whose shallow roots remained, in many cases, fundamentally European. "Africa's own history" nevertheless refused to go away.

In case after case, as the grip of colonial power loosened, ethnic, kinship, regional, and religious ties, both old and new, threatened to demolish the fragile social order left in the wake of colonialism.

Ethnicity's power was felt not only in the newly independent states. The second development leading to the collapse of assimilationism was the experience of the more industrial parts of the world. By the 1970s, even nations in the world's most developed regions appeared to be re-fragmenting and "retribalizing" as ethnic and racial identities reasserted themselves. Intergroup conflicts erupted within populations who ostensibly shared elaborate and long-established civic ties. Perhaps no society offered a better example of this trend than the United States, that self-proclaimed melting pot of populations and cultures. The period from the 1960s into the 1990s was punctuated with ethnic and racial claims, counterclaims, and confrontations.

In retrospect, much of this resurgence of ethnicity and race may seem commonsensical. Certainly the claims that ethnic and racial groups around the world have made in recent decades—for land, jobs, restitution, recognition, autonomy, and so on—have often seemed reasonable or at least understandable to many observers. What made these various manifestations of a resurgent ethnicity so puzzling was the expectation of ethnicity's imminent, eventual, or ultimate demise. During these years, long-held assimilationist expectations came up against persistent ethnic realities. Both the nation-building of the Third World and the nation-maintaining of the First World turned out to be frustratingly complex. The contradictions between theory and reality, between expectation and event, could not have been more obvious or more in need of explanation.

The Search for Alternatives

The result of these contradictions was a flurry—occasionally a blizzard—of scholarly activity. Social scientists turned out an assortment of monographs, case studies, analytical concepts, classificatory typologies, and explanatory models trying to piece together the puzzle (or puzzles) of ethnicity. As ethnic and racial groups mobilized across the globe, the amount of social scientific information available about them burgeoned. The range and diversity of the ethnic types, categories, and processes that various analysts of the topic have examined or proposed suggests the explosion of interest.

In 1976, for example, William Yancey, Eugene Ericksen, and Richard Juliani (1976) described the ethnic identities apparently produced or fostered by developing industrial societies as "emergent ethnicity." Herbert

Gans (1979) argued that contemporary third- and fourth-generation European-descent groups in the United States—the contemporary manifestations of the immigrant groups studied by Yancey and colleagues—were carriers of "symbolic ethnicity." Charles Ragin (1977) and others wrote about "reactive ethnicity" as they tried to account for ethnic resurgence in the industrial countries of the world, while Stephen Stern and John Cicala (1991) titled their collection of essays on contemporary ethnic life in the United States "creative ethnicity." Scholars took up the topics of ethnogenesis (Taylor 1979), ethnic competition (Banton 1983; Olzak 1992), ethnic conflict (Horowitz 1985), ethnic mobilization (Nagel and Olzak 1982), ethnic chauvinism (Patterson 1977), the invention of ethnicity (Sollors 1989), and the political construction of ethnicity (Nagel 1986), among other things. Various classification schemes identified ethnic traditionalists, ethnic militants, ethnic manipulators, situational ethnics, pseudo-ethnics, and symbolic ethnics (McKay 1982). In the American context alone, David Colburn and George Pozzetta (1994:142) compiled the following list of ethnic designations that have been used in both popular and scholarly discourse: ethnic revival, reawakening, reassertion, resurgence, revolt, revitalization, renaissance, rediscovery, and backlash; and the new pluralism, the new ethnicity, reactive (or reactionary) ethnicity, ethnic chauvinism, and the invention of ethnicity. We could add many more.

Each of these terms carries a certain set of assumptions and judgments regarding the nature of ethnicity and ethnic relations (Colburn and Pozzetta 1994). Some analysts believe that ethnicity never went away; others argue that contemporary ethnic forms are entirely new. For some, ethnicity is malleable or even negotiable; for others, it is resilient and unchanging. By some accounts, ethnic identities and connections provide a refuge for persons alienated by modern society or struggling with the costs of social inequality; by others, they constitute a resource to be used as a basis of proactive mobilization, linking people together and firing their passions on behalf of a common interest or cause. Some treat ethnicity as a social form with a logic of its own; others, as a social category or set of categories that individuals can use, manipulate, transfigure, or work with according to their own logics and by their own lights. By some accounts, ethnic identities are self-consciously chosen by those who carry them; by others, they are so deeply embedded as to be beyond choice or even consciousness.

From one perspective, material interests drive ethnicity. Ethnic identities are utilitarian: They come to the forefront of social life when there are payoffs attached to them, when people think that they can gain something politically or economically by organizing and acting on ethnic terms. From another perspective, shared cultural practices drive ethnicity. Ethnic identities are not tools for the pursuit of gains but products of the distinctive ways that people live, act, speak, eat, worship, and celebrate. It is our cultural practice, not our agenda, that makes us ethnic. From yet another perspective, what drives ethnicity is the cognitive schemes by which people think about, understand, and negotiate the world around them. Ethnic identities are embedded in the conceptual models of the world and of the self that people learn—from parents, from peers, from experience—and then use to organize their actions and account for what happens to them and to the world at large. However ethnicity may be described or explained, there are those who celebrate it as a haven in a heartless world or as the fountainhead of a human diversity that should be cherished and preserved. To them, it is the key to a better future. There are others who see ethnicity as a threatening and ultimately destructive force whose emphasis on human differences and group entitlements already bears responsibility for a remarkable share of avoidable human tragedy.

This conceptual richness and confusion has drawn on an equally rich and diverse empirical base. As ethnicity and race have captured more and more attention, no part of the world has been ignored. Scholars of ethnicity and race have wandered through a good deal of recent history and around the globe, from Oceania (Linnekin and Poyer 1990) to the states of the former Soviet Union (Khazanov 1995), from Italian and Latino communities in the city of Tampa, Florida, in 1985 (Mormino and Pozzetta 1987) to the German community in the Czech city of Prague a century earlier (Cohen 1981), from the copper mining region of Zambia (Epstein 1978) to Sri Lanka (Tambiah 1986), from Los Angeles and Mississippi (Light and Bonacich 1988; Loewen 1988) to Ecuador (Whitten 1976). It is difficult sometimes to see how all of these concepts, categories, and cases fit together or just what solution they provide to the puzzles of ethnicity and race. In the aggregate, they describe an enormous degree of variation in ethnic and racial phenomena, but do they explain it? They also point to the continuing power of ethnicity and race, but do they account for it?

The Split Response to Assimilationism

The problem has been not so much escaping the assimilationist model— the last major work situated explicitly within the assimilationist tradition was Milton Gordon's *Assimilation in American Life* (1964)—as reaching consensus on what should follow it. The widening gap between assimilationist theory and ethnic reality produced two seemingly contradictory scholarly responses. One, which came to be known as primordialism, suggested that the fundamental, intractable power of ethnicity had derailed the assimilation train. The other response, which came to be known as circumstantialism or instrumentalism, claimed the opposite: that ethnicity's malleability and flexibility were to blame, the fact that it was so easily affected by changes in circumstances and could be used for so many purposes. The first said ethnicity survives because it is fixed, basic to human life, "given" by the facts of birth. The second said it survives because it is fluid, superficial, and changeable, a product of the circumstances of the moment and therefore useful. One said it survives because it is in the blood; the other, because it is in the circumstances or the interests.

Much scholarly discussion has seen these two approaches as mutually exclusive, even diametrically opposed, and in many ways they are, but they also have strengths and weaknesses that are in some ways complementary. In the remainder of this chapter, we explore these two paradigms, investigating what they have to offer to the puzzle of ethnicity and race, and what they leave unanswered.

Primordialism

In 1975, political scientist Harold Isaacs published a book titled *Idols of the Tribe*, which treated ethnic identity as a form of what Isaacs called "basic group identity." This, he wrote, "consists of the ready-made set of endowments and identifications that every individual shares with others from the moment of birth by the chance of the family into which he is born at that given time in that given place" (1975:38). Isaacs was building in part on work by other scholars (Geertz 1963; Shils 1957) that identified such endowments and identifications as "primordial attachments," stemming from "the assumed 'givens'" of social existence. This notion of primordial attachments gave birth to primordialism, the idea that ethnicity is fixed, fundamental, and rooted in the unchangeable circumstances of birth.

Isaacs went on to elaborate eight elements that directly contribute to a person's basic group identity: the physical body (including size, shape, skin color, and so on); a person's name (both individual and family); the history and origins of the group one is born into; one's nationality or other group affiliation; the language one first learns to speak; the religion one is born into; the culture one is born into; and the geography and topography of the place of birth (Isaacs 1975). These elements carry a distinctive power by virtue of their primacy: They happen to us first, and they happen before we have the opportunity or capacity to make meaningful choices. The ethnic identity created by these elements is therefore incomparably resilient and enduring. According to this argument, assimilation came to grief because ethnic ties are far more deeply embedded in the human psyche and in human relationships than we realized.

Isaacs's version of primordialism was the most elaborately worked out in the scholarly literature, but it is also representative in that it asserts the givenness of ethnic and racial identities and acknowledges a common understanding of that givenness in many societies and within many ethnic and racial populations. This colloquial understanding may not involve the same breakdown of elements that Isaacs offers, but it often ends up in much the same place, viewing ethnic attachments and characteristics as basic, enduring, and somehow natural. It is common in many societies, for example, to attribute certain behaviors or attitudes to ethnicity or to race, as if such behaviors or attitudes were acquired somehow at birth or were inevitably produced by membership in the group. If not carried in the genes—"those Mexicans are hot-blooded"—then such stereotypical characteristics at the very least are seen to have deep cultural roots that are difficult to escape, even when one wants to escape them. "See that temper? That's the Irish coming out in him." This fundamentally primordialist conception tends to dominate, often unconsciously, much of the discussion of ethnicity in everyday life. As we will see, it is a crucial factor in interethnic relations and in the formation of ethnic and racial groups. In the meantime, we have to ask whether it makes any sense.

The Weaknesses of Primordialism

The problems with primordialism should be readily apparent. For example, a student of ours, when asked to describe his ethnicity, had the following to say:

> This is a very muddy topic for me. I don't have a pure ethnicity. For
> the record, my mom is German and Irish and my dad is Chinese but was
> raised in Indonesia. Although he is Chinese, every bit of culture (mostly
> food) that he gave me was Indonesian. He taught his kids no language but
> English and tried to raise us like "regular" American kids. Consequently,
> I feel white around whites and Asian around Asians. I suppose I'm a bit
> schizophrenic in the way I try to blend in with everyone. I'm happy about

it though. I like being multi-ethnic. I just hate being asked to bubble in my ethnicity on forms. "Fill in only one bubble please." No can do.

A statement such as this one—by no means unusual in the United States of the 1990s—makes "basic group identity" seem an elusive concept. When this person thinks of himself in ethnic terms, what he ends up with is not one identity but several. If an ethnic identity is primordial and therefore primary or "basic," what are we to think of the person who claims two or three or even more ethnicities? Can all of them be basic at once?

The student we quoted may never think of himself in ethnic terms outside of our asking him, which raises another issue. Isaacs's argument implies that ethnic identity is more "basic" than what Isaacs calls "secondary identities," such as occupational or class identities. For some people, however, ethnic and racial identities may be less compelling and important than other identities. Nothing, for example, has led to more carnage and bloodshed throughout human history than religion. Religious beliefs seem repeatedly to unite human beings, often across ethnic boundaries, in extended conflicts with other human beings who are similarly united. Isaacs includes religion in his list of elements of basic group identity, but what about situations where religion and ethnicity do not perfectly coincide, where ethnic identities cut across religious ones or vice versa? Which one is "basic"? Other bases of identity may also sustain high levels of commitment and inspire dramatic action. Class, for example, has compiled an uneven but still substantial record as a foundation of collective action in the industrial nations of the world. These examples suggest that the primacy of ethnicity is variable, not static. Just why ethnic and racial identities should be more or less compelling in certain situations or for certain persons is an important question, one that we will pursue in subsequent chapters. For the moment, however, the point is that primordialism has difficulty accounting for those persons who attach little importance to their ethnicity.

More important, it is difficult to cope with change and variation from a primordialist point of view. By definition, primordial "givens" are not supposed to change or to vary much within the group. In the primordialist vision, "man is seen as a leopard who cannot change his ethnic spots" (McKay 1982:398). Both ethnic categories and the intensity of an individual's attachment to them, however, clearly vary across situations and over time. Furthermore, many individuals experience identity shifts, sometimes intentionally, over the course of their lives. For example, some Pathan tribespeople of Afghanistan, on joining nearby Baluch tribes, permanently abandon their Pathan identities in favor of Baluchi ones (Barth

1969). Elsewhere, entirely new ethnic groups have emerged in recent years. Is Latino political mobilization—involving Mexican Americans, Puerto Ricans, Cuban Americans, and others—the activation of primordial ties or the mobilization of an identity freshly minted in the United States? Just how primordial, how deeply embedded, or how fundamental and irreducible could such apparently ephemeral or newly discovered attachments be?

The Yorubas of Nigeria are another case in point. Today, Yoruban roots are salient not only in popular consciousness in West Africa; they also are increasingly claimed as the basis of an African diaspora in the Americas. To be Yoruba is to connect to something ancient, to share in group ties with deep, inescapable, and compelling roots, yet there were no Yoruba, in the sense of a distinct, self-consciously Yoruba population, before the early 19th century. In fact, "Yoruba" was a virtually meaningless category until the term was given prominence by European missionaries in Nigeria as an umbrella designation for several groups that shared certain linguistic practices. Over time, the label came to be used not only by missionaries but also by local peoples themselves. Today, Yoruba has become an ethnic label of considerable symbolic and practical power (Peel 1989). A number of other, well-known ethnicities in Africa have generically similar histories. Today's Zulu and Tswana identities, for example, are products of the encounter of certain peoples with colonialism, an experience that marked their passage "from humanity to ethnicity" (Comaroff 1991).

Westerners have invented ethnic and racial identities not only for others but also for themselves, often with far more tragic and devastating consequences. Hitler's concoction of the Aryan master race is the most infamous and horrifying example. A more recent example is the fratricidal collapse of the former Yugoslavia and the devastating warfare over Bosnia. Much of the blame for the conflict among Serbs, Croats, and Muslims has been laid at the feet of centuries-old ethnic identities, rooted in primordial attachments of long duration, that were submerged under the weight of imperial and then communist domination, only to reemerge explosively when the control of these authoritarian regimes was removed (cf. Kaplan 1993). The facts, however, leave one wondering. Historical research suggests that most of the ethnic attachments so viciously pitted against one another in Bosnia were little more than distant memories or ancient myths for many of the people of Yugoslavia before they were rediscovered and reinvigorated by the disempowered intelligentsia that emerged in the wake of the communist downfall (Banac 1984; Woodward 1995).

The point of these cases is that the supposedly elemental "givens" of social life often do not appear to have quite the deeply embedded, enduring, set-in-stone quality that a strict interpretation of primordialist logic seems to require or that common usage often claims. There is simply too much change and variation in ethnicity and race around the world to support the primordialist account. As a result of these and other problems, primordialist views have been the target of sharp and sustained criticism (see, for example, Comaroff 1991; McKay 1982; Thompson 1989).

The Power of Primordial Ties

Although it does not seem helpful in understanding ethnic change and variation, one strength of primordialism is its effort to confront the power of ethnic ties. The primordialist argument was occasioned by the fact that ethnicity had turned out to be far more powerful and compelling than the assimilationist expectation allowed. Primordialism accepted this, insisting that ethnicity is something deeply meaningful and uniquely powerful, irreducible to other social forces or phenomena. What could be the source of this power?

That ethnic attachments often carry a powerful emotional charge and can compel a high degree of commitment from group members is amply demonstrated in the history of ethnic conflicts. Surely numerous factors are at work in such events as the Rwandan genocide, the Jewish Holocaust, or "ethnic cleansing" in Bosnia. Regardless of their complex origins, these events demonstrate the capacity of ethnicity and race to arouse the emotions, sometimes to the point of homicidal fury. Meanwhile, the tenacity with which some ethnic groups cling to their identities despite the economic and political costs of doing so suggests that ethnic roots on occasion go very deep indeed (see, for example, Blu 1980; Wahrhaftig 1978).

The great strength of the primordialist vision is that it zeroes in on this peculiar power (Alexander 1988; McKay 1982). It focuses on the intense, internal aspects of ethnic group solidarity, the subjective "feeling of belonging" that is often associated with racial or ethnic group membership. Clifford Geertz (1963), one of the first scholars to discuss primordial ties, argues that such ties often are seen by those who share them

> to have an ineffable, and at times overpowering, coerciveness in and of themselves. One is bound to one's kinsman, one's neighbor, one's fellow believer, *ipso facto*; as the result not merely of personal affection, practical necessity, common interest or incurred obligation, but at least in great part

by virtue of some unaccountable, absolute import attributed to the tie itself. (p. 109)

These ties, according to Geertz, "seem to flow more from a sense of natural—some would say spiritual—affinity than from social interaction" (p. 110). Given that these ties are experienced by many people as among the most basic elements of human life, it is no small wonder that some people are willing to fight and even die in their defense.

Why, though, are they experienced that way? How do primordialists explain the power and persistence of ethnic ties as opposed to merely describing their substance? To answer this question, we have to turn to the original sources of the primordialist argument, in particular sociologist Edward Shils and anthropologist Clifford Geertz.

Both Shils and Geertz acknowledged the human need for communities of interaction and meaning based on something other than rational, utilitarian interest. Shils (1957) introduced the concept of "primordial" ties as a counterargument against the widespread assumption that in the modern world, small-scale, face-to-face human communities were likely to dissolve or at least lose their relevance to most human beings. One of the reasons assimilationists had been confident that ethnic and racial identities would disappear was their belief in the steady progress of rationality and science. They expected universal values and utilitarian interests to replace local tradition, folkways, and blood ties as the glue holding society together. In their view, the twin revolutions of democracy and industrialism would produce rational, individualized societies in which small-scale, face-to-face communities such as ethnic groups would no longer serve any useful purpose.

Shils disagreed. He invoked a distinction made originally in 1887 by German thinker Ferdinand Toennies between *Gemeinschaft* forms of society or community (small-scale, affective, and intensely solidary) and *Gesellschaft* forms (expedient, individualistic, more rational and voluntary).

> Modern society . . . is no *Gesellschaft*, soulless, egotistical, loveless, faithless, utterly impersonal and lacking any integrative forces other than interest or coercion. It is held together by an infinity of personal attachments, moral obligations in concrete contexts, professional and creative pride, individual ambition, primordial affinities and a civil sense which is low in many, high in some, and moderate in most persons. (Shils 1957:131)

Far from disappearing, the *Gemeinschaft* ties associated with premodern, tribal societies were an important part of what held large-scale, modern societies together.

Shils's thinking was affected in part by his research on the behavior of soldiers during World War II. Shils and other researchers found that combat effectiveness and troop morale in wartime had little to do with soldiers' patriotic zeal, their attachment to the state or its policies, or their belief in some abstract ideology. It was affected far more by the personal attachments among soldiers themselves. These attachments were particularly powerful at the level of the squad or platoon where, over time, small numbers of soldiers shared in an immediate and very personal way the danger, hardship, brief victories, lasting loss, and degrading horror of war (Shils and Janowitz 1948). Shils and his colleagues concluded that even in the most rationally organized settings, such as the military, a great deal of social life still revolved around relationships that were not, strictly speaking, rational. It was not remote individuals and abstract ideas that motivated human beings, thought Shils, but immediate experience and intensely personal relationships. These were more powerful sources of social solidarity, and they were capable of meeting human needs for communion, connection, and meaning (Shils 1957).

Solidarity of this sort could be found wherever shared experience and interdependency tended to build intimate bonds among persons. The leading example of such solidarity was the family. As Shils saw it, attachment to other members of one's kinship group carried a particular power that developed not just through interaction among members. It was a product also of the sense among family members that they shared something unique and compelling. This relationship "could only be described as primordial . . .," a product of the fact that "a certain ineffable significance is attributed to the tie of blood" (Shils 1957:142).

Primordialism and Ethnicity

Shils's main purpose was not to elaborate a primordialist theory of ethnicity. His point was that individual identity and social organization were more dependent than many analysts realized on kinds of ties that he called primordial. It was only a short step from the meaningful attachments that Shils described to those often observed among members of ethnic and racial groups.

A number of students of ethnicity were quick to take that step. For example, although he does not use the term *primordial*, Donald Horowitz's understanding of ethnicity as "a family resemblance" relies on a primordialist conception and on the significance of real or assumed blood ties. Horowitz argues that what makes ethnicity meaningful is the birth connection, or at least the fact that a group accepts someone as if that person had been born into it. "The language of ethnicity," he says, "is the language of kinship" (1985:56-57). Indeed, according to Horowitz, a powerful sense of ethnic identity is difficult to maintain without strong family ties. He argues that this explains the greater prevalence and power of ethnic affiliations in much of Asia and Africa, where family ties tend to be more elaborate, than in the West. Horowitz cites Joshua Fishman on kinship and ethnicity. Kinship, says Fishman, "is the basis of one's felt bond to one's own kind. It is the basis of one's solidarity with them in times of stress. It is the basis of one's right to presume upon them in times of need. It is the basis of one's dependency, sociability and intimacy with them as a matter of course." Ethnicity, says Fishman, "may be the maximal case of societally organized intimacy and kinship experience" (quoted in Horowitz 1985:59-60).

This line of thinking suggests that "primordial" relationships are functionally important. Even in large-scale industrial societies, individuals need relationships that engender feelings of deep and lasting connectedness. Furthermore, these subjective feelings of profound, even inexplicable attachment to the members of a family or a social group are potent bases of collective identity and action (Alexander 1988; Connor 1978).

Ethnic and racial ties often satisfy this need for primordial attachment; however, it is not the actual circumstances of birth that are important. The key is the claim to primordiality that ethnicity typically makes—its presentation of itself in terms of blood ties. Perception and attribution are more important than the presence or absence of a genuine blood connection. Clifford Geertz made this explicit in his discussion of primordial ties. "By a primordial attachment is meant one that stems from the 'givens'—or, more precisely, as culture is inevitably involved in such matters, the assumed 'givens'—of social existence" (1963:109). Such "givens" include kinship connections and common participation in a religious or cultural community. Those who share primordial ties, said Geertz, are linked to each other "in great part by virtue of some unaccountable absolute import attributed to the very tie itself" (p. 109). Thus, both the primordiality of ethnicity and the emotional charge it often carries lie not in the "givens" of social life but in the significance group members attach to them. For example, instead of beginning with blood ties that in turn produce an ethnic identity that therefore has power, we begin with an identity that we claim is rooted in ties of blood and we thereby give it power. As one of the characters in Tennessee Williams's play *Camino Real* (1953/1970) puts it, "the most dangerous word in any human tongue is the word for brother. It's inflammatory" (p. 21).

The criticism of primordialism largely missed this point, reducing the perspective to a claim that ethnic and racial ties really are primordial: given by birth, fixed, unchanging, and ultimately beyond analysis (for example, Eller and Coughlan 1993). It has tended to ignore the grounded conception that Shils and Geertz actually put forward, which found primordialism not in ethnicity and race but in the significance attributed to them. The weaknesses of primordialism are readily apparent, but, despite them, it offers an important key to the puzzle of ethnic power.

Circumstantialism

Primordialists responded to the apparent failure of the assimilationist model by emphasizing the deeply rooted, enduring aspects of ethnic attachments and affiliations. Another, much larger group of social scientists responded with a very different focus. For them, it was not the deep roots of ethnic and racial identities that accounted for their persistence but their practical uses. These in turn were derivative of the circumstances and contexts in which ethnic and racial groups found themselves.

The Utilitarian Logic of Ethnicity and Race

In 1963, Nathan Glazer and Daniel P. Moynihan published *Beyond the Melting Pot,* a study of the ethnic and racial populations of New York City. Glazer and Moynihan challenged the idea, prevalent not only in assimilationist models but more generally in the social sciences, of ethnic groups as primarily cultural groups, held together by shared cultural practices that lay at the core of their identities. Shared culture continued to be important in some cases, they suggested, but the members of ethnic groups were linked as well by ties of interest. The ethnic groups of New York and, they suggested, those in the rest of the United States are also, even primarily, interest groups. Ethnic groups, they said, "are continually recreated by new experiences in America" (1970:17), including experiences that put them in positions in which it makes sense—that is, is in their interest—to organize and act as ethnic groups.

At about the same time, anthropologist Abner Cohen was making a similar argument about ethnic groups in Africa (1969, 1974). Cohen studied urban ethnic groups in Nigeria. "Ethnicity," he wrote, "is fundamentally a political phenomenon. . . . It is a type of informal interest grouping" (1974:97). Interaction between ethnic groups was not likely to lead to the disappearance of ethnicity, said Cohen. On the contrary, ethnicity in the modern world "is the result of intensive struggle between groups over new strategic positions of power . . . : places of employment, taxation, funds for development, education, political positions and so on" (p. 96). Ethnicity was the medium through which various groups organized to pursue their collective interests in competition with one another, interests that were products of the circumstances in which those groups found themselves.

The idea of ethnic groups as interest groups turned out to be a compelling interpretation. Clearly, one reason why the salience of ethnic identities changes is that changing circumstances alter their utility. Any identity is potentially a resource or a handicap; it has potential benefits and potential costs. At the level of individual behavior, for example, the Hutu slaughter of Tutsis in Rwanda in 1994 dramatically raised the potential cost of being Tutsi, but when Tutsis reassumed power in 1995, the costs dropped and the benefits rose. The first set of circumstances encouraged desperate Tutsis to try to pass themselves off as Hutus to survive. Later, the roles were reversed, and some Hutus, fearing Tutsi revenge and unable to escape the country, tried to pass themselves off as Tutsis.

A utilitarian logic is often apparent in group behavior as well. Ethnic ties can be used as the basis of collective political mobilization or of claims to certain resources. This function was at least partly apparent, for example, in the resurgence of ethnic identity among European-descent groups in the 1960s in the United States, which came close on the heels of the Civil Rights Movement. As Black Americans began to challenge the denial of equal rights and equal access to economic and political opportunity, they appeared to those who already enjoyed such privileges—that is, to Whites—as a threat. After all, competition for pieces of the resource pie was bound to heat up if Black Americans were allowed to join on an equal basis. As the Civil Rights and Black Power movements began to break down the barriers that had kept African Americans out of certain jobs, neighborhoods, services, and organizations, one response was a heightened sense of ethnic and racial identification among Whites. They began to mobilize as well, often along the ethnic boundaries that still characterized many urban neighborhoods. As Blacks made their claims, Italian Americans, Irish Americans, Polish Americans, and others made counterclaims. Ethnic identification and mobilization, in other words, seemed to follow the logic of interests (see, for example, Steinberg 1981). This response to the Civil Rights Movement was one of the developments that led Glazer and Moynihan to their own interest-based conception of ethnicity.

During much the same period, government policies such as affirmative action began to redistribute certain social goods by (among other factors) racial or ethnic categories. In response, those with an interest in such redistributions organized along those boundaries. "Ethnic groups emerged so strongly because ethnicity brought people strategic advantages" (Roosens 1989:14).

Things other than government policy or interethnic competition may be at issue in such calculations and transformations. The key might be as simple as a drive to succeed or prosper. In a comparison of ethnic dynamics among Chinese immigrants to the Caribbean countries of Jamaica and Guyana, Orlando Patterson argues persuasively that a marked divergence in patterns of Chinese immigrant adaptation was determined by their divergent socioeconomic interests and opportunities. In Jamaica, a limited set of economic opportunities encouraged Chinese newcomers to concentrate in the retail sector of the Jamaican economy. As they became established and began to expand their economic activities, it was in their interest to consolidate along ethnic lines, exploiting for economic purposes the social and communication networks that ethnic connections made readily available. Being Chinese offered a distinct advantage in the effort to exploit the available economic options. In Guyana, on the other hand, a more diverse set of economic opportunities encouraged a wider dispersion of Chinese immigrants through the economy. Ethnic networks offered no particular advantage to Chinese in Guyana, who were able to succeed individually without such supports. The result was that Chinese identity remained vibrant in Jamaica, while in Guyana it began to fade (Patterson 1975).

In short, by the circumstantialist account, individuals and groups emphasize their own ethnic or racial identities when such identities are in some way advantageous to them. They emphasize the ethnic or racial identities of others when it is advantageous to set those others apart or to establish a boundary between those viewed as eligible for certain goods and those viewed as ineligible. Thus, they might deny persons of a particular race or ethnicity access to jobs or housing or schools. Similarly, they ignore ethnic and racial bonds when circumstances change and other interests, poorly served by an ethnic or racial boundary, come to the fore. Ethnic and racial attachments are not necessarily superficial—"Where ethnic allegiance is in individuals' own best interests, intense feelings will be attached to it" (Patterson 1977:116)—nor are they necessarily easy to mobilize. It is not always simple to figure out which bases of identity and action best serve individual or collective interests or to act effectively on those bases even when their advantages are clear. Both identity and action, however, are mediated, if not determined, by the circumstances and contexts in which individuals and groups find themselves.

This last is an important point, suggesting as it does that ethnic and racial identities are not fixed and unchanging but are instead fluid and contingent, responding to the needs of the situation or the moment. This point also implies that these identities come in different forms, vary greatly in their prominence from situation to situation and from time to time, and may serve a number of different functions. What they have in common is a circumstantially driven utility.

Circumstantialism and Instrumentalism

The centrality of utility in the circumstantialist approach to ethnicity has led many scholars to identify it as *instrumentalism*. Ethnicity and race are viewed as instrumental identities, organized as means to particular ends. We have opted for the more general term *circumstantialism* for two reasons. First, it points to where an analysis of such identities needs to begin: not with interests, which are subjectively determined, but with the circumstances that put groups in particular positions and encourage them to see their interests in particular ways. It embeds identities in changeable social situations instead of in the unchanging attachments that often lie at the heart of primordialism, and it captures the reliance of this approach on social change as the motor that drives the logic of collective identification. In fact, most analysts who work in the "instrumentalist" mode concern themselves much more with circumstances and social change than with processes of interpretation.

Second, the broader term allows us to acknowledge the fact that social change and circumstances sometimes encourage or produce ethnic and racial identities without the intervening mediation of interests. Circumstances may create ethnic and racial groups and identities not through a logic of interests so much as through a logic of social organization. For example, even in the absence of a clear set of economic or political interests, immigrant groups sometimes find themselves concentrated in housing areas or jobs or social institutions. Accordingly, they may come to see themselves as a distinct ethnic or racial population simply by virtue of their circumstances, which tend to sustain daily interactions among them and discourage interactions with others. Ethnic persistence among some European-descent groups in the United States, for example, is a result not only of explicit economic or political interests and calculated strategies but also of the changing circumstances of urban work and life (Yancey et al. 1976). Many immigrant groups entering American cities found themselves residentially and occupationally concentrated. Only certain jobs or residential spaces were open to them. This may have resulted from intentional exclusion, but it also resulted at times from a lack of sufficient skills or connections to obtain other jobs or from the cost of housing and the tendency to settle among friends, family, or fellow language-speakers. Ethnic identities crystallized under conditions that either maintained traditional kinship and friendship networks or sustained new networks that group members then interpreted in ethnic terms. Although these groups may have shared political or economic interests, such interests were not necessary to the development or maintenance of an identity. The circumstances encouraged it on their own, either supporting preexisting identities or fostering new ones.

An important aspect of such circumstances, as we will see in Chapter 6, may be the classification schemes of the receiving society. It typically has its own conceptions of who the newcomers are, employs that conception in its relationships with them, and thereby helps to sustain or change their own sense of who they are. Its conception may be embedded in material interests, but that is hardly necessary. Many such classifications are simply attempts to reduce the complexities of the social world.

Common to circumstantialist approaches, regardless of the degree to which they focus on interests or instrumentality, is the idea that ethnic groups are largely the products of concrete social and historical situations that—for a variety of reasons—heighten or reduce the salience and/or the utility of ethnic and racial identities in the lives of individuals and groups. Sometimes circumstances even create new group ties by placing previously unassociated persons or groups in common situations over extended periods. Interests and utility remain, in most cases, central features of this approach. The important point, however, is that in the circumstantialist view ethnicity and race are dependent variables. They are less independent forces than products of other forces, less creators of circumstances or situations than products of them (Nagata 1981).

Competition and Conflict

In the last 30 or so years, most social scientific studies have turned to circumstantialist perspectives to make sense of ethnic and racial phenomena across the globe. The major analytic project of circumstantialist approaches has been to identify the economic, political, social, and historical circumstances that form or reproduce ethnic or racial groups, crystallize their interests or the relationships within and among them, and launch them into competition or conflict with one another.

In fact, competition and conflict have been at the core of the circumstantialist account from the beginning. The fundamental premise of this approach is that ethnic and racial identities become bases of collective conception and action when distinct populations are thrown into competition with one another for relatively scarce resources, such as jobs, housing, political power, or social status (see, among others, Banton 1983; Bonacich and Modell 1980; Feagin and Feagin 1996; Hannan 1979; Nagel 1995; Olzak 1992; Olzak and Nagel 1986). This focus on intergroup competition has an impressive sociological pedigree, reaching back to the German social theorist Max Weber. Weber long ago observed that it is common for members of one or another group in the society to try to protect access to scarce resources by restricting other people's access to those same resources. He called this process "social closure."

> Usually one group of competitors takes some externally identifiable characteristic of another group of (actual or potential) competitors—race, language, religion, local or social origin, descent, residence, etc.—as a pretext for attempting their exclusion. It does not matter which characteristic is chosen in the individual case: whatever suggests itself most easily is seized upon. Such group action may provoke a corresponding reaction on the part of those against whom it is directed. (1968:342)

Social closure describes a wide array of situations, from the effort members of some professions make to limit competition by setting up elaborate licensing and training requirements to the efforts of Anglo workers in California in the late 19th century to deny jobs to Asian Americans by encouraging legislation limiting Asian immigration and through systematic discrimination in hiring.

Ethnicity and race have been common bases of social closure for one of the same reasons that they are common bases of mobilization: They tend to be visible. Race typically involves more or less readily identifiable physical differences, and ethnicity often has corresponded with cultural differences—patterns of language or accent, modes of dress, behaviors—that make ethnic boundaries easy to establish and observe. Competition thus often leads, via social closure, to an emphasis on ethnic or racial boundaries, and is thereby likely to reinforce and reproduce them.

Early in this century, the Chicago School of sociology also emphasized competition in much of its thinking about intergroup relations. Robert Park, for example, viewed competition as a key process in the organization of society, determining how people are distributed geographically and occupationally. In Park's race relations cycle, global processes such as migration bring previously separate populations into contact with one another, a contact typically followed by competition as those groups struggle for territory or jobs (Park 1926/1950). Park expected competition to "naturally" sort out individuals—not necessarily groups—into their appropriate, individually merited positions, thus rendering ethnic group categories unnecessary and irrelevant. This mixing and sorting process would level the cultural differences between groups. Ethnicity and even race eventually would disappear.

In contrast, more recent analyses have emphasized the ways in which competition and conflict reinforce preexisting ethnic or racial boundaries or even, in some cases, generate them anew. Most focus on the ways that the highly stratified systems of social organization that appear in modern, capitalist societies sustain ethnic or racial boundaries or allow or encourage certain groups to assert ethnic or racial dominance over others. Some of these analyses have become widely used to describe situations of ethnic conflict or competition, or to account for the persistence of ethnic or racial groups.

- *Internal colonialism:* One such approach views some ethnic and racial relations in terms of "internal" colonialism. It draws on perceived parallels between European domination and exploitation of Asian, African, and other colonies, which might be seen as "external" colonialism, and the situations of certain ethnic and racial minorities within some contemporary industrial states. Internal colonialism exists to the extent that a richer, culturally dominant core group subordinates an ethnically or racially identified minority or "periphery" group within the same country. Where apparent or attributed cultural differences coincide with differences in economic development, the two become mutually reinforcing; ethnicity and class are superimposed upon each other. The term *internal colonialism* has been used to describe the situation of Black, Native American, and Latino groups in the United States and of Celtic groups, such as the Welsh, in Britain (Blauner 1969; Hechter 1975). In both cases, ethnic or racial boundaries coincide with economic or class boundaries (see also Barrera 1979; Carmichael and Hamilton 1967; Nairn 1977).

- *Split labor market theory:* Different from internal colonialism but still falling within the circumstantialist concern with conflict and competition is split labor market theory. Whereas internal colonialism sees ethnic and racial boundaries and class boundaries as more or less coincidental, split labor market theory focuses on competition between ethnic and racial groups that are in the same class. For example, employers from a dominant racial or ethnic

group sometimes have the opportunity to replace high-cost workers from their own group with immigrant workers or workers
from subordinate racial or ethnic populations who are willing to
do the same work for less. When they do so, the high-cost, dominant-group workers, fearing job losses or reductions in wages,
have an incentive to protect their privileges by discriminating
against lower-cost, subordinate-group workers. In effect, they engage in social closure, using ethnic or racial boundaries to identify
and act against those within their own class whom they wish to
exclude from the competition for scarce jobs. Split labor market
theory has been used to explain some of the persistence of Black-
White racial conflict in the United States (Bonacich 1976).

■ *Middleman/enclave theory:* Another circumstantialist approach in
which competition and conflict play a significant role is the middleman or enclave model. It focuses on the positions that ethnic
or racial groups, in particular immigrant groups, are able to carve
out for themselves within the larger economy. Entrepreneurs in
such groups often develop dense, concentrated networks of small
businesses. They employ members of their own group and either
serve their own or other minority populations as "middlemen"
traders (Bonacich 1973; Dahya 1974) or compete in the larger
economy, sometimes in business niches to which dominant-group
entrepreneurs are paying little attention (Light and Bonacich
1988; Portes and Bach 1985). For example, Cuban, Jewish, and
some Asian groups in the United States have forged distinct social
spaces for themselves by means of small businesses (such as gar-
dening, small-scale merchandising, and low-budget motel or res-
taurant operations in the latter two cases) and specialized ethnic
economies (such as light industrial manufacturing in the Cuban
case). Ethnic or racial boundaries are reinforced by the particular
and often limited economic opportunities that these groups face
and by the availability within such groups not only of workers
but of preexisting networks of trust that can be turned into entrepreneurial resources.

These competition- and conflict-oriented approaches to intergroup relations indicate many of the most important insights of circumstantialism. First, they show effectively how intergroup conflict and competition
often promote ethnic and racial boundaries, upsetting the assimilationist
process. Clearly, the organization of modern societies can as easily generate

and reinforce such boundaries as dissolve them. Second, they also make clear the importance of power in ethnic and racial processes. It is not simply the distinctive, situationally derived interests of ethnic or racial groups that give prominence to these boundaries. It is also the fact that some groups have the power to make such boundaries effective bases of social stratification and collective action. Third, they typically introduce a class dimension into the analysis of ethnicity. A crucial aspect of the ethnic or racial dynamic in these models is groups' relative positions in the economy, either in the market (in the middleman or enclave conception) or in the process of production (in split labor market theory and internal colonialism). Attention to economic or political position is essential, for example, in understanding the White ethnic (and, fundamentally, racial) resurgence of the late 1960s and early 1970s in the United States. That resurgence was in part a backlash directed against Black assertions of equal rights and equal access to jobs and housing, assertions that threatened the advantages enjoyed by many Whites. By paying explicit attention to the dynamics of inequality and power, circumstantialism has been able to come a lot closer than assimilationism to solving the puzzle of ethnic persistence and variation.

The Limits of Circumstantialism

The competition- and conflict-oriented approaches also indicate limitations in the circumstantialist account. Although the emphasis on power and production affords insight into the forces often driving formation, reproduction, and transformation of ethnicity and race, it also can miss or mistake some aspects of these processes. Split labor market theory, for example, may explain the persistence of racial antagonisms in South Africa or the American South, but it is hard-pressed to account for the resilience of ethnic attachments that appear to be economically and politically disadvantageous—as, for example, among some Native American groups (Cornell 1996; Wahrhaftig 1978). The internal colonialism model may make sense of the persistence of ethnic differences in voting patterns in parts of Britain by attributing them to growing class awareness on the part of exploited groups (Hechter 1975), but it is less able to account for the emergence of separatist identity politics among the relatively affluent French-speakers of Quebec (See 1986; Taylor 1993) or for the mutually destructive pattern of interethnic politics in the former Yugoslavia (Davis 1996). What makes such examples problematic for circumstantialism is that they are forms of ethnicity not based strictly on utilitarian interest or not predicated on a clearly stratified social system.

There is a further problem. The circumstantialist account has difficulty dealing with ethnicity in and of itself. It attributes the resilience of ethnicity to something outside the realm of the ethnic, to some other set of forces, such as economic or political interests. If the forces that precipitate intergroup competition and shape such interests were not busily at work, ethnicity—by circumstantialist reasoning—would indeed disappear, just as the assimilationist model predicts, for there is nothing left to keep it going. Circumstantialism thus suggests that what is wrong with assimilationism is not that it misunderstands ethnicity but that it misunderstands the non-ethnic forces that determine ethnic outcomes. Like assimilationism, it sees ethnicity as hostage to circumstances, but it views circumstances and their effects with a more jaundiced and less optimistic eye. The liberal expectation becomes a liberal lament.

Some scholars have been more self-conscious about these shared assumptions than others. One school of thought, for example, suggests that the modernizing forces expected to dissolve ethnicity were simply less evolved (and ethnic attachments themselves more deeply entrenched) than previous generations of assimilationist scholars realized or could have predicted (see, for example, Steinberg 1981; Thompson 1989). Although they hardly see themselves as assimilationists, these thinkers insist that the mere persistence of ethnic ties does not necessarily invalidate the fundamental assumption of assimilationism (and circumstantialism), that ethnicity is the child of underlying economic, political, and social forces that ultimately determine its fate. Some have gone so far as to deny the significance of ethnicity altogether. Stephen Steinberg (1981), for example, describes ethnicity in the United States as a "myth," redefining it in explicit class or caste terms. Such thinkers conclude, in effect, that their assimilationist predecessors were not so much wrong about the ultimate demise of ethnicity as mistaken about the timing and the dynamics of that demise, and mistaken as well about what assimilation actually looks like. The end result of assimilation is not necessarily harmony and equality. Thanks to forces that have little to do with ethnicity, a group might well share in the common cultural and institutional life of society but, like others who are less well off, still occupy a disadvantaged position.

Most scholars working in the circumstantialist vein have shied away from such bold endorsements of the assimilationist expectation, however, and instead have opted for one of two positions:

- Ethnicity and race are manifestations of other, more fundamental social, political, or economic forces, such as the dynamics of capitalist production relations or colonialism (for example, Gordon, Edwards, and Reich 1982).

- Ethnicity (and, by implication, race) is a form of false consciousness. It is either an idea "imposed" on unwitting populations by opportunistic elites who see ethnic ties as a tool for political mobilization (for example, Stein and Hill 1977), or it is a self-delusion on the part of ethnic group members themselves, who fail to see the real logic of their social positions (for example, Patterson 1977).

In the first vision, ethnicity and race are by-products of other, more basic interests or processes. In the second, they either are conveniences used by elites to energize populations and advance political agendas or are the failed and mystifying results of ordinary people's attempts to understand the world around them. Both approaches tend to see class relationships as basic and ethnicity and race, in contrast, as obfuscations. Neither sees ethnicity and race as fundamental and to some degree independent phenomena, forces in and of themselves. They fail to take ethnicity or race seriously (Omi and Winant 1994), and rather than explaining them, they explain them away.

Trying to account for ethnic and racial dynamics through a search for non-ethnic or non-racial forces that drive those dynamics raises two problems. First, approaches that rely largely on contextual factors for their explanations ignore the sentiments and experiences of many ethnic groups themselves. They allow sociologists either to neglect or to dismiss the understandings and interpretations of ethnic actors, or to interpret them in ways that ignore their impulse and import in the lives of those who identify themselves in ethnic terms. Second, circumstantialist accounts have difficulty answering the question of why it is ethnic attachments—as opposed to other potential bases for collective identity, such as class, occupation, sex, region, or religion—that so often motivate human beings. Why do so many communities appear to favor ethnic identities instead of identities based on the economic and political forces that are supposed to constitute the "real" underlying logic of their situations? In short, the circumstantialist approach has a great deal to offer in understanding ethnic and racial change and the mobilization of ethnic and racial identities. It has less to offer in accounting for the distinctive power that ethnicity and race so often exercise in people's lives and, consequently, in the society as a whole. Our own approach, as subsequent chapters will show, has one leg firmly planted in circumstantialist logic, which we find necessary but insufficient in accounting for ethnicity and race.

Primordialism and Circumstantialism Compared

Figure 3.1 summarizes the circumstantialist and primordialist models of ethnicity. In essence, circumstantialists see ethnicity as fluid and contingent and, therefore, as ultimately ephemeral; primordialists see it as relatively fixed and unchanging. Circumstantialists tend to see ethnicity as either a residual remnant of a premodern era or as the outcome of very modern economic and political processes; primordialists see it as an almost timeless aspect of social life. Primordialists claim ethnic identities to be irreducible and "basic"; circumstantialists see them as manifestations of other forces or label them as false consciousness. And so on.[1]

The continuum suggested in these formulations also provides a way to make genealogical sense of the study of ethnicity. Twentieth-century scholarship on ethnicity has moved back and forth between the two poles represented by the circumstantialist and primordialist perspectives. On one hand are theories and thinkers that have styled ethnic differences as fixed and unchanging; on the other are those that have portrayed them as variable and fluid. Figure 3.2 provides a timeline placing these ideas historically, beginning with the fundamentally biological under-standings of the 19th-century social Darwinists and ending, for the time being, with the circumstantialist arguments that have dominated the field during much of the last few decades.

Conclusion

It may be tempting to respond to the contradictions between primor-dialism and circumstantialism by choosing one or the other as a "truer" account of ethnicity. After all, if an ethnic identity is contingent and thus fluid, how can it also be fixed or primordial? Such a choice is inadequate. Focusing solely on the circumstantial components of ethnicity ignores the personally felt power of many ethnic identities and the socializing process that often produces ethnicities; emphasizing only its primor-dialist aspects neglects the social and historical conditions that generate, maintain, and transform ethnic and racial identities. What, then, are we to do?

FIGURE 3.1

Circumstantial and Primordial Models of Ethnicity

	Circumstantial	*Primordial*
Rationale for group formation	Either utility (access to political power, economic resources, status) or organizational experience (conditions sustain interactions)	Blood, kin, family; cultural connections rooted in circumstances of birth
Orientation of ethnic identities	Toward political, economic, and status interests	Toward local community interests, often not material but ideal
Key explanatory variables or terms	Circumstances, history, structured inequality	Nature, biology, culture, socialization
Nature of the ethnic tie	Instrumental, expedient, convenient—a matter of circumstance and choice	"Given," deeply rooted, not a matter of choice but of circumstantial inheritance
Relationship to history	Product of history, changing, variable	Rooted in history and tradition, stable, permanent
Relationship to circumstance	Product of circumstance	Unaffected by circumstance
Relationship between ethnicity and class	Often serves class interest	Prior to and preemptive of class interests
Role as social scientific variable	Dependent	Independent

We began this chapter with a brief account of genocidal conflict between Hutus and Tutsis in Rwanda. That account raised the question we have arrived at here: Is ethnicity fixed and unchanging, as both Hutus and Tutsis seem to assume, or fluid and contingent, as history seems to suggest? In fact, the Rwandan case is quite clear. As primary bases of organization and action, Hutu and Tutsi identities are relatively recent historical products. Both have very old roots, but until the second half of

FIGURE 3.2

A Genealogical Summary of Scholarly Views of Ethnic Differences to the 1970s

Period	Fixed	Fluid
1880s	Social Darwinism (1880s-1920s) • rooted in biology • Herbert Spencer, early sociologists	
1920s		Assimilationism (1920s-1960s) • rooted in culture, changed via social influence, opportunity • W. I. Thomas, Robert Park, Franz Boas, Milton Gordon (1964), etc.
1950s		Modernization (1950s-1970s) • rooted in "tradition," changed via nation-building • Karl Deutsch, Lucian Pye, etc. (the Western model of development)
1960s	Primordialists (1960s-) Sociocultural view • rooted in socialization, group ties (changes, but slowly via incremental cultural change) • Edward Shils, Clifford Geertz	
1970s	Sociobiological view • rooted in biological circumstances, nature • Harold Isaacs, Pierre van den Berghe, Milton Gordon (1978), etc.	Circumstantialists (c. 1970s-) • rooted in context, history, material interests; changed via rational action • instrumental • Fredrik Barth, Abner Cohen, Orlando Patterson, and many others

the 19th century they organized little of Rwandan life. Sometime around 1860, however, a king named Rwabugiri introduced centralized administrative structures to the region. His reign lasted 35 years, during which the classifications Hutu and Tutsi took on increasing significance. The major feature distinguishing them had to do with political power. Those lineages with lots of cattle and political power became known as Tutsi. Lineages poorer in cattle and political power became known as Hutu. The boundaries of these two classifications were relatively porous, but as state power grew, Tutsi power grew, and movement into the ranks of Tutsis became more difficult.

European colonialism further elaborated and rigidified this boundary. When Germans at the start of the 20th century and Belgians after World War I took control of Rwanda, they gave their own allegiance to the Tutsis. They viewed the Tutsis not only as physically more attractive than Hutus but also as more refined and intelligent, and as having a superior form of social organization. They concluded that, compared with the Hutus, the Tutsis were a superior race. Acting on this conclusion, they implemented policies that supported Tutsi domination of the Hutus, favored Tutsis in schools, and promoted Tutsi economic interests. The Belgians eventually instituted a system of identity cards that listed the ethnic classification of the bearer. The cumulative result was the specification and rigidification of a sharp ethnic boundary. That boundary coincided with a class boundary, but it had typically ethnic and racial assumptions attached to it. To the Europeans, and increasingly to Rwandans as well, Tutsi and Hutu differences were rooted in blood and culture. When, in the mid-20th century, the Belgians shifted their allegiance from the Tutsis to the far more numerous Hutus, it only further emphasized an ethnic divide that had come to organize more and more of Rwandan life and to gain increasing significance in the thinking of Rwanda's peoples. By late in the 20th century, many Tutsis and Hutus had internalized the model elaborated by the colonizers. Not only were there concrete economic and political interests attached to these two identities, but they also had come to carry a powerful emotional charge, asserting the existence of immutable blood ties within each group that compelled ethnic allegiance and support (Destexhe 1995; Newbury 1988). When a Hutu attacked a Tutsi, or vice versa, it was not an individual affair. The ties of blood made it an attack on an entire people. What had been instrumentally created had become emotionally compelling.

The Rwandan case suggests the need for a more complex understanding of ethnicity than either a fixed primordialism or a fluid circumstantialism alone can offer. These two accounts are in many ways mirror images of each other, the strengths of one reflecting the weaknesses of the other. Each contributes insight where the other seems blind, but we need both sets of insights. Ethnicity "is made of neither stone nor putty. . . . The mutability of boundaries does not mean that ethnic affiliations are merely strategic, that they can be called forth whenever it is convenient to do so in the quest for competitive advantage or can be willed into being in the service of economic interest" (Horowitz 1985:66).

What we need is an understanding that fits the Rwandan case—and many others. We need to recognize that ethnicity both is contingent on circumstance and therefore fluid, and is often experienced as primordial and therefore as fixed. In the following chapter, we outline such an understanding.

N O T E

1. For some other comparisons of primordialist and circumstantialist approaches, see Bentley (1987), McKay (1982), Scott (1990), and Yelvington (1991). For one that follows lines somewhat similar to those taken here, see Epstein (1978, esp. pp. 91-112).

4

A Constructionist Approach

In Patrick O'Brian's novel *Master and Commander* (O'Brian 1970/1990:249), Stephen Maturin, an early 19th-century surgeon in the Royal Navy, speaks these lines about his identity: "The identity I am thinking of is something that hovers between a man and the rest of the world: a midpoint between his view of himself and theirs of him—for each, of course, affects the other continually. A reciprocal fluxion, sir. There is nothing absolute about this identity of mine."

Maturin was not speaking about ethnicity or race, but he might have been. Making much the same point, anthropologist Fredrik Barth (1969) long ago argued that both self-ascription and ascription by others are critical factors in the making of ethnic groups and identities. In other words, ethnic groups and identities form in an interaction between assignment—what others say we are—and assertion—who or what we claim to be (Ito-Adler 1980). This interaction is ongoing. It is, indeed, a "reciprocal fluxion," and there is nothing absolute about the process or the end product. Ethnic and racial identities and the groups that carry them change over time as the forces that impinge on them change, and as the claims made by both group members and others change as well.

This is the essence of the constructionist approach that we outline in this chapter. That approach focuses on the ways ethnic and racial identities are built, rebuilt, and sometimes dismantled over time. It places interactions between circumstances and groups at the heart of these processes. It accepts the fundamental validity of circumstantialism while attempting to retain the key insights of primordialism, but it adds to them a large dose of activism: the contribution groups make to creating and shaping their own identities. This constructionist approach also provides the conceptual foundation for the remainder of this book.

The Construction of Ethnic and Racial Identities

In Stephen Maturin's remark on identity, two key statements are especially relevant to ethnicity and race. First, in saying that "there is nothing absolute about this identity of mine," he underlines a point central to the circumstantialist account outlined in Chapter 3: that ethnic and racial identities are changeable, contingent, and diverse. The analysis of ethnicity and race therefore should pay close attention to how their forms and functions vary and how they change over time. For example, we might estimate the role that a given racial or ethnic identity plays in organizing social life in a given situation. We might think of this in terms of the comprehensiveness of an ethnic or racial category. A comprehensive or "thick" ethnic or racial tie is one that organizes a great deal of social life and both individual and collective action. A less comprehensive or "thin" ethnic or racial tie is one that organizes relatively little of social life and action.

At the same time, a second statement in the Maturin remark points to one of the major shortcomings of the circumstantialist approach. Maturin describes his identity as "a reciprocal fluxion." Not only is it continually changing, but change occurs at the intersection of the claims he makes about himself and the claims others make about him. There is a reciprocal relationship at work between these two sets of claims. This reciprocity is missing from circumstantialism, which conceives ethnic and racial identities as largely hostage to external forces and conditions that in effect assign interests and identities to groups. Identities are made in the circumstantialist account, but not by the groups involved. On the contrary, circumstances do the work. Ethnic and racial actors may use their identities instrumentally in pursuit of their goals—this is one of the key points of circumstantialism—but they do little to shape, reinforce, or transform those identities. They simply exploit the identities that situations make available and useful.

These two variables—the comprehensiveness of an identity and the degree to which it is asserted or assigned—offer useful ways to distinguish among identities and to begin to approach the process of identity construction.

The Comprehensiveness of Ethnic and Racial Identities

Ethnic and racial identities vary significantly in the degree to which they organize social life and collective action. In South Africa prior to the

1990s, for example, race was a remarkably comprehensive aspect of social life. It was the organizing principle at the heart of most South African institutions—political, economic, and social. If you were a South African, it determined whom you could marry, where you lived, how you were treated by the police, what your employment opportunities were, how much political power you had, and a great deal more. In short, racial identity was extraordinarily "thick": It dominated layer after layer of social organization with a comprehensiveness and power unmatched by any other dimension of individual or collective identity. Since 1994, however, the new, multiracial South African government has made a conscious effort to "thin" the role of race, to reduce the part it plays in organizing South African society.

For contemporary Italian Americans, ethnic identity is a much less comprehensive organizer of social life. They may celebrate their ethnicity and express it in various ways, but their identity and status as Italian Americans organize much less of what they do and experience than racial identity does for South Africans. Ethnicity, for Italian Americans today, is a relatively "thin" identity. It does not lack significance; indeed, Italian Americans may attach great importance to it. Other dimensions of social life, however—perhaps race or class or gender or occupation or religion—tend to be more powerful shapers of daily life and experience and to play a larger role in what Italian Americans think and do.

This was not always the case. At an earlier time in the history of Italian Americans, soon after their arrival in the United States, ethnic identity was much thicker, playing a much more comprehensive role in their lives. This is one of the ways that identities often change: Over time, they become more or less prominent as organizers of social life and action.

This pattern of change is illustrated graphically in Figure 4.1, which offers a stylized version of Italian American ethnicity at two different points in their history. In both of the diagrams in Figure 4.1, the vertical axis refers to the comprehensiveness of the ethnicity, the degree to which ethnic identity organizes daily life and social relationships among Italian Americans. The higher one goes on the vertical axis, the thicker the ethnicity. The horizontal axis in each diagram represents the population of Italian Americans, divided into percentages, from 0 to 100. Time 1 is early in the history of Italian immigration to the United States, when most Italian Americans are either first-generation migrants or their children. The Time 1 diagram indicates that at this point in their history, ethnicity is very thick for a high proportion of Italian Americans; it organizes a great deal of their life and action and is central to their self-concepts. Only a

FIGURE 4.1

Historical Change in the Comprehensiveness of Italian American Ethnicity (approximate)

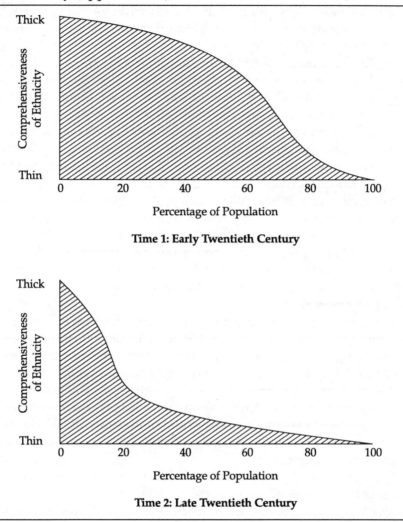

Time 1: Early Twentieth Century

Time 2: Late Twentieth Century

small proportion of the Italian American population—perhaps those who have been in the United States the longest, or those who came as individuals instead of as families, have settled some distance from other Italian Americans, and have tried to mix quickly with the mainstream of U.S. society—experience Italian American ethnicity as thin.

Time 2 is the present. Few first-generation Italian immigrants remain. Most Italian Americans are now of the third or fourth generation in the United States. Many have married non-Italian Americans; many are the children of these marriages. Few speak Italian. Decreasing numbers live in neighborhoods that are heavily Italian American. Most have become part of the economic, political, and cultural mainstream of U.S. society. As the Time 2 diagram shows, their ethnicity has thinned. At Time 2, far fewer Italian Americans experience their ethnic identity as thick. Most may still identify as Italian Americans and may do so proudly, but in fact that identity organizes little of their daily lives. For most of them, it has become the stuff of holidays and stories and old photographs (Alba 1985). To paraphrase Anny Bakalian (1993) on Armenian Americans, whose argument we reviewed briefly in Chapter 1, they have gone from being to feeling Italian.

Not only does this diagrammatic example illustrate historical change in the comprehensiveness of ethnicity or race, but it also suggests that substantial diversity may exist within a single ethnic population. Some portion of that population may experience their ethnicity as very thick while others experience it as rather thin, producing very different manifestations of a supposedly singular ethnicity. Furthermore, these portions may change over time.

The change in Figure 4.1 reflects the assimilation that Italian Americans have experienced in the United States. Not all historical patterns of ethnic change look this way. Assimilation is by no means a necessary or even probable outcome of intergroup relations. Had Italian Americans, for whatever reason, been victims of systematic and sustained discrimination or violence, or had they set out to isolate themselves from the mainstream and preserve distinctive cultural practices and a more powerful collective sense of self, the change in their ethnicity might have been nowhere near as substantial.

In some cases, change might even occur in the other direction, with ethnicity becoming not less but more important as an organizer of daily life. Native Americans offer a U.S. example. As we will see in Chapter 5, at the time Europeans arrived in the United States, the indigenous peoples of North America carried no single, all-encompassing identity. That did not prevent Europeans from viewing them as a distinct race. Over time, however, an awareness of the boundary between themselves and Europeans spread among Native Americans. Eventually, an American Indian or Native American identity became something more than a European perception. It not only organized European and later U.S. policy toward Indians but also became a significant part of Indians' own self-concepts and a basis of indigenous collective action. This pattern of change is the opposite of the Italian American pattern.

Figure 4.2 provides a stylized illustration of the pattern of change in the ethnic identities of the Hutus and Tutsis of Rwanda, whose story we told in Chapter 3. This also moves in the opposite direction from the Italian American one. At Time 1, in the middle of the 19th century, Hutu and Tutsi identities had relatively little influence on the social lives and self-concepts of Hutus and Tutsis. Kinship and residential bonds were much more significant. By Time 2, late in the 20th century, certain changes—the centralization of Rwandan society under Rwabugiri, the rigidification of ethnic boundaries under the German and Belgian colonizers, and the more recent history of ethnic conflict—had made these identities very thick indeed. They had become matters of life and death for huge portions of the Rwandan population.

Why is an ethnic or racial identity thick in one context and thin in another? What drives the change? Circumstantialism is helpful in answering these questions. Its focus on social change; on groups' economic, political, and social positions; and on the interests derivative of these positions tells us a lot about how the comprehensiveness of ethnic and racial identities changes. The constructionist view of ethnicity and race not only shares circumstantialism's basic idea of fluidity—the idea that identities change in their nature and significance across time and situations—but builds on circumstantialism's attempt to identify the specific factors that drive that change. Part of the meaning of "construction" is that ethnic and racial identities are not rooted in nature but are situational precipitates, products of particular events, relationships, and processes that are themselves subject to change.

Assignment and Assertion

Circumstances, however, are not the only factors at work here. As Maturin's remark about his own identity suggests, groups themselves are involved in the dynamics of ethnicity and race. The Maturin statement highlights the importance of self-ascription. Ethnicity and race are not simply labels forced upon people; they are also identities that people accept, resist, choose, specify, invent, redefine, reject, actively defend, and so forth. They involve an active "we" as well as a "they." They involve not only circumstances but active responses to circumstances by individuals and groups, guided by their own preconceptions, dispositions, and agendas.

In recent years, a growing group of scholars influenced by circumstantialism but eager to move beyond its limitations has begun to emphasize

FIGURE 4.2

Historical Change in the Comprehensiveness of Hutu and Tutsi Ethnicities (approximate)

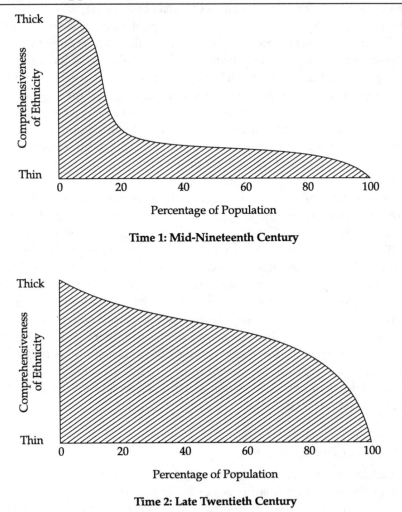

Time 1: Mid-Nineteenth Century

Time 2: Late Twentieth Century

the responses that ethnic and racial groups make to the circumstances they face (for example, Conzen, Gerber, Morawska, Pozzetta, and Vecoli 1992; Espiritu 1992; Leonard 1992; Nagel 1994, 1996; Sollors 1989; Tonkin, McDonald, and Chapman 1989; Waters 1990). These works focus much of their attention on the ways that ethnic groups construct their own identities, shaping and reshaping them and the boundaries that enclose them. Ethnic and racial groups, in this account, may be influenced by circumstantial factors, including the claims that others make about them, but they also use the raw materials of history, cultural practice, and pre-existing identities to fashion their own distinctive notions of who they are.

Joane Nagel's study (1996) of the resurgence of American Indian identity and culture since the 1960s is a good example of this approach. Nagel begins from the assumption that Native American ethnic renewal was made possible both by broad trends in American culture and by changes in federal Indian policy. The success of the Civil Rights Movement made ethnicity both more valuable as a basis of organization and more valued by the society at large. At the same time, the federal government extended to Native Americans an increased degree of autonomy and self-governance. These circumstantial changes on their own would not have produced the particular resurgence in American Indian ethnicity that came in the last few decades. That resurgence, according to Nagel, can be fully explained only by looking at how Indians themselves acted as they took advantage of these broad, situational transformations. Through a number of both tribal and supratribal activities—ranging from individual decisions to follow traditional spiritual practices, to the holding of tribal and intertribal gatherings called powwows, to the organization of political lobbies, to the establishment of systems of tribal governance based on principles of self-determination—Native Americans asserted their own emergent understandings of themselves. In the process, they revitalized both community and culture. The resultant identities were not only products of circumstances; they also were distinctive Indian creations (see also Cornell 1988).

Ethnic communities participate in their own construction and reproduction in many different ways. They may establish organizations, such as the National Indian Youth Council in the 1960s or the American Indian Movement in the 1970s in the United States. They may promote research into ethnic history and culture, as in the endowment of Jewish Studies programs at American universities in the early part of this century or more recently in the development of Asian American research institutes. They may retell official histories in new ways that recognize and celebrate the ethnic group and redefine its past and its relationship to others, as ethnic Georgians did for two or three generations under Soviet rule. They may reestablish defunct cultural practices or invent new ones, as in the revival of the Gaelic language in Ireland or the invention of the African American Kwanzaa holiday. In all these ways and dozens more, ethnic groups play a creative role in shaping their own identities. These are not idle activities. They variously elaborate, reinforce, glorify, specify, or otherwise add to the identity that group members share. They may even affect its thickness. A flurry of such activities may push that identity to the forefront of group members' consciousness. It may encourage them to act in terms of that identity and on its behalf, thereby making it a more comprehensive aspect of their lives.

This creative role lies at the heart of a constructionist approach to ethnicity, but it is not the whole story. The process of construction is an interactive one. Identities are made, but by an interaction between circumstantial or human assignment on one hand and assertion on the other. Construction involves both the passive experience of being "made" by external forces, including not only material circumstances but the claims that other persons or groups make about the group in question, and the active process by which the group "makes" itself. The world around us may "tell" us we are racially distinct, or our experience at the hands of circumstances may "tell" us that we constitute a group, but our identity is also a product of the claims we make. These claims may build on the messages we receive from the world around us or may depart from them, rejecting them, adding to them, or refining them.

This interaction is continuous, and it involves all those processes through which identities are made and remade, from the initial formation of a collective identity through its maintenance, reproduction, transformation, and even repudiation over time. Construction refers not to a one-time event but to an ongoing project. Ethnic identities are constructed, but they are never finished.

It should be clear, then, that the constructionist account does not depart from circumstantialist claims about the fluidity and dynamism of ethnicity and race, nor from its claims about the critical role that circumstances play in collective identification and action. It adds to those claims a creative component, rescuing ethnicity from the prison of circumstance.

This interaction between external and internal forces is not everywhere the same. Circumstances sometimes play a larger or a smaller role. Until the last half decade or so, South African Blacks found themselves caught in a system in which both material circumstances and the claims that South African Whites made about them severely constrained their freedom to build their own identities. They had to struggle to assert and maintain an independent sense of who they were against both the apparent hopelessness of their oppression and the dominant group's power to promote its own ideas of Black racial inferiority through education, the media, and public expression. Some Black political activists in South Africa thought in just these terms, urging their own people to reject the group definitions of the South African regime and to assert their own radically different self-concepts (Gerhart 1978). Native Americans, on the other hand, by the 1970s faced a much less constraining set of circumstances, which allowed them significantly greater leeway in asserting their own conceptions of themselves and in helping them to alter the larger society's conceptions of them.

Boundary, Perceived Position, and Meaning

Whether assignment or assertion dominates the process of identity construction, three primary things are at issue: the boundary that separates group members from nonmembers, the perceived position of the group within the society, and the meaning attached to the identity.

- *Boundary:* Identity construction involves the establishment of a set of criteria for distinguishing between group members and nonmembers. These criteria might include skin color, ancestry, place of origin, a cultural practice, or something else—or a lot of things at once. The point is not the specific criteria used as boundary markers but the categorical boundary they signify—the line between "us" and "them."

- *Perceived position:* Identities emerge in the midst of social relations. Part of identity construction involves situating the group in the context of those relations, specifying its position in a set of relationships and statuses. This may be as simple a matter as establishing that there is a boundary between "us" and "them," the assertion that "we're different." It also often involves specifying the group's relationship to a larger whole or its position in a stratification system, in a distribution of power, status, or other resources. For example, part of Mexican Americans' ethnic identity is the fact that they are Americans. For many of them, part of it also is the fact that they are poor Americans. This perceived relationship to others is part of a group's identity.

- *Meaning:* Identity construction involves the assertion or assignment of meaning. Such meaning may take as simple a form as "we (or they) are good (or evil)" or "we (or they) are inherently superior (or inferior)." It may be far more complex, producing pride or exaltation or dismay or shame. For example, the hypothetical statement that "we are the people who survived a century of oppression but never lost our courage or our belief in ourselves" makes an assertion about the meaning of a particular "we." The

statement that "those people cannot be trusted and are incapable
of governing themselves" assigns a meaning to a particular "they."

Change in boundary, perceived position, or meaning can occur as a result
either of new assertions by the group in question or of new messages
from the environment of other groups and circumstances. Change in
any one of these variously maintains, alters, reinforces, undermines, or
otherwise affects the identity of the group. In short, it reconstructs that
identity.

Identity construction typically involves both assigned and asserted
versions of one or more of these three aspects of identity. The extent to
which assignment or assertion prevails in identity construction generally
depends on the ability of the group to promote among members and in
the larger society an indigenous conception of boundary, position, or
meaning. Where substantial power lies in the hands of outsiders, or where
circumstances have compelling effects on member understandings and
interpretations, the identity is likely to be more a product of assignment
than of assertion. Where outsiders' power is relatively less, circumstances
are ambiguous, or the group has the ability to promote its own conceptions, the identity will be more a product of assertion than of assignment.
Few ethnic or racial identities are entirely the product of one or the other.
Most are products of interactions between the two.

Diversity in Ethnic and Racial Identities

We have made two distinctions so far: one between "thick" or more comprehensive and "thin" or less comprehensive identities, and one between
more assigned and more asserted identities. If we combine these, we
have two axes of variation in ethnic and racial identities. One traces the
degree to which an ethnic or racial identity organizes the social life of the
group, and the other traces the relative importance of external and internal forces in the making and maintaining of that identity.

These two axes are presented graphically in Figure 4.3. We can place
ethnic or racial identities at different points in the four quadrants described by the two crossed axes. For example:

- *Assigned and "thick"*: For a long time, Black South African identity
  was somewhere in the upper left quadrant. South African Blacks
  were carriers of a racial identity assigned to them by dominant
  Whites. That identity organized virtually every aspect of daily life
  and action, and much of what Black South Africans did either reflected it or responded to it.

FIGURE 4.3

Two Axes of Variation in Ethnic or Racial Identity

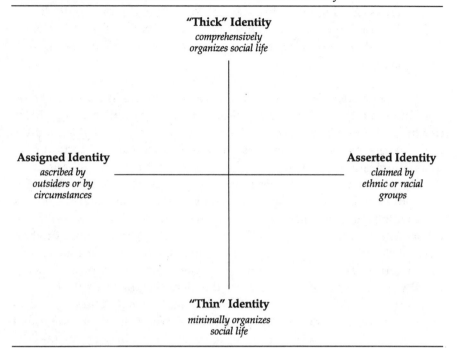

"Thick" Identity
comprehensively
organizes social life

Assigned Identity
ascribed by
outsiders or by
circumstances

Asserted Identity
claimed by
ethnic or racial
groups

"Thin" Identity
minimally organizes
social life

- *Assigned and "thin":* Recent Vietnamese and Cambodian immigrants to the United States carry an Asian American identity that can be found in the lower left quadrant. They are assigned that identity by U.S. society, which often pays little attention to the differences among Asian groups. They still organize much of their own lives in terms of their identity as Vietnamese or Cambodians. Many of those who have come in the last few years still carry cultural practices from their societies of origin, speak their own languages, and live in relatively homogeneous immigrant communities.

- *Asserted and "thick":* One of the White ethnic groups in South Africa is the Afrikaners, to whom we will pay substantial attention in Chapter 5. Their identity can be placed in the upper right quadrant. Both the boundary and the meaning of that identity are fiercely asserted by Afrikaners; it is a crucial part of their self-concept; and it organizes much of their life and action.

- *Asserted and "thin":* Italian American identity began somewhere in the upper left quadrant—it was the receiving society of the

United States that insisted on the "Italian" designation—but over time it has moved toward the lower right. Today, it is increasingly an asserted identity, but it organizes less and less of daily life as Italian Americans have intermarried, moved out of ethnic communities, and entered the mainstream of American society and culture.

We should note three important aspects of the classificatory scheme presented in Figure 4.3. First, individuals who carry more than one identity might be represented in more than one quadrant at the same time. For example, as Asian Americans, these recent Vietnamese and Cambodian immigrants carry a largely assigned and (for them at least) relatively thin identity, but as Vietnamese, they carry a largely asserted and relatively thick one. Similarly, the children of interethnic or interracial marriages might find themselves assigned one identity while they assert another. Alternatively, they may claim both but organize most of their lives—friendships, relationships with parents, cultural interests, and so on—in terms of only one. This four-part scheme, in other words, does not classify groups or persons but rather the identities they carry.

Second, we might find various members of a single ethnic group in more than one quadrant. Although the Asian American identity of recent Vietnamese and Cambodian immigrants to the United States may be largely assigned and thin, there are other Asian Americans—including some Vietnamese and Cambodians, perhaps from earlier migrations—for whom that identity is increasingly asserted and considerably thicker. As time goes on, Asian American identity becomes increasingly important in their self-concepts and organizes more aspects of their lives (Espiritu 1992). For still other Asian Americans, that identity may fall elsewhere along these axes. Similarly, for some Kurds in Turkey and Iraq, Kurdish identity is claimed but thin; it is proudly held but organizes relatively little of daily life, which is lived much as non-Kurdish citizens of those countries live. For others, in particular those involved in the furious insurgency directed at establishing an independent Kurdistan, Kurdish identity is both proudly held and comprehensively experienced; it forms the foundation of individual and collective action and inspires extraordinary sacrifice, often to the point of death. For still others, Kurdish identity may be largely assigned: They are identified by others as Kurds, but they seek to live outside that identity, organizing their lives largely in terms of other interpersonal bonds and identities (McDowall 1996). Much the same is true for an assortment of other groups (see, for example, Albers and James 1986; Cornell 1996; Esman 1983).

This diversity of identities within a single ethnic group is important, for ethnicity is not the only identity, nor even necessarily the major identity, that people carry. Some may take little note of ethnicity or even race, whether their own or others'. Gender, religion, class, occupation, cultural group—these and other dimensions of social life likewise offer bases of personal and collective identification and are often powerful. Part of the analytical task is to understand when and why ethnic or racial identities become most prominent and powerful in social life and in the lives of groups.

The third point about Figure 4.3 is simply the possibility of change. As the Italian American, Asian American, and Rwandan cases that we have discussed all illustrate, the "reciprocal fluxion" that Stephen Maturin spoke of may produce movement and change along either or both of these axes, with an identity starting in one quadrant and moving eventually to another.

The constructionist approach, then, sees ethnic and racial identities as highly variable and contingent products of an ongoing interaction between, on one hand, the circumstances groups encounter—including the conceptions and actions of outsiders—and, on the other, the actions and conceptions of group members—of insiders. It makes ethnic groups active agents in the making and remaking of their own identities, and it views construction not as a one-time event but as continuous and historical. The construction of ethnic identity has no end point unless it is the disappearance of the identity altogether.

The Nature of Ethnic and Racial Bonds

We have considered the comprehensiveness of ethnic and racial identities and the relative influence of internal and external factors on the identity construction process. We have paid little attention thus far, however, to the nature of the bonds that hold group members together. We turn to those now.

Interests, Institutions, and Culture

At a minimal level, an ethnic or racial group is simply a self-conscious ethnic or racial category. Members know a boundary exists and see themselves as occupying one side of that boundary. In this minimalist case, they attach no particular significance to the attendant identity. Such awareness alone has little power to shape action; it is simply another feature of the cognitive landscape. Identities have little influence on group members' actions until they involve more than simply the consciousness among members that they constitute a group. Although the bonds of awareness alone are weak, there are other bonds that may link group members to one another and create a more substantial and potent solidarity. Three such bonds are particularly important: shared interests, shared institutions, and shared culture (Cornell 1996; see also Spickard 1996).

- *Shared interests:* Some ethnic and racial identities are rooted largely in shared political, economic, or status interests. In many cases, what makes ethnicity important to group members is the interests that it serves, whether the pursuit of jobs, resistance to public policies that are seen as damaging, the protection of rights and privileges from the claims of other groups, or something else. To say that these identities are rooted in shared interests means that group members see themselves with common issues at stake and that this perception is fundamental to group identity and solidarity. Many ethnic identities originate just this way. For example, Chinese, Japanese, Vietnamese, and other Asian immigrant groups in the United States realized that they had certain political interests in common. That realization was a key factor in the emergence of an Asian American identity (Espiritu 1992; Vo 1995).

- *Shared institutions:* Groups whose members have common interests often organize in various ways to pursue those interests. They create more or less exclusive institutions: sets of social relations organized specifically to solve the problems group members face or to achieve their objectives. Such institutions may include everything from extended families to credit associations to educational systems to political parties. Group members are bound together in part by their dependence on and common participation in these institutions. Thus, for example, it is in part a set of Native American social service institutions in the city of Los Angeles that binds to one another the members of the Indian population there, who come from perhaps a hundred different Indian nations throughout the country. Those institutions not only help group members solve life problems but also embed their Indian identity in organized sets of social relations (Weibel-Orlando 1991).

- *Shared culture:* Group members may also be bound to one another by their participation in a common culture. By this we refer to a set of more or less shared understandings and interpretations that include ideas about what is important and what is real as well as strategic and stylistic guides to action. Such ideas and guides may be embedded in myths and stories, expressed openly in ritual activity, communicated implicitly in extended processes of socialization, learned through shared experience, or sustained in other ways. They may not only provide conceptual interpretations of the world at large and guides to action in that world, but also specify and exalt the identity of the group. What links group members to one another in such cases is the perception that to a large degree they think alike, or at least view aspects of their own lives and certain critical features of the world similarly.

> What do an Israeli farmer, a New York journalist, and a London businessman have in common? Nothing at all in terms of interests or institutions. Yet once a year they all say the same words at a Passover seder, and that ritual act—that piece of culture—binds them strongly together. Because they share culture, they all see themselves as Jews. (Spickard 1996:5)

Each of these—interests, institutions, and culture—offers a different potential basis of group attachments. Their potency varies. Interests are the least dependable of the three, being most dependent on outside factors. Bonds of interest may be strong, but they are also fickle. Conditions change, and suddenly the shared interests that bound people together are not there anymore. Institutions tend to be a somewhat stronger foundation of group identity because they embed that identity in sets of social relations over which the group exercises some control. Their strength comes also from the fact that they not only offer a reason to act but also facilitate action. Culture tends to be stronger still because, at its most elaborate, it involves a conceptual scheme for making sense of the world. It is one thing to take up a new set of interests or to turn to different institutions to solve life's problems, but it is quite another to turn your back on an interpretive scheme on which you have come to depend for an understanding of the world around you and your place within it. Thus, the bonds of interest tend to be more volatile than institutional bonds, and more volatile still than more elaborate cultural ones.

These bonds are illustrated graphically in Figure 4.4, using four hypothetical groups. The relative salience of each kind of bond varies across groups. Identity and solidarity in Group 1, for example, are based largely on bonds of shared interests. The group has not developed significant institutional mechanisms for pursuing those interests, nor are members

FIGURE 4.4

The Relative Salience of Intragroup Bonds in the Identities of Four Hypothetical Groups

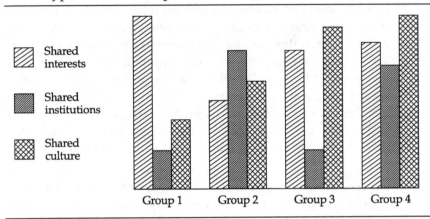

linked to one another culturally by much more than their interpretation of their own position and the interests derivative of that position. Group 2 may have built institutions on which it continues to depend, even as the interests that motivated the building of those institutions attenuate. In the meanwhile, we might hypothesize that common participation in those institutions is beginning to produce a set of shared understandings; the salience of shared culture in the collective identity of group members is rising. In Group 3, both shared interests and shared culture are salient in sustaining the group's identity, but the group is using institutions built by others—perhaps those of the larger society of which the group is a part—to pursue its objectives. In Group 4, all three kinds of intragroup bonds are playing significant roles in collective identity. Not only interests link group members to one another. Members also participate in exclusively shared institutions and share an elaborate set of cultural understandings, symbols, and traditions.

In other words, these different types of bonds are by no means mutually exclusive. Furthermore, they are almost certain to change in salience over time. Indeed, a single identity might fit several of these hypothesized patterns at different times in its history. Generally speaking, although cultural bonds tend to be more powerful than the bonds of shared interests or institutions, solidarity increases as these various kinds of bonds are combined. In Figure 4.4, for example, Group 4 is likely to be substantially more solid than any of the other three. Its ethnic identity has multiple roots, as does its tendency to act in terms of that identity, and those roots have a high degree of salience in the life of the group. This also means that its ethnic identity is significantly more comprehensive—thicker—than are the identities of the other groups shown.

Thus, the constructionist approach to ethnicity and race focuses not only on the factors promoting ethnic and racial identities but also on the kinds of bonds those factors create. Identity construction involves, among other things, the establishment and elaboration of very different links among persons.

Constructed Primordiality

We have paid substantial attention in this chapter to the contributions of circumstantialism, incorporating them into a constructionist approach. But what of primordialism? Where does it fit in?

When groups and circumstances construct ethnicity, what they construct is an identity that typically claims for itself primordial moorings—an anchor in blood ties or common origins—no matter how thick or thin it may be in the practice of daily life or in social organization. Even the thinnest ethnicities tend to be rooted in the kinship metaphor, expressed through reference to common ancestry or origin. They may organize little of life, but they typically retain some of the significance commonly attached to blood ties. This is a crucial source of ethnic power.

Ethnicity and race then emerge as what we might call constructed primordialities (see Appadurai 1990; Griswold 1994:108). An essential aspect of these identities is the fact that, whatever their actual origins, they are experienced by many people as touching something deeper and more profound than labels or interests or contingency. This felt power of ethnic ties seems to be rooted in intimately shared experiences and interactions, in the sense of connection to the past that ethnicity implies, and in the quasi-mystical significance often attributed to blood ties. In the eyes of many group members, this distinctive set of roots lifts ethnicity above other identities as a defining feature of human communities and as a potential basis of action. "Peoplehood," "common origin," and "blood ties," whether asserted or assigned, form in most cultures a uniquely powerful set of interpersonal bonds, but their power is not inherent. It lies in the significance human beings attach to them, a significance that is variable and contingent and altogether a human creation.

We recognize that the understanding of ethnicity we have just outlined presents a potential problem. As a student of ours once put it:

So I know in my head that my ethnic identity is a product of history, of circumstances. But it doesn't feel that way. It feels much stronger than that. To me, it seems beyond circumstances or even the choices that I make. It just *is*. It's part of me and always will be part of me. It feels as if I really don't have any choice in the matter.

Indeed, "constructed primordiality" seems to be a contradiction in terms. How can something primordial at the same time be a construction? And how can the idea a group develops about itself or that other people develop about it—a work, in part at least, of the imagination—arouse such feelings and carry such power?

The power of ideas should hardly be astonishing. At the extremes, plenty of people in human history have accepted physical agony or even death—or have visited both on others—in the name of one or another idea. What often puzzles those students of ethnicity who also carry profoundly felt ethnic or racial identities is the apparent disjuncture between abstract sociological arguments and their own daily experiences, sentiments, and self-concepts. On one hand are the readily demonstrable facts that ethnicities come and go, they vary across space and time, and the forces that drive this variation and change are linked to historical events and to patterns of power and opportunity. On the other hand are the equally real and often more immediately experienced sentiments frequently attached to ethnic identities: the sense of ethnicity's deep and abiding character, of a consciousness that defies choice or change.

This paradoxical situation has parallels with the theoretical divide between circumstantialist and primordialist approaches. The circumstantialist approach often appeals to the mind, and the primordialist perspective captures the heart. The challenge, however, both for theory and for the interpretation of daily experience, is to reconcile these two approaches, finding a way to link the ethnic heart and the social scientific mind.

Our constructionist approach is partly an attempt to answer this challenge. Seeing ethnicity and race as constructed primordialities provides a way both to bring ethnic groups as actors into the heart of ethnic processes and to synthesize the insights of circumstantialist and primordialist approaches. To do so, we have had to abandon "pure" primordialism, arguing that much of the power of ethnicity and race comes not from anything genuinely primordial but from the rhetoric and symbolism of primordialism that are so often attached to them. A contructionism that does not take the primordial metaphor into account loses touch not only with how ordinary human beings in many cases experience their own ethnicities but also with much of what is most potent, distinctive, and revealing about ethnic and racial phenomena.

The Problem of Authenticity

To say that ethnic and racial identities are primordial in only a symbolic or rhetorical sense is to invite a certain degree of skepticism or even outrage from individuals and communities who comprehend their ethnic and racial identities as primordial in the strictest, most literal way. For example, in 1989 an anthropologist named Allan Hanson published a paper titled "The Making of the Maori: Culture Invention and Its Logic." The paper was, among other things, an analysis of a movement known as Maoritanga (Maoriness) or Mana Maori (Maori Power) among the Maori people, the indigenous people of New Zealand. Among the primary objectives of this movement, which has involved both Maoris and non-Maoris, are the reinvigoration of Maori culture and the creation of a more truly bicultural New Zealand in which Maoris are on a political and economic par with Pakehas (the Maori term for European-descent New Zealanders), and in which Maori culture receives adequate respect. At the heart of the Maoritanga movement lie particular understandings of Maori history and culture, including beliefs about the arrival of Maoris in these southern Pacific islands centuries before Europeans even knew they existed.

In his paper, Hanson, who favors Maori Mana, undertook an analysis of Maori understandings about the past and about their own traditions. He made a fairly convincing case that certain key stories, symbols, and events in the Maori oral tradition had origins in the works of early 20th-century Pakeha scholars, who were pursuing their own scholarly agendas. In effect, Hanson called attention to the socially constructed character of certain aspects of Maori identity.

Much to Hanson's surprise and dismay, his argument, which was reported selectively in the press, generated outrage and hostility in New Zealand, not only among Maoris but among local anthropologists as well. They interpreted his research as an attack on indigenous culture and tradition. For these groups, the suggestion that Maori identity was based in part on a myth, on an invented history, was not only an affront to their identity but also an attempt to undermine and discredit the very foundations of Maori culture and community. The argument, they believed, suggested that their own, culturally rooted identity was somehow inauthentic.

Although this was not Hanson's intent, the reaction was not without some justification. There is a kind of sociological and historical debunking or deconstructing going on here, as well as a deliberate provocation. As Hanson later acknowledged, his (and others') use of the term *invention* was to some degree a rhetorical strategy, part of an attempt to open readers "to a point of view that may lead them to understand cultural traditions and their authenticity as something quite different, more dynamic and complex, than they had previously thought. But it is also dangerous, because the word 'invention' predisposes people to think that the author means one thing, while the overall text develops a different and much more subtle meaning" (Hanson 1991a:450). As Hanson also recognized, such rhetoric poses other dangers. For example, ethnic political agendas may be undermined by the misimpression, encouraged by such terminology, that the group in question is merely an opportunistic creation, an invention for purposes of the moment (see Hanson 1991b and the discussion in Nagel 1996, chap. 3).

The attempt to uncover the complex foundations of an identity or culture is not necessarily an attack on authenticity. It may be just what it says it is: an attempt to see where that identity and culture came from, to plumb their complexities. Our own reading is that Hanson was interested in the ways in which cultures and collective identities are constructed, pieced together out of history, tradition, experience, myth, and a host of other sources. The result is no less authentic for being a construction. On the contrary, all cultures and collective identities are constructions of one sort or another; they are changed and reformulated—continually reconstructed—over time. It is this very constructedness that is the source of their dynamism. It keeps them alive.

Furthermore, despite the fact that they are constructions, ethnic and racial ties are seldom, if ever, built on thin air. They are not complete fabrications. Their roots may vary from shared geographical origins to systematically discriminatory treatment at the hands of outsiders, from oral traditions that assert a common history to customary patterns of behavior that distinguish group members from their neighbors, from ancient myths to present realities.

In Chapter 3, we briefly discussed the Yorubas of Nigeria as a classic case of the invention of an ethnic classification, in this case by colonial-era missionaries. The missionaries were not inventing links where none existed. Many of the peoples who eventually would call themselves Yoruba spoke the same or similar languages, shared the same styles of living, carried similar traditions, and organized their political systems by similar principles. Many of these customs either fell short of covering the entire Yoruba-speaking area or were shared with non-Yoruba-speakers in the region. Yoruba-speakers nevertheless stood out in comparison with their neighbors, none of whom developed such a close identification between ethnic identity and linguistic community. The key to the development of Yoruba ethnicity was a political vacuum in the region in the early stages of the colonial era. This allowed Protestant missionaries to promote an explicit regional Yoruba identity based largely on linguistic commonalities. That identity eventually took hold among Yoruba-speakers. Although Yoruba identity did not exist until it was invented by Europeans, it had very real roots in the lives of the people and eventually became the way they saw themselves (Peel 1989). Its origins by no means invalidate its authenticity.

The Yoruba case is far from unique. Despite much talk of the "artificiality" of the colonial boundary-drawing processes that created the new nations of Asia and Africa, many of these colonial territories were put together out of clusters of loosely linked villages and regions. The colonizers often took preexisting kinship and ethnic interests and affiliations into account (Horowitz 1985). In fact, they often drew boundaries in one way only to revise and redraw them later in response to ethnic demands. The artificiality of colonial boundaries came not from indifference to ethnic boundaries but from consolidation. They brought previously independent groups together in political units far larger than the units that preceded them (Horowitz 1985:76).

Many Americans have had their own problems acknowledging the social construction of identity, particularly in the case of race. Political scientist Adolph Reed, after noting that " 'race' is purely a social construction; it has no core reality outside a specific social and historical context," goes on to say that this point "typically elicits a string of anxious, incoherent yes-buts from people all over the official racial map, inside and outside of the academy, across the political spectrum." In Reed's view, "The hesitancy about accepting race's contingency and fluidity shows just how thoroughly racialist thinking—which isn't just bigotry but all belief that race exists meaningfully and independently of specific social hierarchies—has been naturalized in American life, the extent to which we depend on it for our conceptual moorings" (1996:22). The fact that Americans so often believe race to be a given indicates how successful the construction project has been.

That fact also indicates the extent to which, however they are constructed, many ethnic and racial identities take on lives of their own. They are reproduced not by missionaries or European scholars or even, necessarily, by structures of inequality but by their own taken-for-grantedness in the daily lives and conversations of the society. Reproduction has taken this form for the Yorubas, for the Maoris, and for race—both Black and White—in the United States. The best-constructed identities show the least evidence of their construction. Assumed and sometimes even celebrated by those who carry them and by the society at large, they come to seem natural. Those who doubt constructionism verify its success.

In the attempt to understand the dynamics of ethnic processes, the issue of authenticity has little significance except insofar as the concept of authenticity itself becomes the subject of investigation. Authenticity, after all, is a social convention. Some set of group members or outsiders selects a version of an identity and defines it as "authentic," granting it a privileged status. They then use it to distinguish among persons and identities, past and present. The grounds of supposed authenticity, however, are essentially arbitrary. Virtually every people in the world's history has engaged in some sort of contact and interaction with other peoples, visiting, trading, fighting, cooperating, dominating, submitting, and reproducing. They have traded not only goods but also words, ideas, and practices. They have adopted what they found useful and ignored the rest. At what point in that long process of exchange and adaptation have the cultures and identities involved been "authentic," and at what point did they lose their "authenticity"? We would argue that authenticity has been present either at every point or at no point, or simply whenever we or they arbitrarily decide. The key issue is not authenticity but what kinds of identities in what kinds of situations organize human lives and motivate human action and why. The Maori response to Hanson tells us one thing at least: Whatever the authenticity of Maori identity, that identity matters a great deal to Maoris, and they act in its defense. Why and how that happens is the important thing to find out.

The Reconstruction of Circumstances

In the constructionism we are putting forward here, circumstances continue to play a central role. As the social world changes, identities change. Too often, however, the argument is left at that. Even when the construction efforts of ethnic and racial actors are taken into account, circumstance remains the ultimate determinant of the identity-building process. Groups are portrayed simply as responding to circumstantial factors, building identities within the constraints that external forces impose. Identity, however, has its own impacts. Once established, an ethnic or racial identity becomes a lens through which people interpret and make sense of the world around them. It becomes a starting point for interpretation and ultimately action.

If you were a Black, female, and poor textile worker in the American South, you would carry a number of very different identities. It is possible that you would see yourself as all of those things at once. You also might see yourself as first and foremost a woman or first and foremost Black or first and foremost a worker or first and foremost a Southerner. The conclusion you come to about who you are may change as the situations you find yourself in change. Regardless, the identity you claimed would have a profound effect on how you looked at the world around you and your place in it, on how you interpreted the actions of others, on your conception of your interests, and ultimately on your actions. Those actions, inevitably shaped by your conception of who you are, could well have an impact on the circumstances you face.

The same is true of collective identities. A group of people may come to see themselves in a particular way. In time, that self-concept may become embedded in their social institutions and cultural practices and become a constitutive part of how they view the world. That is, the identity may become both asserted and thick. Once it does, it not only gains an inertia that may resist the further impacts of changing circumstances but also may organize action in ways that transform the conditions that occasioned the identity in the first place. As we will see in Chapter 5, this is what happened to American Indians in the 20th century. At one time, most Native American identities were organized at the tribal level, but the federal government and other institutions of U.S. society, once they had confined Indians on reservations, generally dealt with them as a single population. In time, Native Americans saw themselves increasingly not only as tribal citizens but as Indians. They began to develop supratribal, Indian institutions. They began to act politically and forcefully on an Indian basis. In the 1960s and 1970s, their political actions, built on an identity that a century earlier very few Indians subjectively shared, altered the course of federal Indian policy. Thanks in part to these supratribal political assertions, the federal government returned increased power to Native American tribes. That power in turn contributed to a renaissance of identity and culture at the tribal level (Cornell 1988; Nagel 1996).

Ethnic and racial identities can be significant forces in their own right. Although circumstances can construct identities, identities are capable—via the actions they set in motion—of reconstructing circumstances. Ethnic identity, in other words, is not only a product of circumstantial factors (among other things). At times, it produces circumstances of its own.

This attention to the agency of ethnic actors and to the determining role their identity often plays in their actions recognizes the power that ethnic and racial identities potentially wield. It recognizes as well that those identities may carry an intrinsic and irreducible significance, both for those who carry them and for the world at large. Some ethnicities may be merely ways of organizing in pursuit of other interests—as, for example, when some persons organize along an ethnic or racial boundary in pursuit of class interests. They are not necessarily so. They often are neither substitutes for nor reflections of other dimensions of social organization. They have a significance of their own, becoming not a dependent variable but an independent variable in the logic of social change.

The Logic of Ethnic and Racial Construction

It remains for us to review the forces that occasion the construction of ethnic and racial identities, setting in motion their creation, maintenance, reproduction, and transformation. Four such forces are important: interests, meaning, happenstance, and inertia. These underlie the conscious and unconscious processes of construction by which ethnicity and race are born, persist, change, and disappear.

Interests

By saying that interests are a major force in the construction of racial and ethnic identities, we simply mean that collective identities are useful. Richard Alba argues (1990:17) that

> [e]thnicity may serve as a principle of *social allocation;* and it may represent a form of *social solidarity.* . . . To say that ethnicity is a principle of social allocation means that individuals are channeled into locations in the social structure based on their ethnic characteristics. . . . Solidary ethnic groups can be regarded as self-conscious communities whose members interact with each other to achieve common purposes.

Alba's concern is specifically with ethnicity, but the same is true of race. It, too, is used as a principle of allocation and can be a form of social solidarity.

In the case of both allocation and solidarity, interests lie at the heart of the matter. As we remarked in Chapter 3, there is often a utilitarian logic to ethnic and racial identification. When it is advantageous to draw a boundary between one set of claimants to opportunities or resources and another, ethnicity and race lend themselves admirably to the task. When there is a need to mobilize persons on behalf of their interests, the invocation of ethnic or racial bonds can be a powerful call to unity. Consequently, race and ethnicity commonly are called into play in situations of competition over scarce resources: jobs, housing, school access, prestige, political power, and so on.

Social allocation and social solidarity are in some sense complements. When ethnicity or race is used as a principle of social allocation, that fact encourages its emergence as a basis of solidarity. Groups that discover their identity is being used as grounds for major decisions about their lives and opportunities are more inclined to see that identity as important and to make it the basis of their own organization and action. Likewise, groups that already are solidary are more likely to use the identity that most clearly binds members to one another as a differentiator in allocating resources and opportunities, distinguishing, for purposes of allocation, between themselves and others.

Allocation and solidarity also have implications for intergroup relationships. When, for example, Whites impose Blackness (or non-Whiteness) as a principle of allocation, denying jobs or housing or political power to Blacks or others, they simultaneously invoke Whiteness as a principle of allocation, reserving such opportunities to Whites. When some set of people emphasize a common ethnicity as the factor that links them, they also emphasize it as the factor that distinguishes them from everybody else. Any principle of inclusion is also a principle of exclusion.

Meaning

Not only material, political, or status interests are at stake in ethnic and racial construction. For some persons and groups, their sense of who they are and how they fit into the world around them may be at stake as well. In a book written nearly half a century ago, sociologist Robert Nisbet (1953) claims that despite living in an age of economic affluence, dominated by large and powerful states that typically provide an unprecedented degree of security and stability, many human beings feel a profound spiritual insecurity, a sense of alienation from one another and a disconnection from local communities, and a preoccupation with identity. Nisbet argues, much as Max Weber does in the famous conclusion to his work *The Protestant Ethic and the Spirit of Capitalism* (1905/1958), that behind this sense of meaninglessness lie the centralization of power in large organizations and the progressive bureaucratization of function and authority in most aspects of human life. These developments have weakened the traditional institutions—such as the family and the local community—that once provided most human beings with a sense of meaning and connection. Those institutions made them feel linked to each other in secure, personal, humane, and consciously interdependent ways. Such traditional institutions and relationships, says Nisbet, "have become functionally irrelevant to our state and economy and meaningless to the moral aspirations of individuals" (1953:54). Where Weber seems to find such developments ultimately alienating and disempowering, Nisbet suggests that they have energized and inspired efforts to find sources of meaning in the modern world. The most important of these is "the quest for community": a quest for meaningful, intimate attachments that "mediate directly between individuals and the larger world" of economic and political organizations and an often confusing moral life (Nisbet 1953:49).

Nisbet does not mention ethnicity specifically in this regard (but see Smith 1981), and he wrote his book before ethnicity had become so prominent a topic either in the daily news or in social science. He touched, however, on part of the logic of ethnic construction. The blessings of modernity are many, but the preservation of intimate, meaningful communities has not been one of them. Ethnicity, with its sense of historical continuity and its claims to deep and meaningful—even primordial—interpersonal ties, holds out the prospect of communion and connection, of a mediating community between the individual and the large, impersonal institutions that dominate the modern world. If ethnicity does not deliver community in practice, it can do so at least in the imagination. "The members of even the smallest nation will never know most of their fellow-members, meet them, or even hear of them, yet in the minds of each lives the image of their communion" (Anderson 1983:15). This remark, made originally about nationalism, applies to ethnicity as well. It, equally, is a work of the imagination, and its emotional resonance comes not from the material rewards it promises but from the connections it makes.

Not all ethnicities offer such resonances, nor are all ethnicities constructed for purposes of the meanings they have to offer, but some find their logic in just this sort of communion: a connection across social and geographical space and even across time. Part of the power of the primordial claim—the kinship metaphor implied and often explicitly asserted in ethnic ties—lies in its ability to connect across the generations. In our imaginations, at least, the blood tie links the generations to one another. Looking back, we imagine that we carry a blood legacy. Looking forward, we can imagine living on in our kinspeople, in our common blood. "By transforming fatality into continuity," primordialist ties such as those to nation or ethnicity establish "links between the dead and the yet unborn, the mystery of identity (of who we are) and of re-generation (who we yet shall be)" (Anderson 1983).

We mention ethnicity and not race in this regard because this act of the imagination is a classically ethnic act. It is part of the process through which ethnic or racial groups—regardless of what others say or what circumstances may imply—lay claim to meanings of their own. This drive to find or fashion meaning offers a separate logic of identity construction.

Happenstance

Although interests or a search for meaning often drive the process of ethnic and racial identity construction, other factors may play a role as well. Sometimes chance or happenstance is involved. By happenstance, we refer to circumstances that are indifferent to the populations they affect.

For example, one of the ways that ethnic boundaries receive reinforcement or are undermined is through the distribution of positions in the economy. Some distributions are intentionally fashioned. When employers in New York City and elsewhere put signs in their windows in the mid-19th century saying "No Irish Need Apply," or when Anglo workers organized to exclude Chinese from jobs in California late in the same century, they were intentionally denying certain opportunities to Irish or Chinese immigrants; in so doing, they reinforced ethnic or racial boundaries on behalf of their own interests. Sometimes circumstances alone accomplish the same thing. When new immigrants arrive in a society, they may find that few jobs are available to those who lack certain skills; they also may find they are too poor to buy housing in all but a few neighborhoods or that only certain sectors of the economy are growing fast enough to absorb them. Discrimination may be absent in all these cases, yet the ethnic or racial boundary receives support from the circumstances these groups encounter. They form ethnically homogeneous communities because it just so happens that impersonal residential and workplace conditions sustain interactions within the ethnic boundary and discourage interactions across it. Ethnic bonds are supported not by shared interests or by a struggle to find or fashion meaning so much as by the shared experiences of daily living.

Happenstance may seem to give ethnicity in such cases a rather modest foundation, but experience can be a powerful source of collective identification, even when the resultant identity serves few pragmatic interests. The *hibakusha* of Japan provide a non-ethnic example. The *hibakusha* are the survivors of the atomic bombings of Hiroshima and Nagasaki by the United States at the end of World War II. Identity as *hibakusha* may be based on certain interests, and it has been sustained in part by the stigma at times attached to it. What binds these individuals together most powerfully, however, is the fact that they shared an experience that no one else in the world will ever understand in the way that they understand it (Lifton 1967). That experience has become an integral, fundamental part of their self-conception, a profoundly compelling component of who they are. Their identity survives because in many cases they cannot let it go. Something similar can sometimes be found among combat veterans, the survivors of certain natural disasters, or recovering alcoholics, among others.

None of these examples is an ethnic or racial group, but the central point remains. Experience constructs identities. Ethnicity and race are built not only by the rational calculation of interests or the search for communion but also by the incremental contributions of small events that, over time, teach us to think of ourselves and others in certain ways. Those ways of thinking sometimes serve no obvious interest, but they may be no less powerful. In fact, interest-based identities are only as robust as the conditions from which the relevant interests are derived. In contrast, identities rooted in gradually learned ways of viewing the world gain an inertial force that may prove more long-lasting.

Inertia

This point brings us to the last of the forces underlying ethnic and racial construction. Inertia refers to the fact that people are carriers of collective identities all the time. The process of socialization leads individuals to see themselves as connected to other people—and more important, as connected to other categories of people. We are always conscious of sharing more with some people than with others; we are always viewing ourselves as part of some larger body of persons. Because it is part of self-definition, collective identity typically is neither fickle nor merely whimsical. It often has substantial inertial force, all the more so when it is embedded in established relationships and institutions, cultural practices, and ways of seeing the world.

People typically enter new situations or experience social change with collective identities already well established. Whether the origins of those identities lie in rational calculation or in circumstantially shaped experience, once established they become bases of action. In acting on the basis of those identities, people reproduce them. They may even add to the staying power of those identities. Among the many possible actions that people take is the creation of institutions, more or less formally organized ways of solving problems, pursuing objectives, linking some people to each other, and distancing them from others. The identities people take for granted commonly come to be embedded in the institutions they build. The institutions then help to sustain the identities.

Identities rooted originally in inertia may also change. We may find that our actions do not fit the new circumstances we have encountered; over time, we may discover that some other identity makes more sense of the situation in which we find ourselves. Until that happens, the identities we carry are likely to last, in part because they are the ones we have available, the ones that, for the time being at least, we cannot do without.

Conclusion

A constructionist approach assumes that ethnic and racial identities vary across space and change across time. It assumes that societal conditions and social change—the circumstances groups encounter—drive much of that dynamic. It also assumes that ethnic groups are actively involved in the construction and reconstruction of identities, negotiating boundaries, asserting meanings, interpreting their own pasts, resisting the impositions of the present, and claiming the future. Neither actions nor circumstances alone create groups, for our actions depend on how we interpret circumstances, and circumstances ultimately are the products of human actions. Identities are created, elaborated, and re-created in the interaction between the two.

A constructionist approach also assumes that the mutability of identity does not deprive it of power. The power of ethnicity and race lies in the significance we attach to them, both to our own racial or ethnic identities and to the identities of others.

In the chapters that follow, we add some flesh to these constructionist bones. We do so in two ways. In Chapters 6 and 7, we provide more detail on both contextual and group factors that play significant roles in the construction of identities. First, however, in Chapter 5 we explore several cases that illustrate some of the aspects of identity construction that we have described here.

5

Case Studies in Identity Construction

In this chapter, we turn to cases. Here we try to capture construction processes at work. We have selected our cases—they are more like thumbnail sketches—not to support or refute any hypothesis or general theory other than the fundamentally constructionist approach that informs this book. Our purpose instead is to illustrate the diversity of the interactions that take place between circumstances and actors, the ways those interactions construct identities, and some of the various forms and functions that ethnicity and race assume as a result.

Case 1. The Power of Circumstances: Blacks and Indians in the United States[1]

We begin with a comparison of identity construction among two of the oldest minority populations in the United States: African Americans and Native Americans. Today, we tend to think and speak of these two populations in largely monolithic terms, but they did not start out that way, and even today they are nowhere near as monolithic as our common discourse suggests. The terms *African American* and *Native American* refer today to populations that for the most part are seen as distinct and self-contained, that see themselves to some degree in the same way, and that often act on the basis of these identities. The question is, How did they come to be this way? How were these identities established as bases of social organization and collective action?

Part of the answer to this question involves the economic development of the United States, the needs for land and labor to fuel and drive that development, the ways those needs were met, and the steeply stratified society that has been the ultimate result. As the competition perspectives on intergroup relations that we touched on briefly in Chapter 3 suggest, European Americans had much to gain from drawing and enforcing a boundary between themselves and non-European groups, and the power to do just that. Blacks and Indians as racialized "others" were the result, in other words, of particular patterns of domination and exploitation that subordinated both groups in ways intended to facilitate economic growth and national expansion.

What is less apparent from a perspective that focuses largely on competition is the role that these groups themselves played in the process of identity construction, shaping their own identities under conditions of subordination and powerlessness. There is also a puzzle attached to this process. Despite the fact that both Blacks and Indians have constituted subordinated populations within what is now the United States for a very long time, they developed a racial consciousness at very different times. A comprehensive group consciousness appeared early among African Americans. It was apparent early in slavery, flourished in the immediate aftermath of the Civil War, and continues to the present. Despite similarly lengthy and oppressive interactions with European Americans, however, a comprehensive group consciousness took far longer to emerge among American Indians as a common, prominent basis of identity and action, not appearing on a similar scale until nearly the middle of the 20th century. Why was there this difference?

The answer to this question lies in large part in the different circumstances these two groups encountered and in the different mechanisms by which they were subordinated. We begin with a comparison of these two cases, examining the construction of Black and Indian identities as a matter of the dynamic relationship between the specific circumstances each group faced and their own attempts to interpret those circumstances and to claim control over their own lives.

African Americans

The Africans enslaved and transported to the United States in the 17th, 18th, and early 19th centuries came from many different parts of Africa. Most were shipped from the west coast of Africa, from the area known as Senegambia in the north to Angola in the south, and came originally from societies located inland from those coastal areas. That stretch of coast is more than 3,000 miles long. Inland from it lay a vast mosaic of societies, kingdoms, and communities whose languages, cultures, and histories varied enormously. The Africans who came to America constituted no single people but instead an array of peoples, thrust together by the violence of slavery. They saw themselves not as Blacks or Africans but as members of distinct and diverse groups.

Slave traders and slave owners were aware, in at least general terms, of some of these differences. They recognized that they were dealing with many different peoples, although the differences among those peoples mattered to them largely in their implications for how slaves were used. There were common conceptions about the characteristics of different groups of Africans that led slaveholders to believe that certain groups were better suited to some kinds of labor than to others, or were better workers than other groups were.

Although the slave system acknowledged differences, it also tended to destroy them. Slavery is a system of power. It is an extreme form of domination in which the master typically exercises enormous power over the slave, denying the slave not only authority over his or her own person but honor within the society. In slavery, certain persons lose control over their bodies, their labor, their lives, and their fortunes. In the American case, these persons were primarily Africans. Indians at times were enslaved in North America, but never on the same scale.

Undermining Ethnic Identities

In America, slavery reduced Africans to a commodity: individual units of labor available, against their will, for sale. This fact had certain consequences for the group boundaries that framed Africans' own identities. The market for slaves was not a market for groups of persons but for individuals. Although slaves might be bought and sold in "lots"—groups of two or more—the ultimate unit of sale was the individual. For the most part, the market recognized no interpersonal attachments. As different slaveholders bought and sold individual Africans, the ethnic concentrations that had survived enslavement and transportation across the Atlantic Ocean quickly broke down. This market-based dispersion meant that in any given location there was less likely to be a concentration of persons from a single ethnic group than a mixture of peoples. There were exceptions to this, areas in the American South where significant concentrations of distinct African groups survived, but ethnic dispersion and mixing were much more the rule.

The security concerns of slaveholders reinforced this market effect. Where ethnic concentrations survived, African languages were more likely to survive, as were traditional patterns of leadership and of cooperation and action. Slaveholders, many of whom fully understood the outrage and heartbreak that slavery produced among Africans, were afraid such survivals might encourage or facilitate insurrection. By mixing the ethnic origins of their slaves, they believed they could force Africans to give up their own languages and the internal group structures that had survived the passage to America, thereby reducing the chances of revolt. Consequently, many of them systematically split apart persons from similar ethnic backgrounds. These factors rapidly undermined or complicated the identities originally brought from Africa, particularly as the children of the first generation of slaves grew up in ethnically mixed slave populations.

Constructing the Racial Boundary

At the same time, another set of factors was busily constructing a more comprehensive group boundary: the boundary of race. Slavery brought Africans into a society in which race was a fundamental dimension of social organization. In the Southern states prior to the Civil War and in much of the rest of the United States until late in the 18th century, race determined social status, life chances, and political power. To be White was to be free while to be Black was, with few exceptions, to be figuratively and often literally in chains. Slavery created two categories of human beings, free and unfree. Although there were free Blacks, they constituted an exception. The fundamental determinant of which category an individual was assigned to was race. In such a situation, the ethnic identities carried from Africa lost much of their relevance. The significance of race simply overwhelmed them.

Public culture reinforced social and political reality. Although slave traders and some slaveholders may have been aware of ethnic distinctions among Africans, the society at large paid them little attention. The terms of everyday conversation minimized intragroup differences and emphasized the racial divide: Negro, colored, or Black on the one hand, White on the other. The terms were value laden. Race distinguished not only among persons but also among statuses: One race was held to be inferior, by culture or biology or both, to the other. These terms reinforced in language and perception the racial organization of the society.

This combination of ethnic mixing and racial subordination had several effects. To communicate with each other, Africans from diverse origins rapidly developed creole or pidgin languages, and ultimately adopted English. "Bridges of language were the first efforts to link them into one people" (Huggins 1979:62). Not only did Blacks have to find ways of communicating with each other; they also had to develop a set of institutions that could help them to deal with the severe problems posed by slavery itself, among them the maintenance of family, of individual and group dignity, and of simple human pleasure in conditions that often were systematically destructive of the first, flatly denied the second, and made the third a rare and fleeting experience. In other words, they had to fashion a community. Drawing on African roots but also from whatever sources they could find, including some in the society in which they found themselves enslaved, Africans gradually developed kinship systems, religion, customary practices, and forms of expressive culture such as music, song, and storytelling that helped to tie together persons of diverse backgrounds. The housing areas where plantation slaves lived, known as slave quarters, became the heart of the African community, gradually established in thousands of places throughout the South. "With some regional variation, the preparation of food, the songs and stories, the language, and most important, the themes of quarter communities throughout the South were similar" (Webber 1978:243).

These same forces led to the emergence of a powerful racial consciousness. They constantly reminded African Americans of what they shared with each other, and of the gulf—political, social, economic, cultural, and historical—that separated them from Whites.

Thus, Africans encountered a situation in which certain factors—the market organization of slavery on one hand, the racial organization of society on the other—undermined the group boundaries they carried with them and constructed another, racial boundary in their place. Circumstances were primary in this development. The characteristics of Africans themselves—the languages, ideas, traditions, and practices that they brought with them from Africa—contributed a great deal to "the world the slaves made" (Genovese 1976). They contributed little to the process of boundary construction, which was driven overwhelmingly by factors beyond African Americans' control. The primary exception was their color, which served as a boundary marker and became the chosen foundation around which European Americans built their conception of race.

Race in the Aftermath of Slavery

The end of slavery had only limited effects on that boundary, but now Africans' own actions helped to sustain it. Early in the period of Reconstruction following the American Civil War, there was an outburst of Black political and organizational activity throughout the South, much of which asserted an explicitly racial consciousness as African Americans set out to build their own institutions under conditions of freedom. In the process, they challenged much of the substance of the racial identity that had been forced on them. Whereas that identity conceived them as culturally and even biologically inferior to Whites, they asserted their worth and equal capacities as human beings, their equality in the eyes of God, and their right to equal treatment and opportunity in the land that had held them in bondage. Thus, they challenged not the boundary but its significance and its implications for their lives.

That challenge proved largely futile. In the second half of the 19th century and throughout the 20th, American society continued to employ race as a basis of social organization and political power. In the South, the White power structure soon withdrew the political rights Blacks had won in the aftermath of the Civil War and replaced them with the system of discriminatory laws and practices known as Jim Crow. Blacks migrating to industrial jobs in northern cities found themselves victims of discrimination there as well, being excluded from jobs, housing markets, politics, and other social institutions, or being allowed only inferior positions. Formal racial barriers continued to organize the lives and fortunes of African Americans through most of the 20th century. Even when many of those formal barriers were breached, the culture of race survived in interpersonal interactions and in many American institutions, where Black Americans continued to feel the sting of prejudice and discrimination.

It was not until the Civil Rights Movement of the late 1950s and early 1960s that Black Americans were finally able to launch a meaningful strike against the racial caste system in the United States. The social changes this germinal period set in motion have had significant consequences for African Americans. The Civil Rights Movement produced important—if limited—changes in the lives of some Blacks, particularly in the South, where numerous institutional barriers were pulled down and Black Power began to take on concrete meaning in the organization of southern society and in the economic opportunities available to the Black middle class. Although it did not seriously diminish the fundamental significance of race in the United States or end the poverty that a huge portion of the Black population continues to face, that movement and the changes it produced brought Blacks into the political arena and into the ongoing struggle to overcome the institutional and cultural barriers that continue to support a racial organization of much of American life.

The Racial Boundary at Century's End

At the same time, since the 1970s the boundary that once so clearly defined the Black population has begun to show signs of strain. This strain has had less to do with any change in the significance of that boundary for Whites than with the changing experiences of Blacks. Growing divergences in the economic experiences of the Black population, along with differences in the backgrounds, orientations, and fortunes of West Indian and American-born Blacks, have produced divergences in interests, politics, and even self-concepts within the Black population (see Kasinitz 1992; Waters 1994; Wilson 1978, 1987). Such divergences are by no means unprecedented in the Black community. Even under slavery, there were differences in the situationally derived interests of Black Americans, and class cleavages have long been a part of the African American experience (e.g., Dollard 1937/1957). With the growth of the Black population and recent changes in its circumstances, however, those internal differences have become more complex.

Both as individuals and as a group, African Americans have been somewhat ambivalent about these developments. Some believe they indicate that at least a number of African Americans finally have the opportunity to join the American mainstream as other immigrant populations have done. Others worry that as individual African Americans find success in mainstream America, the vast numbers of poor, uneducated Blacks will be left behind, creating an even more insidious class-and-race system of entrenched stratification. Still others think that nothing of fundamental importance has changed at all, while a few find in recent developments evidence of quite radical change and argue that racism is finally disappearing (D'Souza 1995; Steele 1990).

This last hardly seems the case. Systematic racial discrimination remains a feature of American life, albeit sometimes in new forms (see, for example, Massey and Denton 1993), as does a dominant classificatory system in which the racial boundary continues to organize much of the way Americans see and imagine themselves and each other (Bell 1992; Omi and Winant 1994; West 1993). To conclude that racism is disappearing is to confuse race with racism, to conflate Black Americans as a social group (which is in a state of transformation and uncertainty) with Blackness as a cultural category (which may or may not be changing or may be changing in different ways). As different groups of Black Americans find themselves in different situations and carrying different political agendas, neither the future of African American ethnicity nor that of racial ideology in the United States—which has assumed a singular and clearly defined African American community—seems easy to predict.

Native Americans[2]

The pattern of Native Americans' involvement in U.S. society—and the pattern of identity construction among them—looks very different from that of African Americans. Indians, like Africans, were an enormously diverse population when they first came into contact with Europeans. Literally hundreds of distinct peoples populated what is now the United States, speaking often mutually unintelligible languages and, like Africans, carrying very different cultures and histories. Their own collective identities, while complex, tended to focus at the level of the nation or people, the level we conventionally have come to call the tribe: Blackfeet, Oglala, Kiowa, Chickasaw, and so on.

Relations among these groups were in some cases cooperative and in some cases antagonistic. Although they had a pronounced sense of the differences among themselves, and in most cases a powerful ethnocentrism, Native Americans had little sense of the geographical origins that separated them as a general category from Europeans. Cherokee anthropologist Robert Thomas (1968) argues that when most Indians first encountered Europeans, they saw them simply as another variety of stranger—a people they had not previously come across. That quickly changed, but it did so under conditions very different from those that prevailed with Africans, and the result for Native Americans was very different as well.

Labor Versus Land

The different conditions Indians faced had to do first of all with the resources at issue in Black-White and Indian-White relations. Africans were of interest to Euro-American society for their labor; it was the need for a labor force that sustained the slave trade and slavery itself. For a time, Indians also were of interest for their labor, and in some cases, particularly in the American colonies, Indians were enslaved, but most of the labor that Indians provided was very different. In the 17th and much of the 18th centuries, the centerpiece of Indian-White relations in what is now the United States was the fur trade, driven by European demand for animal hides and furs for use in hats, shoes, and other clothing. Indians traded furs to Europeans in return for European manufactured goods. The original acquisition of furs was entirely an Indian enterprise. Only Indians, who still controlled most of the interior beyond the Atlantic fringe of White settlement, had access to the major fur-bearing populations of animals, and only Indians had the hunting and processing skills necessary to the fur trade. The success of the fur trade, in other words, was dependent on Indian labor.

The form and the conditions of that labor, however, differed from the African American situation. Indians entered into the fur trade by choice. The production of furs remained under their control, and they encountered Europeans not in the production of furs—no European oversaw their work—but in the marketplace. The Indian captured the animal, separated the pelt, processed it, and then transported it, appearing at the marketplace (typically a European outpost or settlement such as Albany or Quebec) with fully processed furs in hand, ready to trade.

The Indian role as workers also was temporary. The fur trade had come to an end in much of North America by the latter decades of the 18th century, and as it disappeared, so did the European need for Indian labor. What emerged in place of the need for labor was a demand for land. As the European settler population grew and as the fledgling United States grew increasingly interested in the other economic resources of the continent, land became the focus of Indian-White relations. From late in the 18th century until early in the 20th, the organizing enterprise in those relations was the forced expulsion of Indians from their lands and the westward march of White settlement across the continent.

This shift from labor to land had some critical consequences for the formation of collective identity. Instead of being integrated into the economic structure of emergent American society as individual workers, Indian nations were removed en masse from the lands Whites wanted and were relocated on less desirable lands. This process of removal proceeded through a series of formal treaties signed between the United States and Indian nations. There was a dual aspect to the treaty process. On one hand, many Indians entered into it only under extreme duress following extended warfare and diplomatic resistance to the United States. On the other hand, it was a process that recognized Indian groups as sovereign, if increasingly powerless, nations. This process of expulsion through violence and treaty-making had an ironic result: It often altered but ultimately preserved tribal boundaries. It left Indian communities—impoverished and virtually powerless—on an assortment of diverse and often widely separated lands not desired by Whites, called reservations. It also gradually built up an administrative apparatus that organized Indians by reservation unit, which meant in most cases by tribal unit. In other words, and with some important exceptions, it left the group boundaries that organized much of Indian life to some degree intact, even reinforcing them through a kind of grudging political recognition and the formalization of links between Indian groups and their remnant reservation lands.

Something very different would have been the result had labor remained the centerpiece of Indian-White relations. Presumably, the old group boundaries would have been undermined and perhaps would have disappeared as Indians were moved as individual workers—in response to either coercion or market forces—into the larger economy. Under those conditions, the result might have been either the emergence of a more comprehensive, supratribal, racial consciousness or the assimilation of most Indians into the mainstream of the U.S. population. Assimilation was in fact a recurrent objective in U.S. Indian policy and very much the preferred outcome for many policy makers and other Whites who took an interest in Indian affairs. The process of land expropriation and reservation confinement, the racial antagonism of many Whites, and the desire to teach Indians the ways of Euro-American civilization before integrating them into American society inadvertently produced a situation in which Indian groups could survive as groups, although typically under stress and in execrable conditions.

The general classifications prevalent within most of American society encouraged a more comprehensive boundary. Both U.S. government policy and the popular discussion of Indian affairs conceived Indian populations in largely monolithic terms. The critical boundary in the society at large was the boundary between "Indians" and Whites. Native Americans themselves certainly were aware of this and often used the same terminology. Daily experience, however, carried a very different message. At the start of the 20th century, most Indians still lived their lives within the social relationships of the tribe, on reservations designated as specifically tribal homelands, often speaking indigenous languages and engaged in diverse cultural practices. As late as the early 1940s, the majority of Indian people organized and acted on tribal, not supratribal, terms—that is, not as Indians but as members of distinct, vital, tribal communities.

The Emergence of a Supratribal Consciousness

It was not until World War II and the following decades that a supratribal consciousness began to emerge on a large scale as a common basis of identity and action among the larger part of the Native American population. World War II initiated a substantial migration by Indians into wartime industries and into American cities, a pattern that has continued and grown in subsequent decades. In the 1950s and 1960s, this pattern led to the establishment of significant multitribal communities in urban areas. It also put Indians in a political environment very different from the reservations, one in which tribal identities had little formal relevance. It made more sense to approach the problems of urban Indian populations on an Indian, as opposed to tribal, basis. The Indian boundary was one that public service institutions and policy makers recognized, and organizing on that boundary increased the Indian political presence by aggregating the members of various tribes. By the 1960s, a supratribal Indian politics had begun to emerge in American cities and among a growing number of pan-Indian organizations that saw the more comprehensive Indian boundary as crucial to their own survival and to the survival of the tribal communities from which many of them had come. Those communities and the ethnic boundaries that defined them continued to survive, but in part through a politics that recognized the Indian boundary as an essential adjunct identity, a basis on which to engage the larger society and pursue both tribal and Indian agendas. Today, most Native Americans carry, value, and defend both Indian and tribal identities.

Comparing African Americans and Native Americans

The African peoples who were brought to what is now the United States encountered economic and political systems organized not along sub-racial boundaries but along racial ones, a public culture of race, and a classification system that treated the racial boundary as fundamental. The result was to racialize not only Blacks but the Black experience. In that situation, the more comprehensive group boundary soon became the logical basis of Black group consciousness and action.

American Indians also encountered a public culture of race and a classification system that conceptualized Indians in racial terms. It is important to note, however, that the economic system they encountered for the most part excluded them, having less use for their labor than for their lands. The political system they encountered was built to support the economic one, and ultimately it organized their subordination along tribal lines. Indian experience, therefore, was not racialized in the same way the Black experience was. It still made sense for Indians to organize and act on tribal terms, and thanks to the particular relationships that existed between Indians and the United States, they were still able to do so. Not until the middle of the 20th century, however, did organization on supratribal terms become a compelling and feasible strategy.

Put most concisely,

> In the Black case we have a labour-oriented history of intergroup relations which, over time, undermines a pre-existing set of identities and provides the foundation for another, more comprehensive one. In the Indian case we have a land-oriented history of intergroup relations which, over time, sustains a pre-existing set of identities and inhibits the emergence of another, more comprehensive one. (Cornell 1990:384)

Circumstances obviously are crucial factors in identity construction in these two cases. Both the conceptions of Whites and the material conditions of intergroup relations played determining roles in that construction, although their effects were different in the two cases. Both Blacks and Indians encountered certain opportunities and constraints that profoundly shaped both experience and identity.

Despite the power of assignment, however, the results were not wholly determined by those opportunities and constraints. In both cases, there was agency as well: The groups involved asserted their own conceptions of who they are. Native Americans generally had greater freedom for such assertions than African Americans had. Ever since the latter part of the 19th century, U.S. government policy has encouraged—on occasion forced—Indians to leave the tribal embrace and join the mainstream of American society. Some Indians have chosen to do so; some resisted that pressure and have remained fully integrated into their own tribal communities, which has kept those communities vibrantly alive. The presence of the tribal option was crucial in this development, and that was a product of circumstances. Indian choices also were crucial, and those, at certain times, were freely made. Furthermore, Indians might have organized on a supratribal basis much sooner than they did. After all, the surrounding society took a comprehensive Indian identity for granted, commonly ignoring the major differences that separated Indian nations. A supratribal Indian identity nevertheless emerged on a large scale among Native Americans only when it made sense to them, not when it made sense to Whites.

African Americans also asserted their own ideas of who they were, although for them the alternatives were fewer and the circumstantial constraints—especially under slavery—more severe. Even so, as circumstances enforced a rigid racial boundary and perpetuated their subordination, Blacks challenged the inequalities and negative implications attached to both boundary and position, resisting and reshaping the meaning of their own "blackness" in the process. Within the dehumanizing and debilitating limits of these constraints, Black Americans asserted *their* version of their identity and built a community of their own.

Case 2. Between Assertion and Assignment: Chinese Americans in Mississippi[3]

The American Civil War brought an end to slavery in the United States. In the aftermath of the war, the African American population that had provided most of the labor force in southern agriculture won not only political rights—which meant, typically, that they were voting against the entrenched White power structure—but also freedom of movement—

which meant that many of them could deal with ill treatment at the hands of cotton planters and others by going somewhere else. Many did, choosing to work for other employers, in other industries, or moving to the large cities of the North. These changes confronted those who controlled southern agriculture with a problem. They could not exploit the Black labor force with quite the freedom or in the same ways as they previously had done. What they needed was an alternative pool of workers. One possible source was White migrants to the South, but few Whites could be persuaded to take up sharecropping—the form of production emerging in the region in place of slavery[4]—unless they had to.

The solution, many southern planters thought, was to import Chinese labor. The prevailing view of Chinese in the United States was that they were hard workers and politically docile, and this made them attractive. As foreigners, they could not vote and therefore could not challenge the power structure that kept Whites in firm control of rural southern society. The result was a campaign to recruit Chinese workers as labor in southern agriculture.

Chinese in Mississippi

This campaign was not particularly successful, but it produced a trickle of immigrants. One of the places they settled was in a part of Mississippi known as the Delta, a stretch of rich, low-lying farmland occupying a number of counties along the eastern shore of the Mississippi River. By the early 1870s, a small but growing Chinese population had appeared in the Delta, although it was hardly enough to solve the labor needs of the region. Indeed, the Delta population of Chinese, right up to the 1980s, never much exceeded a couple of thousand people. Luckily for the large cotton planters who dominated the Delta in the 1870s, the labor problem itself was short-lived. In 1876, White supremacists in Mississippi ousted the state government established under northern pressure during the period of Reconstruction after the Civil War, reversed the political and economic gains won by Blacks, and began to put back in place a system of formal and informal controls that would restore much of the old racial stratification system. Faced with diminishing political and economic options and crippled by the rapidly proliferating controls of the Jim Crow system, many Blacks were thrown back into sharecropping and subservience in an increasingly oppressive system of racial domination that remained in place for almost another century.

These developments ended the campaign to recruit Chinese workers, but many of the Chinese who had come to Mississippi stayed, and others occasionally came. Having discovered the economic futility of sharecropping and realizing that they were unlikely to be treated well by the Whites they worked for, they quickly abandoned the cotton plantations and began to look for opportunities of their own. What they found was a classic economic niche. A large number of them opened grocery stores that served the Black population in the towns and cities of the Delta, and there—economically at least—they flourished. Although the move into the grocery business brought the Chinese financial success, however, it did nothing to change their treatment at the hands of Whites or their status in Delta society.

The Chinese and Racial Segregation

When the Chinese came to Mississippi, they entered a racially segregated society. James Loewen, writing about the system the Chinese encountered, comments:

> In its everyday operation, segregation consists of a pervasive system of etiquette. Every movement, every point of contact, every interaction, has carefully detailed alternative sets of norms which can be applied to it, depending upon the race of the other party. Biracial segregation forms a complete set of definitions, expressing and codifying the relationship of dominance and subservience. (Loewen 1988:58-59)

This system of etiquette governs a great deal of day-to-day behavior. "Whites who become 'too familiar' with blacks are subtly corrected, and [Blacks] who presume too much upon the friendship of Caucasians may be roughly brought up short. There is no provision in such a system for a third racial group" (Loewen 1988:58-59). The Chinese constituted such a third group—neither Black nor White—but the system of etiquette was unprepared for them. The racial system, developed over generations of interaction and built into not only social relations but social conceptions as well, had only two available categories. When Whites met Chinese in day-to-day interactions, they needed to know who they were: Whites or Blacks? Which pattern of behavior specified by the informal but rigidly institutionalized etiquette system was called for? Should Whites observe the rules for interacting with one another or the rules for interacting with Blacks? The answer, from the point of view of those who dominated the social system, was not at all complicated. The Chinese had been sought out originally to replace Black workers in a labor system designed to serve White interests. The position they occupied in the society certainly resembled that of Blacks far more than it did that of Whites. Although the

Chinese did not look Black, they did not look White, either. Under those conditions, they could hardly be considered White, but they might easily be considered Black, and that is what they became. They were racialized as Black, assigned the same status as Blacks, and as a consequence experienced essentially similar day-to-day treatment at the hands of Whites.

At this point, the orientation of the Chinese becomes important to the story. Through the early part of the 20th century, most Chinese who came to the Delta saw themselves not, primarily, as permanent residents of Mississippi or even of the United States, but as sojourners, as temporary residents. Life in Mississippi was not an end in itself but a means to a very different end.

> Almost all of the incoming Chinese were young male adults. Their families and their orientations remained in China. Their duty in the new country was to make money, send some home to help support the family, and accumulate some so as to start an independent business and make more money. In a few years, the sojourner hoped to save enough to make a journey back to China, remain for a few months, take a bride, and begin a family. Then after returning to Mississippi he would continue to work and send money home, accumulating for subsequent visits. Eventually he planned to return to China, to retire in the bosom of his family and friends, as a rather wealthy man, and to be buried in Chinese soil. (Loewen 1988:28-29)

The sojourner orientation meant that the Chinese were less concerned with their social status in Mississippi than they might otherwise have been. Economic as opposed to social success was their goal. From the point of view of status, their reference point was not Mississippi but the China to which they hoped one day to return. In absentia, they demonstrated their loyalty to family through their business success and the money they sent home. Knowing they had fulfilled their familial duty, they could expect to return to China one day and enjoy the esteem of family, friends, and community.

That orientation eventually began to change. Among the culprits were time and success: The longer they were in Mississippi and the more successful they were, the more likely the Chinese were to see both their residence and their accomplishments as more than temporary expedients. Building a long-term future in China demanded first building a short-term future in Mississippi, but the more one invested in Mississippi—in adjusting to the local environment and learning its ways; in developing relationships with customers, friends, and neighbors; in developing a business—the less it began to feel like a sojourn, the more it began to feel like a commitment, and the farther away China and the long-term future seemed to be.

Another culprit was family. Some of the Chinese formed relationships with Black women and, in a number of cases, married them and had children, developing more substantial roots in the Delta. Others managed, despite immigration restrictions, to bring wives and family from China to Mississippi. When the federal government relaxed restrictions on Chinese immigration after World War II, more Chinese men brought their wives from China to join them. Once the family had made the move as well, the return to China lost an important part of its rationale, and Mississippi began to look more and more like home.

The result, especially during the 1940s and 1950s, was a gradual change in orientation from sojourner to immigrant, and with it a changing attitude toward the status Chinese occupied in Mississippi. As Mississippi began to look more and more like a permanent home, Chinese merchants began to chafe under the weight of their lowly status. Their concern was not an idle one. Status attributions in the racial system of the South had significant consequences. To be Black was to be denied political power, to be discriminated against in a variety of social institutions from schools to churches to certain stores and public accommodations, to be vulnerable to pervasive daily indignities and implicit threats of violence in interpersonal relations across the racial divide, to experience discrimination in the courts and at the hands of the police, and so on. Having concluded that they were likely to remain in Mississippi, the Chinese then had to confront the greatest handicap that they and their children faced in their effort to succeed in the society they now called home: the fact that Whites viewed them in the same terms—in effect, classified them—as Blacks. If they were to move forward, that had to change. They set out to change it, to make a racial transition. In essence, they set out to persuade the White power structure to reclassify them as Whites.

A Strategy of Racial Reassignment

The key to altering the racial classification of the Chinese was changing the White image of the Chinese. The Chinese pursued this largely in two ways: by altering their own behavior and relationships to more closely fit White models, and by developing a set of parallel institutions that could serve their own community in ways similar to the institutions serving Whites.

The first of these involved ending certain relationships with Blacks and emphasizing their own racial distinctiveness. There were not enough Chinese in the Delta to pose a threat to any White economic interests, so Whites had no economic stake in the classification of Chinese as Black, nor did they object to Chinese retail outlets serving the Black community. Whites did object to intimate social relations between Chinese and Blacks. This violated the core of the concept of racial segregation, suggesting that the differences between Blacks and Chinese were minimal whereas the differences between both groups and Whites were large. The Chinese saw that these relations would have to change. They knew that the racial system classified entire groups by the behaviors of single individuals and that a successful image change would require a high degree of conformity to White norms on the part of the Chinese. The Chinese began to put social pressure on individuals to end Chinese-Black marriages and friendships. The rest of the Chinese community ostracized Chinese men who cohabited with or married Black women. Some of these men broke up with their partners. Others moved away, and some remained and retained their relationships but clearly were no longer welcome among the Chinese. Chinese adjusted their own living situations in other ways to more closely resemble those of Whites. Chinese grocers moved out of living quarters they had long favored behind or upstairs from their stores and began to buy separate houses outside the Black communities where their stores were located. They redecorated their stores to look more like those in the White community. Chinese who had grown up largely among Black Mississippians made a conscious effort to distance themselves from Black culture and behavior and to model their own behaviors on those of Whites.

At the same time that they distanced themselves from Blacks in all but business relationships, the Chinese avoided asking for complete equality with Whites. While ending marriages with Blacks, they made it clear that they had no intention of marrying Whites either, underlining their support for the fundamental White concept of racial separateness and their belief in their own group distinctiveness. They remained deferential toward Whites, asking, in effect, not necessarily to be treated as equals but at least to be treated as not-Black.

The second approach to an altered image was the formation of a set of community institutions that could serve Chinese needs in ways modeled on White institutions. The Chinese established their own Baptist churches and missions; set up schools so that their children no longer had to attend schools set up for Blacks; and established social clubs, youth organizations, and even Chinese cemeteries, allowing them to escape the Black cemeteries they had been forced to use in the past. These institutions often involved Whites as advisers or participants, preaching in the churches, for example, or teaching Sunday school.

The institutions served several purposes. First, they offered settings in which the Chinese could interact with one another and build a sense of solidarity. They also offered settings in which pressure could be brought to bear on those who did not live up to the White standards the Chinese were trying to emulate. Second, they were a vehicle for acculturation, socializing Chinese to patterns of Christian worship, school behaviors, and skills and rituals characteristic of much of White American society. Third, they presented an image of the Chinese doing things familiar to Whites in ways that Whites would recognize and understand, demonstrating that the Chinese were far more like Whites than like Blacks.

This multifaceted effort paid off. Growing numbers of White institutions, particularly in the small Delta towns, gradually began to accept the Chinese. The churches were the first to open their doors, then public accommodations such as restaurants and transportation, and eventually even the schools. By the beginning of the 1950s, nearly all of the White school systems had opened their doors to Chinese American children. Although Chinese continued to be barred from certain activities and organizations, particularly the elite institutions of the larger towns, a major transition was well under way. Writing originally in 1971, Loewen commented (1988:96), "Although they still do not enjoy full equality, the Chinese are definitely accorded white status, affirmed for example by the 'W' in the appropriate blank on their driver's licenses." In essence, the Chinese had succeeded in escaping the assigned identity Black and asserting their own identity—Chinese—and establishing it as close to, if not entirely comparable with, White identity.

The Chinese Success

Why were the Chinese successful? Aside from their own determination, several factors were crucial to their ability to alter the classifications that the larger society made. First, they made clear that they were not challenging the system of racial segregation or classification as a whole, but only their particular place in it. By maintaining the pattern of racial etiquette, being deferential toward Whites and disdainful toward Blacks, and by making clear that they would not challenge the fundamental idea of White superiority, the Chinese made their effort acceptable to Whites. Second, their business record worked in their favor. Chinese groceries on the whole were successful, and their relative affluence "constituted the most far-reaching difference in image that could be imagined, contrasted to the destitute black population" (Loewen 1988:97). It allowed the Chinese not only to support the establishment of their own institutions but also to make notable charitable contributions to White churches and other organizations, and to engage in patterns of consumption that brought their own lifestyles closer to those of Whites. Third, and perhaps most important, the White establishment that controlled the Delta had little compelling economic or political interest in confining the Chinese to the bottom of the racial hierarchy. Certainly the Chinese effort faced opposition from Whites on occasion, and some Whites never abandoned their original view of the Chinese, but at least the Chinese could have an impact on such opposition, for in reconceptualizing the Chinese as not-Black, Whites had to give up very little. This dramatically distinguished the Chinese situation from that of African Americans in the Delta. Even if they had wished to, there was no way that Blacks could emulate the Chinese achievement. In 1940, Blacks represented more than 70% of the Delta's population and most of its agricultural labor force; by 1960 that had changed very little. The Delta economy and, therefore, the economic fortunes of its White establishment depended wholly on Black subordination, on a system of race relations that tied Blacks into sharecropping and long-term debt to Whites, denied them political power, and made them vulnerable to a legal system and a system of racial etiquette in which Whites made the rules, called the shots, and won all the battles. Whites had little to lose from the change in Chinese status but everything to lose from a similar change for Blacks. What the Chinese were permitted, Blacks would never have been allowed.

The Peculiarities of Assertion

This story is hardly typical of the larger population of Chinese Americans in the United States, many of whom likewise have struggled with prejudice and discrimination, phenomena that have characterized much of the Chinese experience in America. Other portions of the Chinese American population have had to find ways to respond to situations that denied their political and economic freedom and defined them as less worthy—sometimes less human—than Euro-Americans. They have responded differently, in part because their situations have been different. The distinctive social structure of Delta society powerfully shaped both the experience of the Mississippi Chinese and their singular response to it. They faced a limited set of choices within that society. Those limited choices meant that the only way they could both remain in the Delta and escape their subordinated position was to become supporters of the larger racial system that was the foundation of Delta society. In essence, they had to tacitly buy into the racism at the heart of Black-White relations in the American South.

In the Mississippi Chinese case, we can readily see assertion at work. Once they decided to remain in the Delta, the Chinese set out to change the way Delta society saw them. They undertook a form of "ethnic reorganization" (Nagel and Snipp 1993): They reorganized their own social relations and altered the norms governing those relations, in this case to make them better conform to the expectations of Whites and in resistance to the identity that Whites had assigned them. In the process, they also set out to alter the White interpretation of Chinese identity, to change the meaning that Whites attached to it. Finally, they attempted to alter the system of racial categories itself. What began as a two-category system eventually moved closer to a three-category system. Although White and Black remained the dominant categories organizing Delta society, the Chinese managed to establish a much sharper boundary between themselves and Blacks and to make the boundary separating them from Whites far less clear and onerous than it once had been.

Case 3. From Thick Ethnicity to Thin: German Americans

Germans who came to the United States in the 18th and 19th centuries found themselves in a situation dramatically different from the rigidly stratified, biracial caste system that confronted Chinese immigrants upon their arrival in the Mississippi Delta. The country the Germans entered treated them—and White people generally—very differently from Chinese, Indians, or Blacks. German immigrants could look forward not only to sharing the riches of the New World but, after the founding of the United States, to full and equal citizenship. This more welcoming environment hardly seems promising ground for the construction of an enduring ethnic identity, but Germans were not entirely free and unconstrained. An Anglo culture and an English-speaking populace dominated the United States, and the promise of citizenship carried with it the expectation that Germans would shed those things—language, custom, even identity—that marked them as distinctive and made them who they were.

Many of the early German immigrants to the United States were willing to pay this price, but the transition was easier said than done: The cultural practices of everyday life are not easily shed. Furthermore, as

German migration expanded in the 19th century, fewer Germans were willing to accept the costs. Some 19th-century German immigrants believed that the United States not only should help to sustain German culture in America but also should promote it as a rich and invaluable contribution to American society. Many of them set out to sustain a consciously and culturally distinct ethnic identity. Resisting the assimilative demands of the receiving society, they were determined that German culture should flourish in the cities and farmlands of America. Their determination was a source of tension between them and their hosts. Out of this tension, a distinct and elaborate German American identity eventually emerged, only to be abandoned when societal conditions changed.

Two German Migrations

At the start of German migration to America, most migrants had little interest in maintaining distinctive communities or collective identities. In what we might label the colonial period, from the 17th century until about 1815, the number of Germans moving to America was not large, numbering between 65,000 and 100,000 persons for the entire period. They came for a number of reasons: religious freedom, economic opportunity, even the sheer adventure of new and abundant frontiers. For the most part, however, they came with individual or family interests in mind. Most wanted and expected to make their way into the mainstream of American society, taking advantage of the opportunities that the New World offered. If the immigrants themselves were not entirely successful, then they at least would prepare the way for their children, whom they fully expected to thrive in North America.

Most of these early immigrants realized that this would mean leaving much of their Germanness behind, and they were prepared to do so. Communities with distinctively German characteristics nevertheless quickly began to emerge in America. The immigrants brought with them ways of living, thinking, and communicating that were different from those of most other Europeans living in the New World, and different from the dominant Anglo culture. Given these differences, it made sense for successive immigrants to settle among those who had already come, who spoke their language and shared their ways of life, and with whom they shared, in many cases, familial or friendship relations. Contrary to romanticized images of immigrants as huddled masses of isolated individuals or families who arrived impoverished and disoriented in an alien land (cf. Handlin 1973), most German immigrants were "chain migrants" (Kamphoefner 1987): They followed in the footsteps of family and friends who had gone before them. They knew where they were going and much of what awaited them once they arrived.

The welcome they received, although certainly better than what Blacks, Indians, or Chinese experienced, was not entirely positive. There was some anti-German prejudice among the English-speaking populace. None other than Benjamin Franklin complained about the "Palatinate Boors" who were threatening to "Germanize us instead of our Anglifying them, and [who] will never adopt our Language or Customs" (quoted in Kamphoefner 1996:152). Despite such views, these early German communities were less the products of discrimination or prejudice than of inertia and convenience: the inertia of already existing language and custom, and the convenience of settling with friends and compatriots.

Inertia, however, is a poor foundation for an ethnic community in a world that expects and encourages assimilation. These communities were small, and they had neither the resources nor the collective will to sustain themselves (Waters 1995). Most were little more than way stations whose main function was to help newly arriving immigrants and their children adapt to the conditions of life in the New World. Most immigrants soon moved on, searching out opportunities on the frontiers and in new communities that were less likely to have significant German populations. Furthermore, the Germans who came to America in this period were far from united. The Germany they came from was not a unified country but a group of states variously linked to one another. It was a large territory that would not be politically unified until 1871. Immigrants came from various places within it. They shared some cultural attributes and a common language, but they spoke several different Germanic dialects. They were divided further by class, education, and religion. There were numerous Catholics, significant numbers of Protestants, anticlericals, and a small number of Jews. In short, the migrants of the colonial period had little sense of themselves as a united people.

That changed after 1815. In the 19th century, a second and quite different wave of German immigration headed for the United States. Three characteristics distinguished this second wave. The first was its sheer size. In the 100-year period beginning in 1815, more than 5.5 million Germans came to the United States, by far the largest foreign-language immigration of the period and one of the largest in all of American history.

The second distinguishing characteristic of this wave was its extraordinary diversity. Although internal differentiation had made it difficult for colonial-era immigrants to recognize their broader commonalities and interests, it became a source of strength in the second wave. German employers and employees, skilled and unskilled workers, Catholics,

Protestants, Jews, entrepreneurs, teachers, and numerous others poured into the United States. For the first time, German immigrants had little reason to seek out associations with non-Germans. Their numbers and diversity were such that they could find what they needed in rapidly growing German neighborhoods and communities, and they depended little on the non-German society they were entering. United by a broad commonality of language, immigrants in this second wave quickly formed organizations of various kinds, everything from welfare groups to cultural organizations to fire companies, building their own institutions to meet their own needs and overcoming the various differences that divided them (Conzen 1976). Population size and diversity, in other words, went hand in hand, allowing Germans to turn not only small towns and villages but even entire sections of major cities into "Little Germanies," institutionally complex communities that included a major portion of the German population of the United States.

The third distinctive characteristic of this second wave was the fact that many of these later immigrants wanted to retain their Germanness. Toward the middle of the century, there was a growing nationalist movement in Germany, an effort to create a stronger and more unified country. This movement, fueled by German romanticism, culminated in the failed revolution of 1848. Many of the Germans who came to the United States in the mid-19th century were either supporters of the nationalist movement or had been influenced by it. In the aftermath of the failed revolution, they headed for America, intent on nurturing and sustaining German identity and culture. Although they eagerly sought the economic opportunities that the United States had to offer, they were far less interested in the cultural mainstream than earlier immigrants had been, or in making the cultural adjustments earlier ones had made. On the contrary, many of these new immigrants felt that the descendants of their colonial-period predecessors had abandoned "German virtues while acquiring only American vices" (Conzen 1985:135). As far as the newcomers could tell, the Germans who had come before them had little coherent identity or meaningful culture, and they had earned little more than contempt from the host American society.

In contrast, these new immigrants wanted to build a world of their own in America, a world in which the highest praise for anything was that it was *gerade wie in Deutschland*, which, roughly translated, means "as good as in Germany" (Wittke 1952). The nationalists among them set out to restore what they saw as a lost appreciation of German culture and heritage among earlier immigrants and their children, and they began promoting German language and nationalist thought among Germans in the United States. Some went so far as to propose German ethnic separatism, hoping to establish isolated settlements where German culture could be reproduced and preserved. Some proposals even called on Germans to assume the control of an entire state or to found a new colony somewhere on the frontier, beyond the western boundaries of the United States (Hawgood 1940).

Cultural Preservation

The separatist impulse brought by the new nationalists had only limited impact, but the preservationist impulse flourished. Economic interest undermined the former. Confronted with a choice, most of the hundreds of thousands of Germans pouring into the United States preferred the economic opportunities that came with integration to the cultural autonomy that separatism might afford. Even those who were most committed to joining the economic mainstream of American life, however, were determined not to leave their culture entirely behind. Among other things, they had a strong conviction that German culture was in many ways superior to what they encountered in the United States, and they believed that the qualities of that culture should be welcomed and supported. Many felt they had a "special right . . . to support an ethnic existence in America because of the special gifts that they would ultimately bring into the melting pot" (Conzen 1985:139). Although they appreciated Americans' practical achievements and their aptitudes for business and politics, they found Americans lacking in appreciation "for the higher things in life. Germans, by contrast, were dreamers, artists, thinkers, impractical perhaps, but able to enjoy life and cultivate warm, personal relationships." They would bring to America "the gifts of sociability, public morality, and an appreciation for the good, the true, and the beautiful" (Conzen 1985:139). Making such gifts required that Germans preserve their community and culture. Instead of being absorbed and overwhelmed by the American mainstream, they would have to gradually unite with it as major contributors. In short, they would have to become and remain *German* Americans.

At the heart of this movement to cultivate and preserve a distinctly German presence in the United States was a group of liberal intellectuals known as "Forty-Eighters," the so-called "Refugees of Revolution" (Wittke 1952), who had come to the United States after 1848 hoping to promote in America the dream of a unified German civilization that they had failed to realize in Germany itself. Energetic and entrepreneurial, they reinvigorated German cultural life in the United States, founding a series of voluntary associations, historical societies, singing groups, and other organizations designed to foster German culture and identity.

Among the more distinctive of these organizations were a set of social clubs devoted to physical culture known as "Turnvereins" (Barney 1994; Lipsitz 1991). These were a German import. In 1806, the French emperor Napoleon had conquered certain German territories. Bemoaning defeat and fragmentation at the hands of the French, patriotic German reformers set out to improve the strength and character of the German people through—among other things—physical fitness. The Turnvereins were one result. Among the Forty-Eighters were numerous Turners, as the members of these clubs were called, and they set out to establish Turnvereins throughout the German communities of the United States. By the end of the 1850s, there were nearly 160 of these clubs in Boston, New York, Philadelphia, Baltimore, and other cities. They had spread up and down the Ohio, Missouri, and Mississippi River valleys and had attracted a membership of some 10,000 people (Barney 1994).

Turnvereins in the United States were at first primarily centers of German-style sport (a combination of gymnastics and calisthenics) and recreation, but they quickly took on much broader functions. Under the guidance of the educated, idealistic Forty-Eighters, they became centers for instruction in the German language and offered adult education classes in German politics, philosophy, and history. They presented dances, concerts, and plays; hosted arts and crafts classes; and were home to all manner of German meetings, special interest groups, and associations. In many cities, the halls where Turners met also provided a place for the public consumption of alcoholic beverages and for recreation on the Sabbath. Nativist, prohibitionist local governments prohibited both of these practices, much to the dismay of German immigrants who were largely united in their desire to enjoy themselves in traditional German fashion, not excluding their Sunday recreation. Aside from the persistent use of the German language, Germans' views on alcohol and Sunday leisure probably antagonized the Anglo-American population more than anything else about them. Turners were active as well in numerous political causes, among them the neutralization of the growing U.S. nativist movement directed against foreigners and the abolition of slavery. In St. Louis, for example, Turners lobbied to keep the state of Missouri loyal to the Union and to antislavery ideals during the Civil War. Although it is difficult today to recapture how controversial some of these issues were in the 19th century, all of them, from abolition to Sabbath recreation, were connected in one way or another with the effort to preserve and cultivate German ideals and customs in the face of an often unsympathetic and unyielding Anglo culture.

Also contributing to the preservation and cultivation effort was a huge network of German-language publications. By the 1860s, at least 16 American cities had German-language daily newspapers; some had two or more in competition with each other. In 1850, New York City had four German-language dailies, more than Berlin or even Leipzig, the German publishing center. At their peak in 1894, there were nearly 800 German publications in the United States, including 97 daily newspapers, providing news, features, and community information in the mother tongue (Kamphoefner 1996:156). These publications also were vigorous participants in the political debates of the day, especially those having to do with assimilation and the preservation of German culture. Well-known journals such as *Die Abendschule* (The Evening School), published in Minneapolis and distributed widely to German families across the United States, were influential in helping German immigrants develop and retain a sense of themselves as German Americans (Peterson 1991).

Many German immigrant children retained fluency in German, often greater fluency than in English (Eberle 1987). This was the result not only of family influences but also of German-language elementary schools. Many of these were church based, but public schools were almost as important. Nearly half of all elementary students who learned German in 1900 did so in public schools at public expense. Some municipal public school systems, such as those in Indianapolis, Baltimore, Cleveland, and Cincinnati, established fully bilingual systems where German was the primary language of instruction (Kamphoefner 1996:157).

These preservationist efforts did not go uncontested. In the 1870s, for example, when Germans demanded that the schools of Buffalo, New York, teach the German language, they met with hostility from nativists and others. When a tally of births in the city of Buffalo revealed that in 1878 nearly 2,000 out of 3,700 newborn children were German, a Buffalo newspaper urged Americans to "realize in what a contemptible minority they are in this Teutonic city" (quoted in Eberle 1987:78). Such opposition had only limited effects. In 1910, there were 150 German organizations in Buffalo (Eberle 1987:84), and Germans were involved in all parts of the city's economy, politics, and civic culture. Much the same was true in other cities.

All this activity masked an underlying trend that was moving the other way. German ethnicity, in the language of Chapter 4, was gradually "thinning," organizing less and less of German American life despite the efforts of its strongest supporters and the effects of cultural organizations, German-language media, and schools. The fact was that many Germans continued to put economic opportunity ahead of cultural preservation, making the cultural sacrifices necessary to take full advantage of the economic opportunities available to them. Most were in frequent, if not daily, interaction with non-Germans, speaking English, carrying on business transactions, talking to non-German customers, and adjusting to the needs of the larger economy and to well-established American ways of life. German culture was becoming less and less relevant to ongoing daily activities. It was more and more a matter of history and heritage, symbols and memories. Simply put, as the years went by and their participation in institutions of the larger society increased, German Americans became less German and more American.

Change, however, was not entirely in one direction. At the same time, much of America was becoming more German. As the 19th century wore on, growing numbers of Anglo-Americans began to adopt German practices, from the public consumption of alcohol to Sunday leisure activities and publicly sponsored sport and recreation. Conflict over these issues diminished not so much because German Americans were adjusting to Anglo-American views as because the dominant Anglo-American culture was coming around to German (and other immigrant) ones (Kamphoefner 1996). By early in the 20th century, much of the United States had adopted practices that had once been alien. In some ways, Benjamin Franklin had been right: The immigrants and their descendants had "Germanized" a number of aspects of American life.

The Triumph of Assimilation

Then came World War I. The anti-German hysteria that the war generated in the United States sounded the death knell of the cultural preservation movement. When the United States entered the war in 1917, German Americans' status plummeted. Public school systems dropped the study of German language and literature, libraries removed German books from their shelves, and municipal officials changed German street names. The war presented German Americans with a choice: Are you *German* Americans or Americans who happen to be of German descent? Quite abruptly, the first option became unacceptable. German organizations and culture quickly lost their appeal. German Americans found themselves plastering over German-language cornerstones and adopting English translations of their German names. Buffalo's German American Bank, one of the city's leading financial institutions, became Liberty Bank, dachshunds became "liberty pups," and hamburger, named after Hamburg, Germany, became Salisbury steak (Eberle 1987:82). The preservationist movement collapsed.

A little more than two decades later, in 1941, Germany and the United States went to war again. What was left of the cultural romanticization that once had fueled the drive to sustain German community and identity in America collided with the grim horrors of Nazism, German expansionism, the rise of Adolf Hitler's Third Reich, and the Jewish Holocaust. For German Americans, the assimilation that Anglo culture had promoted from the start had already become the strategy of choice. World War II only affirmed what they already realized. What mattered was to be Americans after all.

In recent years, there has been something of a resurgence of interest in German American ethnicity in the United States, accompanying a general resurgence of interest in European-descent ethnicities. On the 1990 census, some 58 million Americans (up from 49.2 million in 1980) reported at least some German ancestry, making it the largest ancestry group in the United States. Whereas German American ethnicity certainly still exists, however, it is far thinner than it was in the 19th century. It has become what Herbert Gans (1979) calls "symbolic ethnicity," an identity that is invoked on occasion—on holidays or at family gatherings, for example—and that clearly has some meaning for many of those who share it, but has little influence on most people's daily lives. It organizes self-concepts for many German Americans, but it organizes little of what they actually do.

There is irony in the German American story. On one hand, German Americans consciously sought to maintain an ethnic culture and community. They built their own institutions dedicated to that end. On the other, they also pursued economic and political integration into the American mainstream. Their success at the latter eventually undermined their efforts at the former, but it did not destroy them. That was left to changing circumstances—two world wars—that dramatically altered the environment in which German Americans found themselves.

Thus, assimilation may have triumphed in the end, but it did not do so easily. Particularly in the massive second wave of immigration, Germans came to the United States with clear ideas about who they were and little interest simply in becoming Americans. Well equipped with numbers, skills, and community resources, they entered a society that to a large extent, albeit sometimes grudgingly, allowed them to pursue their own objectives and even, in certain areas such as language instruction in public schools, lent those objectives its own support. As a result, they succeeded for a time in accomplishing their goal: to be Americans, but of an emphatically German sort. Had not World War I intervened, the history of the German community in the United States might have been different. Barring the two world wars, their ethnicity might have remained a thicker, more vibrant aspect of many German Americans' lives well into the 20th century.

It certainly was vibrant for a time. Through the 19th century and beyond, Germans successfully asserted the identity they wished to maintain. That they were able to do so and to play so large a role in the construction of their own ethnicity was the result of several things, not least of them the fact that they were White. Although they encountered antagonism and occasionally intense pressures to conform to the Anglo majority culture of the United States, they experienced nothing like the violently imposed subordination that Blacks faced or the enforced acculturation with which many Indians had to deal. Some Anglo-Americans saw German immigrants as a threat to their own cultural dominance, but few saw them as racially inferior or treated them as such. As a result, Germans were able both to be themselves and to become Americans—to maintain their distinctiveness even as they took full advantage of economic and political opportunities that few Blacks or Indians or Chinese would have for another century.

Ironically, this degree of opportunity and acceptance by the larger society would surely have been their downfall in the long run. Although they built institutions designed to preserve German culture and community, German Americans were never dependent on those institutions for their own well-being or to solve the urgent problems that immigrant communities often face. The institutions of the larger society also were available to them and were better able to serve one of their primary objectives, which had to do with building economically viable lives in America. Consequently, their efforts at cultural preservation were faltering even before global conflicts stepped in to make that preservation indefensible. Faced with few obstacles to the realization of their interests, possessing a set of institutions that were peripheral to their most basic needs, and carrying a culture that became increasingly acceptable to Americans even as they tried to preserve it as a thing apart, German Americans were unlikely to remain a separate people for very long.

Case 4. Constructed Primordiality and Ethnic Power: Afrikaners in South Africa[5]

At the southern tip of the African continent lies the Republic of South Africa. For many years, South Africa was a pariah state to much of the world, thanks to the rigid racial organization of the country in which a small European minority, largely of English and Dutch descent, exercised enormous political and economic power over a far larger African, Coloured, and Indian majority, brutally suppressing their efforts to gain control of their own lives and a more equitable share of the country's vast riches.[6] This stark racial divide and the lethal governmental policies used to enforce it became a focus for much of the world's critical attention, particularly since the 1960s as Black resistance mounted, as government policy became more vicious, and as racial barriers in other parts of the world began to fall. In the early 1990s, thanks both to the economic and political pressures exerted by other nations and to the persistent, frequently suicidal resistance of the Black population, significant change finally came to South Africa. Racial equality achieved constitutional status, although the economic differences between Whites and other South Africans today remain enormous. In 1994, Nelson Mandela, who had spent much of his life imprisoned by the South African government as a leader of the political resistance to the White regime, became the country's first Black president.

Throughout this period, however, the European-descent population was by no means monolithic. For the study of ethnicity, one of the most interesting aspects of the South African experience has been the persistent division and conflict between English-descent Whites, on one hand, and the so-called Afrikaners—descendants of Dutch, French, and German settlers—on the other. In the fall, rise, and ultimate triumph (until the last decade) of South Africa's Afrikaners we can see another ethnic process at work: the marshaling of symbolic resources by an ethnic community on behalf of its own solidarity and survival.

Afrikaners and English

The Dutch were the first Europeans to settle in what is now South Africa, establishing a settlement on the Cape of Good Hope, at the southernmost tip of the continent, in 1652. By the first decade of the 18th century, the European population of the area had grown to nearly 2,000, including not only Dutch but also French and Germans. Over the next few decades, growing numbers of Dutch-, German-, and French-descent farmers, known to themselves as Boers and eventually as Afrikaners, arrived at the Cape and began to move inland in search of land, trading with the various African peoples they encountered, enslaving some, employing others as farm laborers or servants, and occasionally fighting with them as Africans resisted European encroachments. As this resistance grew, so did a racist ideology among the Afrikaners, one that held the indigenous African peoples to be both fundamentally different from and inferior to the Europeans.

The Afrikaners were not the only Europeans to come to South Africa. Late in the 18th century, growing numbers of British settlers began to appear at the Cape, and in 1806, in the aftermath of the Napoleonic Wars, Britain wrested control of the Cape Colony from the Dutch. Both British administration and English culture were very different from the Afrikaner equivalents. Eventually, the British set out to reorganize the Colony's social and political institutions after British models, and to Anglicize the Afrikaner population. That population was heavily rural and agricultural (the word *Boer* means farmer), whereas the English dominated trade and commerce and were concentrated in the towns. Over the next couple of decades, the British administration made English the official language of the Colony, placed English teachers in the country schools that served the Afrikaner population, put pressure on Afrikaner families to give up their own language and cultural practices, and even brought in Scottish ministers to teach in the Dutch Reformed Church that dominated Afrikaner religion. Official positions were reserved to English-speaking persons. Because of their lack of English proficiency, most Boers were excluded even from juries, including those by which they themselves were to be judged.

British cultural impositions and institutional domination led to tension between the two groups, as did more liberal British policies toward Blacks. The British angered Afrikaners when, for example, they abolished legal distinctions between Whites and the Khoikhoi, the indigenous people of the Cape area, and angered them again when they created a circuit court to hear the complaints of Black servants against their Boer masters. The end of slavery in the British colonies undermined the agricultural economy of the Afrikaners, while British policies made it difficult for Boer slaveholders to receive compensation for the loss of their labor force.

By the middle of the 1830s, Afrikaner discontent with British rule was widespread. Some leading Afrikaners saw British domination as a threat to the Afrikaner way of life and talked about the need to maintain an Afrikaner "nationality" or ethnicity, distinguished by language and religion and a singular view of the proper place of the Black population in South African society. Combined with this discontent was the desire of Afrikaner farmers for more land than was available in the Cape Colony as its population grew. Afrikaner eyes began to turn northward, and by 1838 4,000 Afrikaners—the number would rise to 12,000 over the next few years—had left the Cape Colony in search of freedom and a home "in the unknown wilderness of the North" (Reitz 1900:92, quoted in Moodie 1975:5).

This inland migration came to be known in Afrikaner folklore as the Great Trek. As the Afrikaners moved north, they encountered not only the hardships of what to them was a wilderness but also the resistance of the African populations for whom that wilderness was home. Leading that opposition were the Zulu people. In 1838, a column of Afrikaner emigrants, moving north, set their sights on the heart of the Zulu kingdom. On December 15, they encamped in a defensive formation on the banks of the Ncome River in Zulu territory. The next day, a massive Zulu army attacked them there. In a furious battle, known afterward as the Battle of Blood River, the Afrikaners defeated the Zulus, killing some 3,000 of them, and broke the back of Zulu resistance to their advance. This victory paved the way for the eventual establishment of the independent Republic of Natal.

Over the next few decades, however, the British refused to leave the Afrikaners alone, sending a military expedition to occupy and annex Natal. The Afrikaners moved on, founding two new republics to the west, the Transvaal and the Orange Free State. In 1899, continuing British efforts to control these two states and to force the Afrikaners into submission led eventually to all-out war. The Boer War of 1899-1902, which the Afrikaners ultimately lost, was a bitterly fought conflict that devastated Afrikaner communities. In 1910, the victorious British established the Union of South Africa, bringing together the Afrikaner states with Natal and the Cape Province in what is known today as the Republic of South Africa.

The end of Afrikaner independence did not produce the degree of social and cultural integration among the descendants of Europeans that the British—and some Afrikaners—had hoped to see. The "union" was primarily a political entity. Within its confines, the early decades of the 20th century witnessed instead the emergence of a powerful Afrikaner nationalist movement. That movement gradually attracted growing numbers of Afrikaners to its cause, and in 1948 the National Party, standard bearer of Afrikaner nationalism, was voted into power. Over the next few decades, Afrikaner-dominated governments elaborated the system of *apartheid*, or racial separation, that came to characterize all of South African society. Afrikaners established themselves as the dominant social and political force in South African life. For a time, at least, Afrikanerdom was victorious, and it would remain so until the revolutionary transformations of the late 1980s and 1990s, which finally brought its power to an end and introduced a genuinely multiracial South Africa.

The Race and Class Alternatives

At the heart of the 20th-century Afrikaner political resurgence, leading eventually to electoral triumph in 1948, lay the development of Afrikaner ethnicity. Afrikaner collective identity itself is not a puzzle. In this all-too-brief historical summary we can easily find the raw materials of ethnic construction. Language, religion, and national origin, for example, offered ready boundaries between English and Afrikaner populations; economic concentrations divided them; governmental policy under the British, although much of it was designed to denationalize and Anglicize the Afrikaners, instead reinforced the ethnic boundary by singling out them and their interests for differential treatment. There were other logics of collective identity at work, however, ones that might have led to very different outcomes. One logic argued, in effect, that what mattered in South African life was class: the distribution of persons through the economic structure of the society, and in particular the gap between wealthy capitalists and exploited workers. The relevance of this for Afrikaners came from systemic changes in the South African economy. In the 20th century, changes in agriculture and the shift toward an industrial economy forced much of the essentially agricultural Afrikaner labor force to migrate to the cities. There they joined unskilled Black workers at the bottom of the economic ladder, below the typically more appropriately skilled English workers and at the service of a wealthy capitalist class, itself largely—but not exclusively—English. A class-based logic of group formation suggested that Black and White workers of all groups should join across the racial divide, forge a common class identity, and organize against those who controlled the country's wealth and governed their lives.

The other logic argued, in effect, that what mattered most in South African life was race: the fundamental divide between Black and White. Certainly the potential boundary was clear enough: the physical distinction of color. A race-based logic of group formation suggested that Afrikaners and English of all classes should join together to protect their status and power against the rumblings of outrage among the disfranchised darker populations of the country, submerging Afrikanerdom in a larger racial alliance.

In the long run, the second of these turned out to be far more compelling than the first. A class-based alliance between White and Black workers faced not only the problem of racism, already deeply embedded in South African history and in both English and Afrikaner cultures, but also the fact that unskilled Black and White workers were often in competition with each other, with Blacks typically willing to work at wage levels Afrikaners were unwilling to accept. A race-based alliance between English and Afrikaner, although a more likely outcome and the one that, by the middle decades of the 20th century, certainly prevailed, faced problems of its own. Afrikaners saw themselves as victims of British imperialism; much of their history was a record of efforts to escape British domination. Furthermore, the economic gap between English and Afrikaner populations was wide: It was English wealth that dominated the emergent industrial economy of South Africa. Any interethnic alliance was likely to find the English playing the leading role, calling the shots, and reaping much of the benefit. These factors made a racial alliance problematic. Another potent factor contributed to the survival of Afrikaner ethnicity: the self-conscious effort at self-preservation on the part of Afrikaners themselves.

The Symbolic Construction of Ethnicity

Beginning in the 1870s, and in reaction to the policies and power of the British colonial regime, some Afrikaners set out to articulate and promote—in essence, to construct—an elaborate and positive sense of Afrikaner identity and peoplehood. At the heart of this effort was a loosely linked set of what Crawford Young (1976), writing about ethnicity generally, has called "cultural entrepreneurs." These typically are persons drawn usually from the professional middle class and the intelligentsia who engage in "the ideologization of identity," an effort to assign to a particular identity a unique history and future and to generate a stock of cultural symbols that can serve to mobilize and unite group members on the group's behalf (pp. 45-46). In the South African case, these cultural entrepreneurs set out to tell the Afrikaner story in their own way, to make of that story the foundation for an enduring Afrikaner nation, a potent narrative of Afrikanerdom that would solidify the ethnic allegiance of its people.

The first effort to give written form to such a story came in a book produced by a small Dutch Reformed Church congregation in the agricultural town of Paarl in 1877. The title of the book translates approximately as "the history of our country in the language of our people." That language was Afrikaans, the spoken language of the Afrikaners and a derivative of Dutch. This was the first book ever published in Afrikaans. More important,

> It was the first book to treat all Afrikaners, dispersed as they were among British colonies and independent republics, as a single people. It was, too, the first book to set out the rudiments of a national mythology, with the overt purpose of encouraging Afrikaners to think of themselves as forming a distinct people with a common destiny and to resist the pressures for assimilation into British culture. (Thompson 1985:31)

As the publication of this book suggests, one of the arenas of resistance to assimilation was language. In elements of expressive culture such as poetry, Afrikaners not only could retell their story in new ways but also could do so in a linguistic medium of their own. The poetic reframing of the Boer War offers an example. The devastation and brutality of the war had left a legacy of profound bitterness among Afrikaners, but in the first decade of the 20th century a new generation of lyric poets transformed the war into a powerful symbol of solidarity, sacrifice, and suffering. In their words, written in Afrikaans, Boer pain and anguish became a testament to patriotism and peoplehood. "By articulating and universalizing the Afrikaner fate, this new Afrikaans literature helped to formulate a clear consciousness of national identity" (Moodie 1975: 42-43). It gave dignity to suffering and heroized what had seemed a futile calamity. It also "proved that Afrikaans could be a language of true artistic worth and beauty . . . awakening a realization of the lyricism and essential linguistic validity of the *patois* of home and hearth" (Moodie 1975:45-46).

Such poetry contributed to the growing Afrikaner effort to resist Anglicization and build their own sense of peoplehood through the promotion of Afrikaans as the daily language of Afrikanerdom. This effort was linked intimately to the Afrikaner nationalist movement. Before the Boer War, many South Africans, including some Afrikaners, had viewed Afrikaans with disdain, viewing it as merely a simplified and inferior form of Dutch. In the aftermath of the war, it became a symbol of the politically vanquished but culturally resilient Afrikaner nation. To speak Afrikaans and to insist on its use in places of business became acts of patriotism. Afrikaner clergy, journalists, teachers, and others, concerned that growing numbers of Afrikaners moving to the English-dominated cities would abandon their language and with it lose touch with their Afrikaner roots, began to lobby for recognition of Afrikaans as an official language. As urban Afrikaner populations grew, they became large enough to have their own schools and churches, which then became settings for the promotion of Afrikaans and the support of Afrikaner solidarity. By the late 1910s and the 1920s, Afrikaner teachers had succeeded in having Afrikaans adopted in the junior grades in schools in some areas, and in 1925, the language movement triumphed when Afrikaans replaced Dutch as the country's second official language and was written into the country's constitution as the legal equal of English.

Afrikaners memorialized the suffering of the Boer War in a more material way as well. In 1913, they unveiled the Vrouemonument ("National Women's Monument"), dedicated, according to the plaque on the monument, to "the memory of the 26,370 women and children who died in the [British] concentration camps and to the other women and children who perished as a result of the War of 1899-1902" (quoted in Moodie 1975:18).

> Within a circular enclosure stands a sandstone obelisk. At its foot is a statue . . . of a bareheaded woman holding a dying child. Another woman . . . stands beside her staring resolutely out across the Free State veld. On either side of this group are two bas-relief panels. On the left panel, under the caption "For freedom, volk [folk] and fatherland," we see women and children entering a concentration camp. . . . On the right panel is depicted an emaciated child dying in a camp tent with his mother by his side. (Moodie 1975:19).

The Vrouemonument soon became one of the holy places in the emerging history of Afrikanerdom, an icon capturing both the tragedy and the determination of Afrikaners.

A Chosen People

A critical element in this emerging Afrikaner conception of themselves was the notion of Afrikaners as a special, even "chosen" people, engaged in the realization of a grand, divinely fashioned design. This notion had its roots in the Calvinist theology of the Dutch Reformed Church, in particular in the Old Testament idea, supported by John Calvin, that an entire people might the be called by God to serve as his particular servants. One of those who did the most to advance the idea of Afrikaners as such a chosen people was Paul Kruger, president of the South African Republic (the Transvaal) from 1881 until its conquest by the British in the Boer War, and a man of considerable prestige among Afrikaners. "This formidable president laced his speeches with explicit comparisons between the history of the biblical Israelites and the history of the republican Afrikaners," asserting that Afrikaners were, indeed, the elect of God (Thompson 1985:32).

Afrikaners found signs of their election in the history of the Great Trek—their inland migration in search of a homeland of their own and an escape from British domination in the 1830s and 1840s—which in time became the centerpiece of their national narrative. This epic represented for them a demonstration of the divine hand in their history. They had been led out of the Cape Colony, were tested again and again by hardship, and were beset by enemies, yet God delivered them. He did so in response to their own commitment. A few days before the Battle of Blood River in 1838, the Afrikaners made a pledge that if God would give them victory in the struggle they knew was coming, "they would build a memorial church and they and their posterity would always celebrate the anniversary of the victory, to the honor of God" (Thompson 1985:144). The leader of the Afrikaners, Andries Pretorius, reported that following the battle they

> decided among ourselves to make known the day of our victory, being Sunday, the 16th of this month of December, among our entire community, and that we shall consecrate it to the Lord, and celebrate it with thanksgivings, since, before we fought the enemy, we promised in a public prayer that should we manage to win the victory, we would build a house to the Lord in memory of his name, wherever He shall indicate it; which vow we now also hope to honor, with the help of the Lord, now that He has blessed us and heard our prayers. (quoted in Thompson 1985:154).

Toward the end of the 19th century, as the threat of British conquest of the Afrikaner republics grew, December 16—known eventually as the Day of the Covenant—became the occasion for annual ceremonies at which Afrikaners would remind themselves of their commitment, made at Blood River, and remember the sacrifices of those who had come before, who had overcome the wilderness on behalf of God and the Arikaner nation. Among certain members of the clergy and political leaders such as Kruger, the victory at Blood River was a miracle, clear evidence of God's intervention on the Afrikaners' behalf. In the first half of the 20th century, the Great Trek, the Battle of Blood River, and this covenant between the people and their God each found a prominent place in written histories of the Afrikaners. They were staple features of the history taught in Afrikaner schools. In 1938, the centenary of the Great Trek, a column of oxwagons replayed the exodus from Cape Colony. Stopping at towns throughout South Africa, in December they converged on Pretoria, where a huge crowd of Afrikaners observed the laying of the cornerstone for a monument to the Voortrekkers (those who took part in the Great Trek). Moodie writes of the completed edifice (1975:19-20):

> This monument is a vast granite temple visible for miles around. Broad steps lead through a bas-relief oxwagon *laager* [defensive formation] to the main hall. Halfway up, the steps divide to make room for a huge . . . statue of an austere pioneer woman with her two children; this is flanked by four bas-relief wildebeest. . . . The vast domed hall at the top is empty save for a marble frieze on the walls that depicts the events of the Trek, with the covenant oath figuring prominently. In the center of the sanctuary is a circular opening like a well reaching down into the basement. In this lower vault lies a granite cenotaph . . . inscribed with the words: "*Ons vir jou, Suid-Afrika*" ("We for you, South Africa"). . . . Every year at noon on December 16, the sun shines directly through an aperture in the roof of the monument and into the depths below to illuminate the word "*Suid-Afrika*" inscribed upon the symbolic altar.

The building of the Voortrekker Monument and the ritual reenactment of the Great Trek represent a culmination in the effort of Afrikaners to construct a conception of Afrikanerdom sufficiently compelling to overcome alternative bases of identity, such as class and race, among their own people. In their development and mobilization of symbolic resources—language, ritual, expressive culture, material representations of the people and of their suffering and their triumph—Afrikaners kept the sense of their own historical and cultural distinctiveness vibrantly alive.

For much of the 20th century, this symbolic construction of ethnicity prevailed. On the other hand, it flourished in a situation in which racial issues were never far beneath the surface. In 1911, D. F. Malan, a leading Afrikaner, had argued that "any nationality, formed by God through history and environment, has in itself a right to existence . . . God wills differences between nation and nation. And He wills these because he has placed before each people a unique destiny" (quoted in Moodie 1975:71). Malan made this argument in the context of English-Afrikaner conflict; it was an argument for Afrikaner autonomy and cultural identity, but its essentialism and separatism would later prove useful in the White quest for justification of continued oppression of South Africa's Black, Indian, and mixed-race populations. When Afrikaners finally took power in 1948, they turned their own argument for ethnic separatism into a more comprehensive argument for racial oppression. They institutionalized that argument in the *apartheid* system, which rigidified racial identities and organized the strict separation of the races, facilitated the continued exploitation of Black labor on behalf of White wealth, and readily employed the most deadly forms of violence to enforce the dominant White position in South African society. The argument that had served Afrikaners so well in their resistance to the English proved an equally powerful ally as they moved more unequivocally into the oppressor's role in regard to Blacks.

Race had always lain in the background of Afrikaner assertions of identity. For Afrikaners, Blacks were the quintessential Other—the unchosen people, uncivilized, unbelievers, at times scarcely human. As Leonard Thompson points out, however, "Before the second half of the twentieth century Afrikaner mythology was able to assume racism rather than to elaborate it, since similar racist views prevailed in Europe and America and among other white South Africans. Moreover, British imperialism seemed to constitute a greater threat to Afrikaner interests than black resistance" (1985:27).

The Power of History and Myth

Afrikaner ethnicity was not entirely the product of the opportunities and constraints that Afrikaners experienced, although certainly the circumstances they faced were crucial foundations for Afrikaner identity. That identity also was a product of their own efforts to sustain their ethnicity as a basis of solidarity and action in the face of circumstances that argued as forcefully for other such bases. Against such circumstances, they set out to create a narrative of Afrikanerdom that could inspire the allegiance of their people. What was important in that narrative was not so much the events it recorded as the interpretation of those events, their transformation into compelling myth.

That such myths carry significant emotional power was apparent in an incident that occurred more than 40 years after the centennial of Blood River. It was inevitable that professional historians eventually would re-examine the events of 1838. In 1979, a group of South African theologians and historians gathered at a conference in the capital city of Pretoria to reconsider the events that had taken place nearly a century and a half earlier. The opening paper presented at the conference was a secular reappraisal of Blood River and the Covenant entered into by the victors in that battle. The author and presenter of the paper was a prominent Afrikaner historian. His paper questioned both the facts regarding those events and the interpretations that had since come to be accepted as part of Afrikanerdom's national myth. Word of the professor's analysis had leaked out, and only a few minutes into his presentation, a group of 30 or 40 men burst into the hall and, before a stunned audience, proceeded to pour tar and feathers over the speaker. Their leader seized the microphone and read the following statement (quoted in Schutte 1989:217-18):

> As young Afrikaners we have reached the end of our tether. Our spiritual heritage and everything we consider holy to the Afrikaner are being trampled underfoot and desecrated by liberalist politicians, 'stray' academics and false prophets who hide under the cloak of learning and false religion. . . . In this symposium they defile the holiest of holies of the Afrikaner being. This attitude is blasphemous and annuls the meaning of Afrikaner history.

That meaning, of course, was not inherent in the events themselves; it was given to them, an interpretation, a product of cultural entrepreneurship and of the development and skillful use of symbolic resources in the process of ethnic construction. Regardless of its origins, it had become a powerful myth indeed, part of the bond of shared culture that, along with shared interests and no shortage of institutions, linked many Afrikaners to each other solidarity.

Yet the tar and feathers were a rearguard action. By 1979, the meaning of Afrikaner history might still have been fiercely felt by many Afrikaners, but it could no longer hold the line against the growing forces of comprehensive social change. The 1980s would be turbulent, but by their end the whole edifice of White domination would be teetering, thanks to the growing Black and mixed-race resistance that in the 1990s transformed South African society.

Case 5. From Thin Ethnicity to Thick: Basketball and War in the Former Yugoslavia

They came from a country known for its basketball teams, and they made up perhaps the best team it ever produced.[7] In 4 years of official international competition, they never lost a game. In 1985, as 17-year-olds, they won the European Cadet championship; a year later, the European Junior title. They took on the senior national teams of Bulgaria, Turkey, and the Soviet Union, and they beat them all. Three of them eventually became National Basketball Association stars in the United States: Vlade Divac, originally with the Los Angeles Lakers and then with the Charlotte Hornets; Toni Kukoc of the Chicago Bulls; and Dino Radja of the Boston Celtics. Two more went on to international acclaim: Teo Alibegovic with Germany's Alba Berlin, one of Europe's top teams, and Sasha Djordjevic in the Italian League. Djordjevic was named European Player of the Year in 1994. For most of them, as a *Sports Illustrated* story pointed out (Wolff 1996), the high point of their careers remains their 86-76 victory over an American squad that included future NBA stars such as Larry Johnson, Gary Payton, and Stacy Augmon, a victory that won the 1987 World Junior Basketball Championship for Yugoslavia.

What made this victory and this team special, many observers agreed, was not just the athletic brilliance involved. It was the spirit of these young men, their togetherness, their camaraderie. For 4 years, these teenagers, who came from all over the country—Kukoc and Radja from Croatia, Djordjevic and Divac from Serbia, and Alibegovic, a Muslim, from Bosnia—trained together in a way possible only under a socialist sports regime. They lived together, ate together, and traveled together year round. They practiced together, played together, and pulled pranks on one another. They were in many ways a family, close as brothers, thick as thieves. The entire experience, Alibegovic recalls, "was like first love. It stays with you the rest of your life." Their coach, a Serb named Pesic, sent them a team photograph taken on the day they captured the 1987 world junior title in Bormio, Italy, with a message inscribed on the back: "Keep this picture. Never forget what we accomplished together" (Wolff 1996:84).

They surely knew that one day their lives would take them in different directions, but not one among them could have predicted how quickly that day would come, what would bring it about, or how utterly decisive its impact would be. Not one of them could have known that in less than 4 years it would become difficult for many of them to even say hello to each other, much less laugh, talk, reminisce, or play basketball together. What happened to the Yugoslav Dream Team, these Boys of Bormio, is, in microcosm, what happened to the country of Yugoslavia itself, and a powerful if disturbing testament to the creative and destructive potential of ethnic attachments and affiliations.

Kukoc vividly remembers the beginning of the end. It came in the summer of 1991 as the Yugoslav team competed for the European championships.

> The afternoon of the finals Kukoc's roommate, a guard from Slovenia [a Yugoslavian territory on the northeastern edge of the country] named Juri Zdovc, received a fax from the Slovenian minister of sport: If Zdovc played that night, he would be considered a traitor to his people. With a wife and a child back home, Zdovc had no choice. He tearfully bid his teammates goodbye. "I understood," Kukoc says. "It wasn't basketball anymore." (Wolff 1996:88)

It was civil war. Slovenia had declared its independence from the Yugoslav federation 3 days before the tournament semifinal. The Yugoslav National Army had responded by attacking Ljubljana, the capital of Slovenia. The breakup of Yugoslavia was under way.

The fighting quickly spread to Croatia, which also had declared its independence. In September, Macedonia, Yugoslavia's southernmost province, followed Slovenia's and Croatia's lead in seceding from the Federation. The worst, however, was reserved for Bosnia and Herzegovina. Early in 1992, in the face of a disintegrating Yugoslavia, Bosnia and Herzegovina reluctantly took their own steps toward self-determination, seceding from Yugoslavia. Situated uncomfortably between the Croats on one side and Yugoslavia's Serbs on the other, Bosnia and Herzegovina— or simply Bosnia to much of the world—bore the brunt of the violence that had become all-out ethnic war: Serbs against Croats, Croats against Serbs, and both against Bosnia's Muslims. Scenes of death and destruction— much of it directed against civilian populations—became commonplace on television screens around the world. Bosnia became a symbol of the fury of unchecked ethnic hatred, and the term *ethnic cleansing*—the systematic expulsion or extermination of one ethnic group by another, figuratively "cleansing" its territory of the offending group—took its dubious place in the world's vocabulary. In the next 3 years, perhaps as many as 200,000 people died, and the world watched in horror as Yugoslavia fell apart.

Gradually but inevitably, that young championship basketball team found itself broken and divided along similar lines, its members unable, for all their best intentions and efforts, to remain apolitical and above the fray. Kukoc, who saw the houses of numerous friends and relatives in his Croatian hometown of Split destroyed, describes his interactions with his Serbian and Muslim teammates: "It always gets down to asking how's your family, how's mine . . . and when you touch on families, you have to touch on the war, and when you touch on the war, you're on opposite sides" (quoted in Wolff 1996:88). Alibegovic, the Bosnian Muslim, probably lost more family and friends in the war than any other member of that championship team. He captures powerfully the shock and disillusion now shared by many of his teammates. "You know, I never knew what nationality anyone was when we were playing with each other. And I bet you they never knew what I was. . . . Well, now we know" (quoted in Wolff 1996:90).

Ethnic Passions and Ethnic History

What had happened? Where did these ethnic passions come from? Yugoslavia, as we noted in our brief discussion of nationalism in Chapter 2, emerged from the ruins of the Habsburg Empire soon after the end of

World War I. From its very inception, it was a multiethnic state whose peoples shared a largely common language and a great deal of culture but also practiced different religions and had histories and traditions of their own. Some observers of the Yugoslavian collapse in the early 1990s seized on these historical and religious differences as the source of supposedly long-standing animosities that finally had surfaced in ethnic warfare. "It's tragic, it's terrible," President Bill Clinton of the United States told television host Larry King in an interview in June of 1995, "but their enmities go back five hundred years, some would say almost a thousand years" (quoted in Sells 1996:23). In this scenario, Yugoslavia was a potential cauldron of ethnic tensions, divisions, and hatreds that had been suppressed for decades by the tight-fisted control of the communist dictator Josip Broz Tito, who ruled Yugoslavia from the end of World War II until his death in 1980. With Tito's passing and the collapse of communism throughout Eastern Europe at the end of the decade, so the argument went, the ancient ethnic antagonisms—the "Balkan ghosts" (Kaplan 1993)—finally had resurfaced.

History tells a somewhat different story. Although there has been plenty of conflict in the Balkan region of Europe, the boundaries among the constituent groups of Yugoslavia were historically far less fixed and their relations more harmonious than prevailing popular and press accounts at first implied. Like their championship basketball team, the lives, families, businesses, and interests of the Balkan peoples had long been composed of complex mixtures of Croat and Serb, Bosnian and Croat, Serb and Slovenian, and so on. Drazen Petrovic, another of the young Yugoslav basketball players and a budding NBA star in his own right until he was killed in a 1993 car accident, had a Croatian mother and a Serbian father, and he was far from an exception. Not only had these groups lived and worked with one another in relative harmony, but over the years they also had mingled and intermarried to such an extent that to say to which group one belonged was often as much a symbolic choice as an assertion of genealogical fact. In a society in which many people carried multiple ethnicities, there was often an element of arbitrariness in both the assignment and the assertion of identity. If one's family included Slovenes and Croats and Serbs, then how one identified oneself became as much a matter of tradition—"We've always thought of ourselves as Serbs"—as a matter of genealogical reasoning. Multiplicity could be a source of pride. Nowhere was this more the case than in the Bosnian capital of Sarajevo, much of it bombarded into ruins by Serb artillery in the early 1990s. The city had been chosen as host to the 1984 Winter Olympic Games partly on the basis of its well-earned reputation as one of the most cosmopolitan, tolerant, and welcoming cities in Europe.

The differences among these various ethnicities are in fact more modest than earlier responses to the war assumed. Virtually all of the peoples of the war-torn territories speak dialects of the same Slavic language.

> When Orthodox Serbs refer to Bosnian Muslims, for example, it may sound like members of one long established ethnic group challenging the heirs of alien invaders. The fact is that Orthodox Serbs are the Serbo-Croatian-speaking children of Slav ancestors who moved south sometime around the sixth century and converted to Christianity sometime after the ninth, while Bosnian Muslims are the Serbo-Croatian-speaking children of the same Slav ancestors, who moved south at the same time but converted to Islam sometime after the fifteenth century. The proper analogy is that between an English Catholic and an English Protestant. (Davis 1996:xiii).

Once they came to realize the facts about Yugoslavia's and especially Bosnia's pluralist ethnic past, many Westerners dramatically reversed their earlier assessments of the Balkan conflict. President Clinton was one of those. "Bosnia once found unity in its diversity," he remarked. The lives of Muslims, Orthodox Serbs, Catholic Croats and Jews were "woven together by marriage and culture" (quoted in Cohen 1995:A-27). The revised understanding saw the Bosnian conflict as the product of gross political manipulation on the part of ethnic, nationalist leaders who were either crass opportunists or incomprehensible, irrational fanatics. At times, the campaign by other countries to deal with the Bosnian crisis seemed to focus largely on individual leaders of one or another of the groups involved, as if deposing a particular person would somehow restore happier days when ethnicity was little more than an interesting aspect of a person's background and not an excuse for genocidal warfare.

The truth, as so often happens, lay somewhere between ancient antagonisms and pluralist peace. The history of the region is one of periods of harmony punctuated by conflict among groups who see themselves as in various ways different and in various ways alike. Sarajevo, the capital of Bosnia and Herzegovina, was long a center of Serbian nationalism, which figured in the onset of World War I. There have been recurrent nationalist movements among Serbs, Croats, and Slovenes who have competed for dominance or been played against each otehr by outsiders or elites. There have been insurgencies and revolts, and a brutal civil war occurred in Bosnia during World War II. There have been religious tensions as well between the Muslims who make up a large portion of Bosnia's population and their Christian compatriots, both in Bosnia and in other parts of Yugoslavia. There also has been a tradition of coexistence and unity, with the various populations of Yugoslavia living side by side, sharing a largely common culture and joining in common enterprises. An ideology of Slavic unity reached back to the 19th century, when a set of Slav intellectuals, recognizing that the various South Slav groups were much more like each other than like any of their neighbors, promoted the idea that all the Yugoslavs were in reality a single nation.

The coexistence of these varying traditions has offered fertile ground for any number of political agendas to take root and grow. Ethnic nationalists could appeal to historical events, perceived affronts and abuses, to bolster their separatist hopes and claims. Those who envisioned a united and multiethnic Yugoslavia likewise could make their dream resonate with a significant past. The richness and complexity of Balkan history offered something for everyone.

The Thickening of Ethnicity

When the Communist Party under dictator Josip Broz Tito took power in Yugoslavia at the end of World War II, it imposed an authoritarian regime over this diverse collection of closely related peoples. Western powers hoped that Tito would build the kinds of political institutions that would bridge Yugoslavia's ethnic and religious divisions and provide mechanisms through which internal conflicts might be resolved. Such institutions never appeared. On the contrary, Tito himself fanned the flames of ethnic-religious tension when it was in his interest to do so, exploiting the divisions within his country to maintain his own power. In Bosnia, for example, the most multiethnic of the various Yugoslav regions, Tito made ethnicity the basis of formal political classifications. He required Bosnians, who had once informally called one another "Catholic," "Orthodox," and "Muslim," to be known henceforth by ethnic or ethnoreligious designations: "Croatian," "Serbian," and, beginning in the 1970s, "Muslim." He eliminated the designation "Bosnian," which had linked these groups. That category no longer appeared on Yugoslav internal passports (Dragadze 1996:345; see also Beloff 1985; Djilas 1991). In effect, although ethnic identities were less and less important among most Bosnians (and Yugoslavians more generally), they were nevertheless preserved by the state as tools for organizing politics and controlling elites. Ethnicity thus remained alive as a potential basis of identity.

Part of what makes the Yugoslavian tragedy compelling for students of ethnicity is not simply the complexities of the case—which are daunting—but also these processes of ethnic construction. Ethnicity in Yugoslavia emerges less as something people are fighting about than as the weapon they are fighting with: a tool for pursuing territorial, political, and economic objectives. Ethnic history itself becomes a weapon: whether or not the antagonisms are age-old, they certainly are treated as such. The wounds of history—real, imagined, or somewhere in between—have proven convenient justifications in numerous societies for claims to independence, territory, enhanced status, or revenge. Why not in Yugoslavia as well?

By late in the 1980s, with Tito dead and communist regimes beginning to crumble across Eastern Europe, Yugoslavia became an arena in which the focused work of identity construction went on apace, with various nationalist groups and individuals marshaling symbolic resources to mobilize their peoples and support their claims for territory and power in the unknown future that was surely coming. Thus, the Serbs, in pursuit of their nationalist dream of a Greater Serbia, deliberately and successfully revived memories of real and imagined past aggressions and atrocities inflicted on them by Croats and Muslims. At a famous battle in Kosovo in 1389, the Ottoman Turks—Muslims—defeated the Serbs. A Serb prince named Lazar was killed. As presented by Serbian nationalists, the martyred Lazar is a Christ figure, one of whose disciples—a Muslim—betrays him, and this betrayal "becomes the ancestral curse of all Slavic Muslims" (Sells 1996:24). The later conversion of Bosnians to Islam meant that the hands of Bosnian Muslims would be forever stained with the prince's blood, an emblem of the Bosnian Muslim attempt to eliminate the Serbs as a people. In the late 1980s, Serbs used the story of Kosovo and the prince's death to promote the "ethnic cleansing" of Muslims; it became part of the Serbs' story of their own lives and fortunes, the moment when their independence was lost. On June 28, 1989, nearly a million Serbs made a trek to Kosovo for a Passion Play commemorating the 600th anniversary of the battle. Through their account of Kosovo, the Serbs heroized themselves, villainized Muslims, and drew an ethnic boundary right through their history. Croats, Slovenes, Macedonians, and Bosnia's Muslims found their own symbolic ways to accomplish similar things.

In the 1980s, after Tito's death, Bosnia reversed his policies, claiming common, non-ethnic Bosnian citizenship for all individuals within its borders, regardless of ethnicity or religion. Bosnian Serbs demurred, claiming they had too little in common with those who held power in Bosnia's capital Sarajevo, whom they called "Turks," to share a government. In the mid-1990s, with the war in Bosnia raging around him, the leader of the Bosnian Serbs offered an idea of what the city of Sarajevo, once the cosmopolitan jewel of Yugoslavia, would be like, if he had his way, once the war was over. For him, despite all the symbolic manipulations, the enormous scale of systematic rape and expulsions, and the killing on all sides, ethnicity was not yet thick enough. It could be thickened nicely by walls:

"Our vision of Sarajevo is like Berlin when the Wall was still standing. . . . The city will be divided into Muslim, Serbian, and Croatian sections, so that no ethnic groups will have to live or work together" (quoted in Finnegan 1995:6). As basketball player Alibegovic had pointed out, in 1987 the members of the Yugoslav championship team had not known the ethnicities of their fellow members. "Now we know."

The Triumph of Dissimilation

Today, what once was Yugoslavia is a collection of independent republics. Ethnic tensions remain. In Bosnia in particular, the possibility of a return to war lurks just beneath the surface of a tense peace. If assimilation is the coming together of distinct peoples in a sharing of common culture and institutions, Yugoslavia offers us the specter of dissimilation and a sobering lesson in the danger that lurks in claims to "the unimpeachable singularity of national, linguistic, cultural, even racial identities" (Elshtain 1996:52). The ethnicities that surfaced so brutally in Bosnia and its neighbors in the 1990s may have had political and economic interests at their core, but those interests hardly dictated the forms of those ethnicities nor the ferocity of the conflicts among the groups involved. It was not interests alone but their ethnicization that sustained the passions evident in the devastation: the invocation of common blood as a crucial element in a frenzy of bloodletting.

In 1992, as war raged across the region, another basketball team representing a smaller and now largely Serbian Yugoslavia won the European finals again. A Croatian team took third place in that tournament and joined the Serbs and the second-place Lithuanians on the medal platform. But too much had changed. Before receiving their gold medals, the Serbian winners gave the three-fingered salute that nationalist Serbs often flashed during the ongoing war. The Croats, once the Serbs' countrymen and even teammates but now their enemies, saw the salute, turned their backs, stepped off the platform, and walked away.

A Comparison of Cases

Circumstance and utility play obvious and central roles in these cases. The conditions of economic and political development in the early United States and the very different societal interests that emerged from those conditions were powerful causal factors in the divergent trajectories of group and identity formation in the Black and Indian comparison.

Circumstance and utility were similarly determining features of the Chinese effort to escape their position in Delta society. That effort depended on the fact that Whites gained little from keeping Chinese in the same position as Blacks and lost little from permitting some form of reclassification. The Chinese, on the other hand, had much to lose where they started and much to gain where they ended up.

The relative openness of U.S. society to German immigrants allowed a substantial and rapid degree of economic integration into that society, limiting the success of their own efforts at cultural preservation. Those efforts collapsed when World War I precipitated a dramatic change in the U.S. environment and made it very much in the German American interest to abandon the attempt to sustain a prominent and assertive ethnic identity.

In South Africa, Afrikaner identity construction took place in a context of competition with the English, joined later by a defense of racial domination. Afrikaners defended their privileges and their sense of themselves as a distinct and "chosen" people to the bitter end.

Communist control of Eastern Europe and the Balkans crumbled in the late 1980s and early 1990s, leaving an uncertain and unstable situation in its wake. The peoples of the former Yugoslavia were quick to turn to ethnicity as a basis of political mobilization in pursuit of resurgent claims to territory and power.

In all of these cases, social change and the situations it produces drive much of the dynamic of identity construction and of collective action by ethnic and racial groups. The significance of circumstance and utility, however, varies in these cases. Nowhere do they carry the whole explanatory load in the attempt to understand identity construction. We cannot simply "read" identities—neither their boundaries nor their meanings— from circumstances or the interests they produce. Even in the Indian and Black cases, these groups rejected in various ways of the identities that circumstances presented to them. Blacks, for example, could do little about the boundary that White society imposed, but they resisted its meaning, asserted their own conception of who they were, and embedded that conception in institutions and cultural practices that in turn sustained them. We cannot understand the nature of African American identity with reference to circumstances and interests alone.

Even within the dynamic of interest, many groups still make choices. Native Americans adopted a supratribal identity when it was in their interest to do so, but the conditions favoring such an identity were present long before, and the pressures to abandon tribal identities often were intense. The United States bludgeoned them with guns, disease, and administration, but it also welcomed them with open arms. The specified condition was: "Stop being Indian—or Apache, or Hopi, or Cheyenne, or Lummi—and you will be welcome here." They rejected both the pressure and the opportunity, struggling to preserve distinct, indigenous communities that for a long time promised little more than poverty and powerlessness. To explain that, we have to understand not only political and economic circumstances but also the ways Indians looked at the world, the bonds not only of interest but also of interpretation and understanding—the cultural bonds—that linked them to one another.

Choice is readily apparent in the Afrikaner case. It was the intentional, organized efforts of Afrikaner elites and intellectuals that directed identity construction toward ethnicity and away from class and race, either one of which would have found support in the changing circumstances that Afrikaners faced. German Americans likewise had choices. Those choices were a consequence of the circumstances of their immigration, in particular of their relatively welcoming reception by U.S. society. In the 19th century at least, however, those circumstances did not dictate the choices Germans made. Their effort, successful for a time, to preserve a German culture and identity in the United States was freely made, often against the assimilationist pressures of American life.

Identity construction is not passive. People assert identities. They do so within the constraints that circumstances allow, according to their own interpretations of their interests, and with the resources they have at their command.

One other factor plays a role in these cases, more so in some than in others. Quite independently of specific sets of circumstances and interests, these cases suggest the power that ethnicity and race, as categories of collective identity, potentially convey. It is in the interests of Whites to construct a boundary that effectively sets African Americans apart. It is in the interests of Whites to attach a meaning to that boundary and to the categories that boundary creates that can justify denying to African Americans the rights of White Americans. Race meets their needs. The power of race lies in its suggestion that it distinguishes qualitatively different kinds of human beings. By claiming that African Americans form one race and Whites form another—that is, by constructing two separate and distinct races—Whites create a basis for and a defense of slavery and of all the subsequent forms of domination and denial that have shaped Black-White relations in the United States. White actions can be explained by circumstances and their attendant interests, but the impact of their actions can be explained only by race itself.

So, too, with ethnicity. Circumstances and interests play a significant role in the Afrikaner effort to construct an identity compelling enough to sustain their community under conditions of social change. What makes that effort successful among many Afrikaners is the skillful use of ethnicity's potential to tap deeply resonant beliefs in most human cultures. With an appeal to blood and the sanctity of peoplehood, Afrikaners turn their identity into both vehicle and object of community preservation, drawing from ethnicity the full measure of its potential emotional charge.

That charge peaks in Bosnia. Circumstantially produced interests obviously play a central role in the Bosnian tragedy, but they cannot explain the savagery of the actions groups have taken on their behalf. The power of ethnicity lies in its capacity to arouse passion and commitment. In pursuit of their interests, Serbs, Croats, Bosnian Muslims, and others organize along ethnic lines, equating ethnicity and country and even, at times, religion in a potent plea for the defense of peoplehood against the affronts and abuses of centuries. They take full advantage of all the symbolic power that ethnicity has to offer—with horrifying results.

Conclusion

The construction of ethnic and racial identities proceeds quite differently in each of these cases, and the outcomes vary as well. The identities that result are by no means the same, but there are continuities—across these cases and many others—in the factors that typically play a role in identity construction. In Chapters 6 and 7, we turn our attention to those factors. We shift our focus from cases to the variables that shape the construction process, illustrating those variables and their impacts with examples drawn from around the world.

NOTES

1. This discussion is based largely on Cornell (1990) and on references cited therein.

2. We use the terms *Native American* and *American Indian* interchangeably in this book, reflecting the different usages within the indigenous population of the United States. Native American lately has been the preferred term on university campuses and among some supratribal organizations, although the pattern is by no means consistent among such organizations or among

Indian scholars. The term *Indian* is far more widely used and sometimes explicitly preferred in reservation communities.

3. This discussion is based on Loewen (1988).

4. Sharecropping is a system of agricultural labor in which those who own the land employ one or more—sometimes many—families to work the land for them. The owner typically lends the family land on which to live, tools with which to work, seed, and perhaps livestock, and in return receives a major portion of the crop produced. By charging high interest rates on the loan, the owner ensures that the tenant, or sharecropper, is seldom out of debt. As James Loewen writes (1988:11), "Sharecropping operated so as to keep tenants poor and make landowners rich."

5. This discussion is based largely on Giliomee (1979), Moodie (1975), Schutte (1989), and Thompson (1985).

6. As of 1990, the population of South Africa included some 28 million Africans, slightly more than three million "Coloureds" or mixed-race persons, about a million Asians, mostly descendants of Indians brought to South Africa in the 19th century as indentured laborers to work the sugar plantations, and slightly fewer than five and a half million Whites. Of these last, 2.9 million were Afrikaners; the other two and a half million largely English.

7. The basketball story that frames this case is drawn from Wolff (1996).

6

Construction Sites: Contextual Factors in the Making of Identities

These sites are domestic examined from — but the point of view — idea of sites for the has relevance those about in of that I sites constructed is essential identity maintained or might be in region.

The cases of identity construction in Chapter 5 lend support to two of the central themes of this book. The first is the idea that ethnicity and race are products both of social change and circumstance and of human interpretation and action. The second is the idea that they therefore are neither "natural" nor static identities but are variable, diverse, and contingent. But contingent on what? What drives the variation in identities and in the construction process across space and over time?

The cases in Chapter 5 suggested some of the answers to these questions, but those answers were embedded in the specifics of the cases themselves. In this chapter and the next, we attempt a more systematic and more general answer. The question for Chapters 6 and 7 is this: What factors are likely to play a significant role in the construction of race and ethnicity wherever that process occurs? Accepting that some factors will surely play a larger role in some cases than in others, at what set of variables should we be looking if we want to understand ethnic and racial identity construction in general terms?

We divide these factors into two categories. As suggested in Chapter 4, identity construction is driven both by the situations in which groups find themselves under conditions of social change and by the resources and attributes they bring with them to those situations. Group resources and attributes are the subject of Chapter 7. This chapter takes up the situations in which groups find themselves: the context in which identity construction occurs and the contextual factors—aspects of the world external to the group in question—that shape that construction.

Critical Sites

Although identity construction may occur in any part of a society and as an aspect of virtually any set of social relations, we focus in this chapter on six critical construction sites and the forces at work within them: politics, labor markets, residential space, social institutions, culture, and daily experience. Each of these sites is an arena in which identity construction occurs. It is a place where social actors make claims, define one another, jockey for position, eliminate or initiate competition, exercise or pursue power, and engage in a wide array of other activities that variously encourage or discourage, create or transform, and reproduce or ignore identities. Our concern in this chapter is less with the specific actors involved—who vary from place to place and time to time—than with the kinds of forces at work and the social locations where those forces operate and actors act. Our concern is with the arenas where boundaries are established, where some identities become more elaborate or comprehensive and some less, and where patterns of intergroup stratification are established or change, altering the advantages and disadvantages that different identities carry.

Empirically, these arenas or sites are difficult to separate from one another. For one thing, identity construction seldom occurs in only one such site; on the contrary, it usually involves processes occurring simultaneously in many parts of the social order. In addition, these sites often are linked to one another. Politics, for example, may have an impact on labor or housing markets; economic success may change the way outsiders view group members; and culture infuses all these arenas with particular ways of thinking and talking that have implications for collective identities. We separate them here not to suggest that they operate independently of each other—they seldom do—but to make clear the multidimensionality of identity construction and to provide one piece of an analytical framework for thinking about how the process works.

We can describe each of these sites in terms of the opportunities and constraints that groups encounter there. Change in that set of opportunities and constraints has potential implications for identity.

Politics

All intergroup relations can be described in terms of power: the differential ability of human groups to influence the decisions and relationships that have consequences for their lives. That ability is itself a product of both environmental and group factors: of the opportunities and constraints groups face and of the resources that they carry with them. For the purposes of this chapter, it is the former, or contextual, factors that matter: the opportunity or constraint set operative in the political arena.

Situational change often involves changes in the political circumstances groups face—that is, in the formal distribution of power. Power is distributed and operates through informal relationships and processes as well, a number of which we touch on in later sections of this chapter. It is the more formal circumstances that are at issue here.

These circumstances are diverse, but they include such things as citizenship, the franchise, entitlements of various kinds, policy provisions, and the rights groups or individuals have and the vulnerabilities they face. Any or all of these may be altered through social change, in particular by processes such as migration or other comprehensive reorganizations of social relations. In some cases, such changes enhance political opportunities (some migrant groups, for example, are political refugees fleeing constraint for freedom); in others, they reduce opportunities (enslavement is an obvious example, but international migrants often choose, for economic or other reasons, to enter situations where they lack citizenship and their political freedom is limited, and political upheavals often transform power relations between groups). In every situation, political factors have potentially high impacts on identities. Large power differentials between ethnic or racial groups sharpen and reinforce ethnic and racial boundaries, giving increased significance to the identities they define; small differentials, other things equal, blur those boundaries, decreasing that significance.

Political Systems and Boundary Maintenance

This potential for boundary maintenance or reinforcement is inherent in political systems, all of which discriminate in one way or another. They treat certain classes of interests or certain classes of persons differently from others. At the very least, at the level of the state, they grant citizens rights they deny to noncitizens. Most discriminate among citizens as well. The political system in the United States, as in most countries, discriminates against the young: 9-year-olds, for example, do not have the right to vote. Until passage of the 19th constitutional amendment in 1919, which prohibits states and the United States from denying the right to vote on account of sex, that system treated women like 9-year-olds, denying them the franchise. It was not until passage of the Voting Rights Act in 1965 that many Black Americans were free to vote, exercising a franchise that White Americans—men, at least—had taken for granted for generations. As recently as the mid-1980s, some American Indians still had to go to court for the right to representation in some county governments (Thackeray 1985; Wood 1986).

For much of U.S. history, citizenship likewise has been far from universal among the American-born. In 1790, the U.S. Congress reserved citizenship for free White immigrants. Most African Americans achieved full citizenship recognition only with the end of slavery. Although some Native Americans had become citizens through certain treaty negotiations and policy provisions, it was not until 1924 that Congress made all U.S.-born Native Americans citizens in the land they had lost to Europeans. Japanese could not become naturalized American citizens until 1952.

In each of these cases, the distribution of political rights designated and solidified a group boundary. The United States is hardly the only example of the formal political invocation of ethnic or racial boundaries. The country of Malaysia, at one time a British colony but independent since 1957, is a multiethnic society. Although the largest population is Malay (a general term that, as we noted in Chapter 2, unites a number of different groups indigenous to Malaysia), 40% or so of the country's population is non-Malay. Most of the non-Malays are Chinese and Indians, descendants of workers brought to Malaysia by British colonialists in the late 19th and early 20th centuries to meet the labor needs of the rubber plantations and tin mines. Following independence in 1957, the new constitution and subsequent government policies guaranteed to Malays a number of advantages, among them disproportionately generous representation in the political system and privileged access to certain lands, jobs, scholarships, financial credit, and business licenses. The government also set controls on immigration so as to limit growth in the non-Malay population (Jesudason 1990; Lim 1985).

Such policies and provisions have several effects. By controlling the size of different ethnic populations, they control one of the sources of power available to groups. By specifying an ethnically specific distribution of government-controlled opportunities and patronage, they ensure that one group's ability to influence decisions and relationships will continue to grow at the cost of other groups' abilities to do the same. By formally institutionalizing the ethnic boundary in the political structure of the country, they solidify and strengthen that boundary. This last continues a long-term historical process of creating and reinforcing an exclusive and specifically Malay ethnic identity that is as much a product of colonial and postindependence political categorizations as it is of any precolonial indigenous conception (Hirschman 1986; Nagata 1981).

Other countries have done much the same. In the 1950s and 1960s, the government of Romania gradually reorganized power relations in Romanian society under the slogan "Romania for the ethnic Romanians." It permitted emigration by Germans and Jews (this right was denied to others, but the government's hope was that it would reduce the size of these minority populations), withdrew certain rights from the Hungarian minority, and reduced the presence of minorities in governmental positions and in the governing Communist Party. It also partly dismantled a Hungarian-language university, removed non-Romanian names from streets, and initiated policies designed to make Romanian the official language of the country (Brass 1991:59; Gilberg 1980:205-7). The impact of these policies was not only to reduce the influence of non-Romanians in Romanian society but also to increase the salience and significance of ethnic identities. The government used those identities as the basis of the organization and distribution of power, privileging some groups over others.

Such preferential policies are quite common in multiethnic societies. Among the many examples:

> In Fiji, nearly all the cultivable land has long been reserved to Fijians. In Sri Lanka, a policy of "standardization of marks" gave extra points to applicants for university admission who took their examinations in Sinhala, so that Sinhalese applicants were preferred to Tamils. In Indonesia, a specified percentage of the shares in new companies must be held by *pribumis* (indigenes); there are comparable preferences for non-Chinese in government contracts and business loans [since modified]. (Horowitz 1985:655-56).

Policies such as these serve a number of purposes. Some governments adopt them in an explicit effort to overcome economic and other disparities among ethnic populations that may lead to conflict. Others adopt them, in effect, to protect or promote such disparities, serving the interests of some groups against the claims of others. Regardless of the intent, such policies often have led to increased conflict. Racial riots in 1969 in Malaysia, for example, were traceable in part to government policies designed to promote Malay interests against the interests of Chinese and Indians. No one was entirely happy with the government's action: "The Malays were unhappy because it was not producing enough results, the non-Malays because it had gone too far" (Lim 1985:272). Similar policies have played a significant role in recurrent eruptions of Sinhalese-Tamil violence in Sri Lanka (Tambiah 1986).

A variation on this theme of ethnically based governmental policy can be found in the very different governmental receptions accorded by the United States to immigrants from Mexico and Cuba. Mexican immigrants to the United States historically have received little in the way of federal assistance; on the contrary, even legal immigrants from Mexico have at times been the targets of federal and state antagonism. Cuban immigrants, on the other hand, have benefited from an assortment of government resources. In the aftermath of the Cuban Revolution in 1959 and in opposition to the government of Fidel Castro, the U.S. government defined Cuban immigrants as political refugees. Hoping to facilitate their rapid adjustment to the United States and to demonstrate the possibilities of success in a free society, in 1960 the government set up the Cuban Refugee Program in the federal Department of Health, Education, and Welfare. This program set about easing the transition of the first wave of Cuban immigrants—many of whom, unlike later migrations from Cuba, came from elite sectors of Cuban society—into the U.S. economy, helping many of them to find jobs and housing and to solve the myriad problems attached to immigration (Pedraza-Bailey 1985). Although Cubans have experienced antagonism as well, particularly as the class backgrounds of more recent Cuban immigrants have changed and as their numbers have grown, both conceptually and practically, U.S. policy set them apart, not only from Mexicans but also from others, emphasizing this boundary as one of special importance and granting their identity a particular significance.

Forms of Political Organization and Informal Practices

Informal practices may contribute as much to identity maintenance or construction as do formal policy or constitutional provisions. One of the expressed goals and supposed achievements of the Soviet Union was the creation of a society in which ethnic and national loyalties and identities ultimately disappeared, replaced by a much broader allegiance to the Soviet Union and communism. In ethnically diverse Turkmenistan, however, which was part of Soviet Central Asia, ethnic or "tribal" identities continued to be important throughout the Soviet period, and they remain so today. Despite Soviet claims, common political practices helped to sustain them. Under Soviet rule, "it became a common practice for the first secretary of the Communist Party of Turkmenistan to put his tribesmen in prominent and important positions in the government, administration, and even in the scientific and cultural establishment, and regional party organizations sometimes resembled tribal fiefdoms" (Khazanov 1995:125). By using patronage to favor group members, the local party helped to preserve the idea that ethnic identity mattered despite an official policy that sought to eradicate such identities as bases of social organization.

   In addition to the formal distribution of power and the policies that derive from or contribute to it, the particular forms that the organization of power takes also may have an impact on ethnic identities. Jerome Karabel has argued that one of the factors that fostered or preserved ethnic identities among European immigrant populations in the United States in the 19th and early 20th centuries was the decentralized structure of American politics. Much of American politics was urban politics. Particularly in the big industrial cities of the northeast, political machines organized at neighborhood levels dominated most political activity. According to Karabel (1979:217), neighborhoods were "the very levels where ethnic divisions were most salient." Many immigrant workers' "first and primary contact with the political system was via the neighborhood ward boss. Often of the same ethnic group, he would provide them—in return for loyal support of the machine—with jobs, housing, relief, and, when necessary, help in court." To a significant degree, urban politics was an ethnic politics, superimposed on and reinforcing a set of preexisting, spatially organized ethnic boundaries. Thus, the political system lent practical and important support to ethnic identity (see also Katznelson 1981).

During the apartheid era in South Africa, state policy and ideology sought to downplay differences between the two dominant White groups (Afrikaners and English) while putting massive efforts into the reinforcement of ethnic and territorial distinctions among Black groups—distinctions that in many cases were relatively recent products of earlier Afrikaner or English actions. This was accomplished partly through the organization of politics. The enormous and legally buttressed power differential between White and Black emphasized the racial boundary and the commonalities among Afrikaners and English in opposition to Blacks. At the same time, the government organized a set of ethnic "homelands"— ostensibly on a path to independence—for the Black population. The state designated different homelands for different Black groups and confined excess black populations—that is, those not currently needed for their labor in the rest of South African society—to those cramped and impoverished homelands. Thus, group boundaries gained formal political dimensions, designating uniformly powerless but ethnically and geographically distinct populations (Butler, Rotberg, and Adams 1977; Young 1985).

The Political Construction of Ethnicity

What all of these examples point to is what Joane Nagel (1986:97-98) calls "the political construction of ethnicity," a process by which "the rules for political participation and political access" create, reinforce, or alter ethnic boundaries, giving significance to ethnic identities. Some of those rules discriminate among groups, highlighting the political differences between "us" and "them," the fact that "they" have rights or access that "we" do not (or vice versa). Others organize political participation along ethnic lines. On occasion, as in the South African "homelands," the early years of Native American confinement on U.S. reservations, or the case of neighborhood politics, the organization of power has an explicitly spatial dimension. In such cases, boundaries that can be traced in power relations can be traced in physical space as well. Part of what distinguishes "us" from "them" is that we are here, and they are there. What all of these cases have in common is the construction of ethnic and racial identities in the organization and working of politics.

Labor Markets

Labor markets are another common site of ethnic and racial identity construction, and understandably so. Work is a central and essentially universal human activity that is organized in nearly all societies into a variety of categories: industries, occupations, sets of entitlements or vulnerabilities, types of labor, and so on. Every society's division of labor offers a ready-made categorical scheme. As persons are distributed into the categories that the division of labor offers, group identity construction is one eminently possible outcome. By the same token, collective identities offer potential bases for the distribution of persons into categories, a process that reinforces those identities by giving them an organizational dimension in the workplace.

Ethnicity and Occupational Concentrations

One of the most common features of multiethnic situations around the world is the different occupational compositions of the groups involved. Many societies have what amounts to an ethnic division of labor in which certain occupations, industries, or kinds of work have become, for a time at least, the province of a particular group. The most stark examples come from slave societies, in many of which a particular racial or ethnic group is heavily concentrated in one kind of labor—typically manual labor—or in a particular industry such as agriculture. The pattern, however, is hardly peculiar to these situations. In the 1840s, for example, following the end of British slavery, British sugar planters on the Caribbean island of Trinidad, today part of the independent nation of Trinidad and Tobago, had to find replacements for the African labor force that no longer could be forced to work on the sugar plantations. Ultimately, they turned to indentured labor brought in from India. For the next three decades, although some Indians, at the end of their indentures, obtained land and became small farmers, the majority remained attached in one way or another to the sugar plantation economy as laborers, or in some cases as shopkeepers on large plantations. A century after Indians first entered Trinidad in large numbers, they remained heavily concentrated in agriculture, although some had entered commerce and the professions, and they continued to dominate the cutting of sugar cane (Brereton 1993; R. Henry 1993).

A similar process in which Indians displaced formerly enslaved Africans in a sugar economy took place in Guyana over much the same period. While Indians remained heavily concentrated in agriculture and in rural areas, displaced Africans headed for urban areas and public services. By the middle of the 20th century, an ethnic division of labor was still apparent in Guyana, with Indians dominating land development and much of the commercial sector and Africans dominating primary education, the civil service, and the army (Despres 1975; Enloe 1980).

Such examples are common in countries with a history of large-scale importation of labor—which makes them especially common in colonial and formerly colonial societies—but they appear across a wide range of countries. The ethnic division of labor in parts of Nigeria, for example, has been highly specialized. In one area, the largest population is made up of the Ikale people. They control most of the land and dominate farming. Other groups, most of them immigrants moving from adjacent areas of Nigeria at one time or another over the last century, also tend to be concentrated in certain occupations. For example, "the Ijo and the Itsekiri fish and trade in open shops by the rivers; the Urhobo and Isoko are concerned mainly with oil palm produce" (Otite 1975:121). Ethnic and racial occupational concentrations also appeared in western Europe in the 1960s and subsequent decades as rapidly increasing numbers of immigrants flowed into western European cities from southern and eastern Europe and northern Africa. In France, significant portions of the female Spanish and Portuguese immigrant populations entered domestic service, but very few Tunisian women did, being far more likely, if they worked at all, to end up in small-scale commerce, reflecting conceptions they brought with them about the appropriate roles of women. Male immigrants—in particular the Portuguese—were most likely to be in the construction industry, except for Poles, who were more likely to be found in agriculture, fishing, and mining (Castles and Kosack 1973:64).

These last two cases point to a complicating factor in occupational concentrations: sex. Men and women frequently are concentrated in different occupations. In West Germany, for example, in the period from

1969 to 1980 there was a significant shift in the job concentrations of immigrant workers from Italy, Spain, Portugal, Yugoslavia, Turkey, and Greece. The shift was from manufacturing to service sector jobs, but it was dominated by women; men remained largely concentrated in blue-collar work (Castles 1984:129-30). In the United Kingdom in the period from 1966 to 1991, a clear divergence appeared in the fortunes of men and women from Black and Asian ethnic groups, largely Pakistani, Bangladeshi, Indian, West Indian, and Guyanese immigrants and their children. Over the period, Black and Asian men show significantly greater upward mobility in the socioeconomic system than do Black and Asian women. Again, many women entered service sector jobs, but they did so at the low end and showed limited upward mobility. Men, on the other hand, demonstrated greater upward mobility, both from manual to non-manual jobs and within specific occupations, closing much of the gap between themselves and Whites. In fact, gender differences in socio-economic achievement appear to be greater than the differences either among these ethnic groups or between them as a whole and Whites (Iganski and Payne 1996). Two students of gender and work reach a similar conclusion regarding occupational segregation and race in the United States: "Men and women of the same race are more segregated [occupationally] from each other than are African Americans and whites of the same sex" (Reskin and Padavic 1994:57).

Gender stratification in such cases can have significant effects on the construction of ethnic and racial identities, offering other potential bases of identity formation and collective action. Sex in these cases may be as important in shaping individual and collective experience as ethnicity or race, particularly if what happens in other sites fails to lend strong support to the ethnic or racial boundary.

The United States has its own history of ethnic occupational concentrations. The New York City census of 1855 listed 29,470 domestic service workers. All but about 6,000 of them were Irish. Comments Stephen Steinberg (1981:154): "Not only were most domestics Irish, but it was also the case that virtually all Irish women who worked did so as domestics." At various times, Mexicans in America have been concentrated in agricultural migrant labor (many still are), Japanese in farming, Chinese in mining and railroad construction, and Africans, during slavery, in plantation agriculture. Today, significant numbers of Korean immigrants to the United States are in small business. Illsoo Kim (1987:226) estimated that in 1985, 41% of the Korean families in the New York metropolitan area were running small businesses, largely in the retail sector, and found other data suggesting that 70% of the Koreans in New York worked in such businesses. Ivan Light and Edna Bonacich (1988:161) found Koreans "massively overrepresented" in the retail trade in Los Angeles in the early 1980s, with disproportionate numbers—as compared with the population at large—running their own small firms.

The Dynamics of Labor Concentrations

Such concentrations are products of a number of factors, from coercion (as in slavery) to timing (where are the labor shortages—and therefore opportunities—in the current economy?), from the particular circumstances of migration (Irish women often immigrated to the United States alone, and live-in domestic service offered single women a measure of personal security) to the skills or backgrounds of migrants (Urhobo migrants in Nigeria were largely uneducated, meaning they had little basis on which to compete for urban jobs, but they had experience working with oil palms). European and North African migrants to France have tended to go where the jobs are; similarly, Italian migrants to the United States often entered construction, whereas Poles often entered steelmaking, because these were expanding industries when each of these groups arrived. Many Jewish migrants to the United States ended up in the garment industry, partly because they had the necessary skills and partly because it was a growing industry when they came, and it needed their labor (Yancey et al. 1976). As the Jewish case suggests, job concentrations may reflect in part the experiences and skills migrants bring with them. It is only natural to look for work first in something you already know how to do. For many of the uneducated and unskilled, on the other hand, the lowest-wage jobs typically are all they can find. In some cases, job concentrations reflect the movement of information along migrant networks: Early migrants hear of additional jobs in their own industries and pass on the information to relatives and friends in search of work or soon to join them in the receiving society.

Discrimination in employment or in access to economic resources is another major factor shaping ethnic or racial occupational concentrations in many countries. Japanese migrants to the United States at the turn of the century tended to concentrate in agriculture. This was partly by choice and partly the result of union discrimination against them that prevented them from entering other kinds of jobs. Many Japanese soon began to buy land and become small farmers. White farmers in California, seeing Japanese farmers as competition and wanting to keep them in the labor pool, lobbied for passage of laws that would prevent the Japanese from buying land. In 1913, the California legislature passed the

Alien Land Act, which prohibited land purchase and most land leasing by noncitizens; its target was the Japanese (Fugita and O'Brien 1991; Saxton 1971). Nearly all migrant groups to the United States have experienced labor market discrimination of one sort or another at different times, some far more severe than others, with the enslavement of Africans and continuing labor market discrimination against them and other racially distinct groups representing the most extreme version and the largely friction-free entry of northern and western European groups—excepting the Irish—representing the least.

Similar phenomena can be found in other countries. In the decade following World War II, Polish and Italian migrants to Britain found themselves facing discrimination in the labor market. British workers often were unwilling to work with immigrants (Castles and Kosack 1973). Forty years later, much of the antagonism in Britain had turned from European targets to new waves of immigrants from Africa, the Caribbean, and Asia. Widespread, sometimes violent discrimination against these workers kept many stuck in the lowest-wage occupations (Gilroy 1987).

In short, the situational factors encountered by ethnic and racial groups include particular sets of labor market opportunities: differentially limited openings in the occupational structure of the society. Under certain conditions, these opportunities tend to produce ethnic or racial occupational concentrations. Those conditions include structural factors (the characteristics of the labor market, of the larger economy of which that market is a part, and of the timing of group entry into the market), behavioral factors (the actions of groups in positions of power directed toward less powerful populations, as in systematic discrimination, and the choices that ethnic populations make in the labor market), and the characteristics of ethnic and racial groups themselves, including the skills and experience they have and the internal connections among group members, through which job information often moves (we will take up these characteristics of ethnic groups in more detail in Chapter 7). As these conditions change over time, the set of labor market opportunities these groups encounter changes as well.

Such occupational concentrations have obvious identity effects. Not only the experience of discrimination but also the impact of common occupational activity and interpersonal interactions in the workplace may sustain a sense of being somehow different. These effects deserve more attention, but first we turn to another site with identity-shaping potential: residential space. Because labor market concentrations and residential concentrations have some of the same effects on identity, we postpone our detailed discussion to the end of the next section.

Residential Space

As important as occupational opportunity—and frequently related to it—is residential opportunity. Just as they cannot always choose where they work, people are not always free to choose where they live. As with jobs, the discriminatory actions of others may limit residential freedom of choice, as, for example, in redlining: the practice by financial institutions in some American cities of denying loans to African Americans so as to keep them from buying houses in certain neighborhoods (see Massey and Denton 1993:51-55). Prices obviously limit choice, effectively closing portions of the housing market to group members with limited incomes. A labor market that concentrates available jobs in certain geographical areas may thereby limit the range of choices for those who need, for one reason or another, to live close to the workplace. Even where there is a substantially open housing market, residential concentrations may occur simply as a result of the choices people make, for example, choosing to live near friends, relatives, or others who are familiar or of similar background. Whatever the logic of the concentrations, they often have impacts on ethnic boundaries.

Ethnicity and Residential Concentrations

Residential concentrations helped to maintain an Irish ethnic identity in England in the mid-19th century. In 1846 and 1847, the potato harvest in Ireland failed, exacerbating already serious rural poverty. Faced with famine, hundreds of thousands of Irish left the country. In those 2 years alone, more than a half million of them entered the English city of Liverpool. Although as many as half of these eventually moved on to North America and others went elsewhere in England, a significant number stayed in Liverpool, raising the number of Irish from just over a tenth of the city's population in 1830 to nearly a quarter of it by 1851. For the most part, according to Pooley (1992:74), these were "unskilled and impoverished rural peasants moving into an industrial and urban society." The occupational opportunities for unskilled Irish men were limited largely to poorly paid, casual labor, particularly in dockyards. Employment was uncertain, day to day, and competitive. The only way to know when jobs were available and to claim them quickly was to live near the dockyards. As a result, many of these immigrants lived in cheap, decaying housing near the docks where the hiring took place. Among immigrant women who worked, the most common jobs were low-paying sweatshop labor in shoemaking or dressmaking, "reinforcing tendencies which pushed the Irish into low rent housing" (Pooley 1992:75). The result was residential segregation, tied largely to limited labor market opportunities. Such segregation helped to sustain a distinctively and self-consciously Irish population in the city of Liverpool for the rest of the 19th century.

As this example suggests, labor and residential markets often are related—other things equal, better-paying jobs allow greater choice in housing, restrictions in housing can make some jobs geographically inaccessible, and so forth. Changes in economic activity also affect residential concentrations. Early periods of rapid industrial growth, at least in the most developed nations of the world, concentrated industry in city cores. High transportation costs and a common lack of accessible mass transportation meant that workers needed to live nearby. Groups moving to cities to take advantage of increasing demands for labor often ended up in ethnically concentrated neighborhoods close to the industrial cores of those cities (Yancey et al. 1976). Over time, as mass transportation improved and industry itself became less concentrated, some of these ethnic concentrations dispersed, although many ethnic neighborhoods born in the early stages of labor migration survived for a long time.

Again, as with the labor market, there are often network effects on residential concentrations, particularly in migration. Those moving to a new city or society need places to live. They may stay first with relatives or friends and search for housing nearby, or depend on those they already know for information on housing opportunities. In either case, the result is often similar: Ethnic group members concentrate in a particular area. Such concentrations increase the probability of interactions with other group members and add a spatial dimension to the ethnic or racial boundary.

As we suggested at the end of the preceding section, residential concentrations share some identity effects with labor market concentrations. Restricting certain persons—however defined—to particular positions in the labor or housing markets is a boundary mechanism. Whether the restriction has its origins in the impersonal operations of circumstance or in discriminatory or exploitative intent, it both selects a boundary (the basis for distinguishing between eligibles and non-eligibles for jobs or housing) and gives that boundary certain real-life consequences (the specific set of opportunities it creates). In either case, the selected boundary may well be ethnic or racial, as in the intentional exclusion of the Japanese (and others, including Mexicans and Chinese) from certain kinds of jobs in California and of African Americans from some residential locations, or in the circumstantial concentration of Polish immigrants in the steel industry in the United States. It is not, however, always ethnic or racial: The "selected" boundary may be some other group dimension that cuts across or is indifferent to ethnicity and race. High housing prices, for example, discriminate against those with low incomes, and low-wage job opportunities are products of economic forces that may well be indifferent to the ethnicity or race of potential workers. Whatever the origin of the restriction, however, the effect may be the same: to reinforce an ethnic or racial boundary. If jobs of a particular kind are all that are available in a society in which the primary source of new labor is some ethnically or racially distinct group, then the circumstantially produced boundary (that delineating these jobs) and the ethnic or racial boundary (that delineating the group) tend to coincide. The result is that the workplace experience reinforces the ethnic boundary.

Boundedness, Exhaustiveness, and Density

Concentration—whether residential or occupational—is important in identity construction, but it cannot do the job alone. What matters most is the particular kinds of relationships that labor market or residential concentration produce. The key factors are boundedness, exhaustiveness, and density (Cornell 1990). Boundedness has to do with the extent to which the positions in the labor or residential markets available to group members are available only to them and not to nonmembers. A high degree of boundedness means that group members are virtually the only ones in those positions and will be unlikely to encounter nongroup members in similar positions. The typical residential example is the ghetto, a neighborhood inhabited almost entirely by members of a single racial or ethnic population. A labor market example is diamond sellers in New York, an occupation made up almost entirely of Jews.

Exhaustiveness refers to the extent to which a particular position is the only opportunity available to group members. If they have other opportunities as well, exhaustiveness is low; if this particular set of opportunities exhausts the opportunities available to group members, exhaustiveness is high. In the case of Jewish diamond sellers in New York, exhaustiveness is low. Jews may dominate that occupation, but they are not limited to it: Most Jews in the United States are not in the diamond business. In the case of Black ghetto housing in the United States, exhaustiveness historically has been high. During much of the 20th century, for example, Blacks in many cities were effectively denied the opportunity to live anywhere else.

Where boundedness and exhaustiveness both are high, the occupational or residential boundary essentially coincides with the group boundary, reinforcing it. Where one or both is low, occupational or residential boundaries and the group boundary diverge, modifying the reinforcement.

The third feature—density—refers to the extent to which a given occupational or residential opportunity facilitates interpersonal interactions among group members. Centralized workplaces such as factories or dockyards, for example, are more likely to produce frequent and sustained interactions among workers than are dispersed workplaces, such as custodial labor in apartment buildings. They also are more likely to do so than are occupations that involve individual as opposed to cooperative labor, such as sales. Interactions among group members will be more frequent if their work opportunities are geographically concentrated and organizationally centralized, less frequent if they are dispersed or decentralized. Much the same is true, obviously, of residential opportunities, although there is a much lower probability of encountering a residential situation of high boundedness and exhaustiveness combined with low density.

Taken together, what these three features measure is the degree to which group members are likely to have more frequent and dense interactions with other members of the group than with nonmembers. The implications are fairly simple: To the extent that interactions are dense and frequent within the ethnic or racial boundary and dispersed and infrequent across it, the more likely group members are to see their ethnic or racial identity as an important feature of their lives, and to engage in practices particular to the group. The overall effect, then, of labor market or residential concentration where boundedness, exhaustiveness, and density are high is to support the formation or persistence of an ethnic or racial identity and to make it more comprehensive or thick, that is, to organize more of group life in terms of that identity.

Social Institutions

Political institutions are not the only institutions of importance to group formation. Other institutions of significance include schools, churches, social service organizations, sources of financial credit, retail services, and all of the other formally organized mechanisms by which the members of a society solve the various problems of daily living. Social change may disrupt access to such institutions. Some migrant populations, for example, leave many familiar institutions behind and may lack the language skills, familiarity, or information necessary to take advantage of institutions in the receiving society; worse, they may be barred systematically from those institutions. Other migrants, in contrast, may find the institutions of the receiving society both familiar and accessible.

Obviously, this has potentially significant effects on ethnic or racial identities. To the extent that the institutions of the society are available and accessible to all populations within the society, the salience of ethnic boundaries is reduced. To the extent that such institutions are unavailable or inaccessible to one or more populations, or to the extent that special institutions are set aside for them (as in the creation and maintenance of Black-only schools in the American South prior to desegregation), that salience is increased.

Social Institutions and Identity Salience

There are two reasons for the latter effect. The first is obvious: As noted before, discrimination—in this case, the denial of institutional access on the basis of ethnic or racial identity—is a powerful boundary mechanism, whether that access has to do with jobs, housing, political participation, schools, or some other institution. The fundamental message is that you are denied access because you occupy a particular category—because you are Kurdish in Turkey (McDowall 1996) or Tamil in Sri Lanka (Tambiah 1986) or Mexican in the United States (Almaguer 1994) or something else. The category takes on a demonstrable significance in your life, and your sense of the importance of that category rises commensurately.

There is a second reason for increased salience of racial or ethnic identity. Denied access to dominant institutions, populations have to find alternative solutions to life problems, either in institutions created especially for them, in their own already existing institutional repertoires, or by invention. We will have more to say about this in the following chapter, in which we discuss social capital and institutional completeness. The point for the moment is simply that finding institutional solutions within the ethnic or racial boundary increases intragroup interactions, expanding links among group members via institutional participation and the common investments of energy and time in ethnically distinct practices and organizations. To create and use such institutions is to make more elaborate, to weave more thickly, the fabric of a distinct and exclusive community life, a fabric that includes only "us." Finding such solutions within the society at large, on the other hand, increases interactions across the boundary, withdrawing some of the threads from that fabric.

Intermarriage

One of the institutions in which such effects are most apparent deserves particular attention here: marriage. In their study of ethnic and racial groups in the United States, Stanley Lieberson and Mary Waters (1988) point out that ethnic intermarriage

> has consequences for the individuals involved and for the future viability and nature of the ethnic groups themselves. For the individuals involved, intermarriage functions to create more ethnic heterogeneity in their social networks and may possibly lead to a diminution or dilution of ethnic identity. For the individual children of intermarriage the determination of ethnic identity becomes a question and a decision in a way that does not exist for the children of an ethnically homogeneous marriage. (pp. 162-63)

The consequences for ethnic groups, as opposed to individuals, are somewhat less clear. As Lieberson and Waters note (p. 165), it is the central role of the family in processes of socialization that gives to intermarriage so potentially profound an impact on the continuity of ethnic identity. Should intermarriage occur on a large scale in a single generation, it could be followed by a rapid decline in the number of persons for whom a single ethnic identity is central to both self-concept and social relations. It is within the family, after all, that many people first learn the feelings, practices, and understandings often attached to ethnic identities and come to see themselves in particular ethnic terms. Marriage across the ethnic boundary potentially complicates these processes.

At the same time, other factors—the attitudes of other persons, prevailing ideas in the society about the generational transmission of identity (such as the widespread and often official assumption in the United States that the children of Black-White marriages are Black), and so on— also may have an impact on the felt identities of marriage partners and their children. Nonetheless, Lieberson and Waters (1988:165) note that "if a group experiences high levels of intermarriage, this can be viewed as a potentially important factor working against the long-run maintenance of the group as a separate entity."

High levels of intermarriage, however, as these same authors point out (p. 205), depend at the very least on levels of opportunity, and these have varied from group to group and society to society. Opportunity has two dimensions. One is spatial and obvious—most marriages, other than arranged marriages, are the products of contact: People have to be able to meet each other. Physical proximity, then, is important. The other dimension is sociolegal: Both legal and normative prohibitions against marriage across ethnic, racial, or religious boundaries have been common at various times in many parts of the world. From the 13th to the 19th century, for example, intermarriage between Christians and Jews was against either sacred or secular law in much of Europe (Spickard 1989). In Japan, the Japanese for a long time have actively discouraged marriage between themselves and members of Japan's Korean and Ainu minorities (De Vos and Wetherall 1974). Beginning in 1850, a series of California laws prohibited interracial marriages of various kinds, including White marriages with Asians, who generally were classified as non-White. Some of these not only prohibited such marriages but voided existing ones (Frankenberg 1993). Although not always enforced, these laws had teeth: "In 1914 a Japanese man was convicted of White slavery and his White bride threatened with deportation when it came to light they had taken an ocean cruise in order to get married outside territorial waters and thereby avoid the law" (Spickard 1989:70). The first laws against racial intermarriage in what is now the United States were adopted in Maryland in 1661, prohibiting White marriage with Africans or Indians. In time, 38 states eventually adopted laws of one kind or another against interracial marriages, and it was not until 1967 that the U.S. Supreme Court declared such laws to be unconstitutional (Frankenberg 1993:72).

Such prohibitions create or reinforce ethnic and racial identities in three ways. First, by designating categories of eligibles and ineligibles, they construct a specific boundary between populations. Second, because prohibitions against intermarriage invariably involve statements—explicit or implicit—of the relative worthiness of the respective groups, such prohibitions attach differing value to the categories on either side of the boundary: Not only are they different, but one is unworthy of the other. They thereby reinforce the boundary. Third, through their practical effect on the marriage pool, they encourage marriage within the ethnic or racial boundary, thereby avoiding the dilution of felt identity that intermarriage often fosters.

Less formal social controls may have similar impacts. Whites who succeeded in marrying Asians in California during the years when such marriages were proscribed often were ostracized by their families. To marry across the White-Asian boundary was to risk certain social relationships—friendships, the support of kin—on behalf of the marriage. Although the interracial boundary typically was the focus of legal sanctions, less comprehensive boundaries were often the object of less formal modes of control. Paul Spickard notes cases in the 1920s, for example, in which both Chinese Americans and Mexican Americans objected to intermarriage with Japanese, ostracizing women from their own groups who dared to cross that boundary. "With such a pattern of nearly universal nonacceptance, Japanese men and women had to think very carefully before entering into interethnic unions" (Spickard 1989:71). Punjabi immigrants from India—all of them male—encountered similar opposition when they married White or Mexican women in California. In the 1910s and 1920s, Mexican opposition to Punjabi-Mexican marriages led on occasion to violence, although such opposition subsided over time (Leonard 1992).

Both formal and informal prohibitions may change over time and generations. Change in formal prohibitions is illustrated by the Supreme Court's 1967 ruling that laws against interracial marriage were unconstitutional and by the actions of numerous states prior to it. As for the informal prohibitions, Spickard traces changing Jewish, Japanese American, and Black attitudes toward intermarriage in the United States. For first-generation Japanese immigrants, for example, intermarriage with Whites or Chinese was conceivable but unlikely; intermarriage with Filipino Americans or Blacks was unacceptable. By the third generation, intermarriage with Whites or Chinese had become acceptable, and Filipino or Black intermarriage, although unlikely, had become at least conceivable (Spickard 1989:354). As such normative or legal prohibitions change, the ethnic or racial boundary becomes more or less porous.

Population densities can affect these patterns. Among third-generation Japanese-Americans, for example, intermarriage rates tend to be lowest where Japanese American population densities are highest (Fugita and O'Brien 1991). Assuming no substantial restrictions on intermarriage, population dispersal tends to increase intermarriage rates as the chances of engaging in sustained interactions across the ethnic or racial boundary rise.

The Effect of Intermarriage on Ethnicity and Race

At the same time, as we suggested above, the effect of intermarriage on ethnicity and race—its effect on identity—though often conceived as assimilationist (e.g., Gordon 1964), is not entirely predictable. Intermarriage among Asian ethnic populations in the United States, for example, has been a factor in the emergence of a pan-Asian ethnicity (Espiritu 1992): a change in ethnic boundaries but not necessarily a decline in the significance of ethnic identity generally in the lives of Asian Americans (nor in the significance of the separate Asian ethnicities that make up the Asian American population). Racial and ethnic intermarriage are high among Native Americans (Snipp 1989), yet there are significant regional differences in the choice of identity for the children of those Native

Americans who are intermarried. In some areas, Indian intermarriage with Whites and others is a much less reliable predictor of assimilation than in others, as significant numbers of intermarried couples designate a tribal or Indian identity for their children and continue to live in predominantly Native American communities (Eschbach 1995). In a study of ethnic identification among European-descent groups in the United States, Alba and Chamlin (1983) found that persons of mixed ancestry were still likely to identify with only one of those ancestries: Single ethnic identities, in other words, remained salient, despite the linking of identities through intermarriage.

Again, however, not all intermarriages increase the choices available to parents or to children, and the key example is interracial marriage. The degree of choice is significantly diminished in interracial marriages and generally has been denied altogether in the case of interracial marriages involving Blacks, at least in the United States. As we noted in our discussion of race in Chapter 2, the children of these marriages are almost invariably classified as Black by the larger society, which tends to invoke the one-drop rule, a rule not generally applied to the children of White-Native American, White-Asian, or White-Latino marriages, who generally are considered "part" Asian, Indian, or Latino (see Davis 1991; Hollinger 1995).

There is evidence, nevertheless, that in many cases—probably in most—exogamy (marriage across the ethnic or racial boundary) undermines solidarity in the minority population, whereas endogamy (marriage within the ethnic or racial boundary) sustains it (Lieberson and Waters 1988; and see, for example, Alba 1985, 1990; Fugita and O'Brien 1991; Kamphoefner 1987). Certainly this is what one would predict under "other things equal" conditions: As formal and informal proscriptions against intermarriage decline, the group boundary itself loses one of its supports, making movement across the boundary easier, complicating the transmission of identity, and making single component identities less salient in people's lives.

Culture

Human beings live not only in the midst of material relationships and sets of opportunities—political, economic, social—but also in the midst of ideas and understandings. The social world is an interpreted world, as much conceptual as it is concrete. Interpretations, ideas, and understandings are part of culture, and culture is an identity construction site of uncommon importance.

This should be obvious. Although collective identities may be firmly embedded in relationships and institutions, they begin as conceptions, as people's ideas of themselves and others. Ethnicity and race are built not only in concrete relationships but also in the ways we think about, imagine, and articulate ourselves and one another and in the ways we think about and express the world in which we live. Indeed, the institutions and relationships in which collective identities typically are embedded are themselves, to some extent, products of interpretive processes through which we organize the world, first in our heads and then in practice. Culture is sense-making, and collective identities are products of that process.

The culture at issue in this chapter is the culture of the society at large, of the society of which a given ethnic or racial group forms a part. If, in the construction of an identity, people come to a particular understanding of who they are, they do so in part by discovering how other people see them, by experiencing the constructions that other people make—that is, in an encounter with the assumptions of the encompassing culture of the society at large. That culture is unlikely to be seamless: It may embrace quite different sets of ideas in dialogue or in conflict with one another. The interest here is in those ideas and understandings that appear to be dominant or privileged, even if contested, in a given situation, that is, in the dominant culture's assumptions about relevant differences among groups. Three of these are particularly significant in identity construction: first, the categories of ascription that dominate the conceptual organization of group life; second, the group classifications made by dominant populations, or what we might call classification schemes; and third, the status attributions the dominant culture makes: the statuses it attaches to its own group classifications.

Categories of Ascription

By categories of ascription we refer to the broad bases used by the culture at large to conceptualize and talk about groups. These categories reflect that culture's assumptions about what the "natural" or appropriate bases of collective identity, group organization, and collective action are in that society. What is at issue here is not the specific identities involved, such as Neapolitan versus Italian or Puerto Rican versus Latino, but the kinds of identities or differentiators that are commonly in use, such as ethnicity, race, class, region, and so on. When a society assigns people a collective identity, does it tend to do so in terms of race? In terms of class? In terms

of some other differentiator? How is the culture at large inclined to identify people?

Historically, for example, many new migrants to the United States entered a society in which there was—and to a large degree remains—a
"culture of ethnicity,"[1] a set of understandings about the world that gives
prominence to ethnicity as a basis of group categorization and action.
This "culture of ethnicity" is itself a product of a distinctive immigrant
history. Most immigration to the United States has not involved random
individuals moving singly to a new land. On the contrary, at different
times it has been dominated by very different populations and source
societies—northern Europeans of one kind or another from the 17th to
the mid-19th century, southern and eastern Europeans in the later 19th
and early 20th centuries, significant Latino and Asian immigrations at
different times in both the 19th and 20th centuries, and so on—such that
the result was never a mishmash of diverse individuals but a changing
collection of identifiable migrant populations and their descendants. As
each group came and its numbers grew, it became in turn the object of
observation and discussion, opprobrium or praise, discrimination or so-
licitation: a new, ethnically defined "them."

Interwoven through this culture of ethnicity and often overwhelming
it, there also has been a culture of race, rooted originally in the stark divide between enslaved African populations and suppressed Native
Americans, on one hand, and White, European-descent populations on
the other. This culture is amply evident as well in the racialization of various immigrant populations, a process sponsored by the federal government but supported by an assortment of racially White constituencies.
The process found its foremost expression in legal restrictions on immigration from, at various times, southern and eastern Europe, Mexico,
Asia, and elsewhere (Carter, Green, and Halpern 1996; Takaki 1989). Although the social understandings of race have changed over time and
some groups have moved across the racial boundary, as the Irish, Jews,
and even the Chinese in Mississippi did (Ignatiev 1995; Loewen 1988;
Sacks 1994), the organization of American society along lines of color has
remained firmly entrenched, conceptualizing Latino and Asian populations, for example, not only in ethnic but also in racial terms. Combined
with the absence, through much of American history, of an ongoing conversation or politics organized in terms of class boundaries and differentials (Karabel 1979)—that is, of a culture of class—and with persistent (if
changing) socioeconomic and political differences among many of these
ethnic and racial populations, these cultures of ethnicity and race have circumstantially encouraged the identification of both selves and others in

ethnic and racial terms. Today, as ethnic differences within the European-descent population continue to decline in importance, the long-established culture of race appears to be ascendant in American life.

Such categories of ascription not only foster certain kinds of identities—the Black and Indian comparison in Chapter 5 offers two examples—but also discourage others. In the mid-19th century, as Chinese immigrants arrived in California, they encountered prejudice and discrimination not only among Whites but also among the Californios, the Mexican population who had been displaced, socially and often geographically, by the United States invasion in 1846. Some members of this population, embittered by their own losses of land, status, and power, turned their anger against the Chinese and, to a lesser extent, African Americans. They did so in part because they hoped to establish their own superiority, but also, as Rosaura Sánchez argues, because they were caught up in the particular discourse of the times, the ways that group relations were conceptualized. "Forged in a race- and caste-based society, the Californios unfortunately fell back on these operative categories, incapable of constructing an interethnic identity and alliance on the basis of class and ethnic oppression" (1995:302).

In contrast to much of the history of the United States, the categories of ascription in England historically have been class based. At least until recent years, class has provided the most readily available and intuitively appealing terms for organizing and thinking about personal and group experience. Since the middle part of this century, with the influx of racially distinct populations to Great Britain, drawn largely from former colonies in Africa, Asia, and the Caribbean, this has begun to change, with the racial dimension of identity becoming an increasingly powerful element in how people think about themselves and others (Carter et al. 1996; Gilroy 1987; Katznelson 1976). A culture of race is joining the culture of class as a foundation of collective identification in Britain.

The Netherlands likewise has experienced significant immigration in recent decades, with Turks, Greeks, Surinamese, Pakistanis, and others coming to the Netherlands to work. There, however, the language of intergroup relations and categorization has tended to employ either specific ethnic categories or to refer to immigrants more generally as "foreigners," "migrants," or "non-indigenous" peoples (Verkuyten, de Jong, and Masson 1995:257).

A culture of ethnicity or race does not necessarily compel organization on ethnic or racial lines, but it certainly facilitates it. For those trying to make sense of new situations, the prevailing understandings already present in those situations—manifest, typically, both in the ways that people talk and in the ways that institutions are organized—provide a ready-made and (in most cases) demonstrably relevant set of terms and interpretations. At the very least, the actions and categorical assumptions of dominant populations or, as we saw in the section on politics earlier in this chapter, of dominant institutions such as the state are disproportionately influential in shaping the organization of the society. As a result, they are likewise disproportionately influential in shaping the experience of other groups within that society. If the prevailing categories of ascription do not at first appear relevant—as, for example, to an immigrant population—they very well may in time.

Classification Schemes

What groups often encounter, however, is not only broad categories of ascription but also specific group classifications that also play a part in constructing identities. Prevailing classification schemes figure in identity construction most clearly for migrants, who in moving from one society or set of social relations to another often simultaneously enter a new classification system, different from the one they have shared or been accustomed to. James Ito-Adler (1980) has provided an example. The Cape Verde Islands lie in the Atlantic Ocean off the western coast of Africa. Formerly a Portuguese colony, Cape Verde became an independent state in 1975. Both before and after independence, small numbers of Cape Verdeans began migrating to the United States, many of them settling in eastern Massachusetts. Most of these new immigrants thought of themselves either as Cape Verdeans or, in some cases, as Portuguese, but they were viewed quite differently by the society they were entering. The numbers of Cape Verdeans were small, and the local classification system—the informal conceptual categories used by members of local communities to organize the world around them—did not have a Cape Verdean "slot." It had a Portuguese "slot," because Portuguese have been coming to the area for decades, and they and their descendants form a substantial population in southern New England. The newcomers, who spoke Portuguese, might have found a place there. Unlike the Portuguese, however, Cape Verdeans are Black. There was uncertainty in eastern Massachusetts about how to classify Cape Verdeans—Portuguese-speaking Black people—but, given the preeminent significance of race in American culture, local custom eventually classified them as Blacks. This had little effect on the self-concepts of the migrants themselves, who had grown up in the Cape Verde Islands and formed their identities there, but it had a telling effect on their children—the second generation—who

grew up, went to school, and began to launch adult lives amid the classificatory messages and racial tensions of the United States. According to
Ito-Adler, second-generation Cape Verdeans, following the practice of
the locally dominant population, also began to think of themselves as
Blacks.

This pattern is not unusual. The experience of second-generation immigrants from the Cape Verde islands resembles that of the children of
Haitian migrants to the United States. Their experience of Haiti is second-
hand. Increasingly comfortable in both African American and more general American cultures, and more powerfully influenced by the assumptions of the receiving society, they, too, have come to see themselves as
Black (Woldemikael 1989).

These two cases illustrate as much the power of the American culture
of race as the power of more specific dominant classifications, but non-
racial classifications can have similar effects. For many European migrants, entry into U.S. society involved an encounter with classifications
different from those with which the migrants came. Jonathan Sarna
(1978:372) points out that the classificatory ideas of "outsiders"—of the
receiving society—were a primary factor in the "ethnicization" of often-
fragmented European immigrant groups. Among "outsiders" he includes not only the dominant elites in the United States but also other
immigrants who had already arrived from other countries, who once in
the United States often found themselves caught up in a classificatory
chaos of dozens of identities and origins tied to different immigrant
groups. In an attempt to make sense out of that chaos, they frequently
assumed the presence of self-conscious national identities where, in fact,
such identities did not exist. Few of the rural and poorly educated peas-
ant populations that made their way to the United States in the late 19th
and early 20th centuries carried with them a sense of membership in
what today we think of as long-established European nations. Lithuanians, for example, for the most part had little sense of Lithuanian identity,
while many Poles were more likely to identify themselves as Silesians,
Goralis, or Kashubes than as Poles (Connor 1990). Events in Europe, such
as the involvement of many of these nations in World War I, often had an
impact on the self-concepts of immigrant populations, who for the first
time saw their homelands, via newspaper reports, as "national" actors on
the world stage. The classifications of the receiving society, manifest in
the mass media, in public talk, and often in official pronouncements or
actions, also were important. Lucanians, Calabrians, Neapolitans, and
the like, for example, over time came to see themselves as Italians or Italian Americans partly because that was how they were viewed, officially

and unofficially, in America (Alba 1985). They and other European immigrants also quickly recognized themselves as White, adopting both the racial categories of ascription of the receiving society and its specific racial classification scheme.

Similar processes were apparent among Asian migrants to Hawaii. Immigrants from northern, central, and southern China, sharing little in the way of common identity, discovered on arrival in Hawaii that the various elements of the receiving society viewed them as Chinese. Over time, they came to see themselves the same way (Glick 1938).

Such patterns are common around the world. For example, rural migrants to the city of Port Moresby, capital of the island nation of Papua New Guinea, typically come from small rural social units based on closely related kin, with little sense of more comprehensive collective identities. Once in the city, however, they encounter the classifications of established residents, many of them previous migrants, who tend to label newcomers in terms of general ethnic categories that combine numerous villages or areas. They do so in part because they simply cannot keep track of all of the various village identities that newcomers carry. As newcomers interact with established residents, they gradually begin to make use of the same classifications. The labels begin to stick, and soon the migrants begin to see themselves in the terms already in use in the city, and to act accordingly. The labels become identities, and the identities organize action (Levine and Levine 1979).

Although the impact of classification may be most apparent in the case of migration, it appears elsewhere as well. In the middle of the 19th century, for example, a distinctive ethnic identity began to emerge among the well-established German minority in Bohemia, especially in Prague, today the capital of the Czech Republic. Disruption of another kind was involved in this case. In the first half of the 19th century, an organized movement of Czech nationalism began to appear in the multiethnic society of Bohemia. Its purpose was to achieve equality for the majority Czech population, resentful of the economic and political dominance of the German-speaking minority in the population, but at its center was a vision of a Czech national society and a dream of Czech dominance in Bohemia. By the 1850s and 1860s, this movement had established a considerable presence in the city of Prague (Cohen 1981).

At the time this movement emerged, the German-speaking minority in Prague had little sense of itself as an ethnic group. Along with language differences, class distinctions were important to German speakers—they dominated the middle and upper strata of Bohemian society—and most of them "saw their social position defined by their leading roles in the economy, government and education and not really by virtue of belonging to a separate German people" (Cohen 1992:269). The Czech nationalist movement changed that. Partly in an effort to defend their position, German-speakers began "to accept the Czech argument that two distinct peoples inhabited Bohemia" (Cohen 1981:30). In other words, as Czechs began to identify and organize along an ethnic boundary, distinguishing their own "us" from a German "them," Germans responded accordingly, increasingly seeing themselves as Germans. As this suggests, the discovery that "we" are their "them" can have identity-constructing effects of its own.

Classification and Government Policy

Some of these examples underline the fact that not only the public at large but also official practices and conceptions often play a role in the classificatory construction of ethnic boundaries. Here the links between the political and cultural sites are obvious. Joane Nagel (1986:96) argues that the most powerful ascriptive force in any state is the central government. Not only does it structure political participation in particular ways, as we have seen, but it also often is the source of changing classificatory terms adopted by publics as part of their own ways of viewing the world. The fact that any government has some control over the resources of the society gives extra weight to its classificatory decisions—to the bases on which it distributes those resources—and it is this link between classificatory terms and real-world consequences that makes governmental classification so powerful in the construction of identities.

This is perhaps nowhere so evident as in the period when many African and Asian countries were colonies of European powers. The classification systems of the colonizers determined the ways they organized not only government but also the experiences of the colonized, thereby encouraging or discouraging the salience of particular identities. In Uganda, for example, according to Crawford Young (1985), British colonial administrators often mistakenly assumed that linguistic or other cultural similarities among indigenous peoples were indicators of comprehensive group structures and collective identities. They put together administrative apparatuses that reflected their assumptions, combining previously unrelated groups in administrative units, and in the process—essentially by political fiat—they invented ethnic groups. Uganda was hardly an unusual case. Such administrative creations were common, in one form or another, in much of the colonial world, where the colonial state, says Young, in some cases "breathed life into quite novel categories of identity" (Young 1985:74).

U.S. history has its own versions of these processes. We have already seen, in Chapter 5, how federal classifications encouraged the emergence of a supratribal American Indian identity among Native Americans. In the 19th century, the federal government had an impact on less comprehensive Indian identities as well. In the process of negotiating treaties of land cession and confining Indian groups on remnant reservations, the government often combined distinct groups into single categories. Following extended warfare, for example, the federal government forced a number of culturally similar but politically distinct bands of Comanche Indians onto a single reservation in the Indian Territory, now Oklahoma, designated in their collective name. Before long, according to William Hagan (1976:133), members of these bands, faced with the daily reality of federal and public use of the name "Comanche," began to see themselves "more and more as Comanches rather than as Quahadas or Yamparikas" or other band identities, which long had priority over "Comanche" in their own sense of themselves.

In more contemporary times, affirmative action programs have had some similar effects in the United States, specifying certain group boundaries as appropriate for certain purposes. In the process, they encourage the perception of those boundaries as enduring and appropriate bases of identity and action, thereby reinforcing them. Felix Padilla (1985) argues, for example, that the effort to take full advantage of affirmative action policies and city programs designated specifically for "Hispanics" brought Puerto Ricans and Mexican Americans together in Chicago in the 1970s, stimulating an explicitly Latino ethnic consciousness and political mobilization along explicitly Latino lines. The changing terminology of the federal decennial census has done much the same, giving names to certain racial boundaries, such as Hispanic or Asian American, encouraging those names as group identifiers, and linking the numbers counted under those names to funding levels in some federal programs. The terminology thereby encourages the identities it already assumes (see, for example, Espiritu 1992; Oboler 1995; Waters 1995).

As all these cases suggest, and as Espiritu (1992:6) points out, "categorization is intimately bound up with power relations." Some groups have the power to draw the boundary lines where they wish, and thus to successfully classify both themselves and others within the dominant system. Others lack that power and find themselves either struggling against dominant classifications or adjusting to them. Either way, the classification system and the identities it proposes become part of the world with which they have to deal, and at times part of their own conceptual schemes.

Status Attributions

Closely related to the classifications that populations encounter are the statuses attached to those classifications. Status differentials solidify boundaries, whereas status attributions flag identities as attractive or unattractive. The classification Black in the United States traditionally has marked much more than color. In the dominant culture, it signified a divide between qualitatively different kinds of human beings: superior Whites and inferior Blacks. This difference was particularly onerous because it was assumed by many to have genetic roots.

In other words, classification into distinct categories is only one aspect of identity construction. To the extent that in the prevailing culture the resultant categories also mark status differentials, and to the extent that those differentials are assumed to be substantial, consequential, and inherent, the boundary-creating effect of classification tends to increase. At each point, the boundary becomes more emphatic and imposing, and the information it conveys about the persons within the categories it defines becomes more detailed and elaborate.

This, of course, has effects across a number of identity construction sites. For example, as status differentials between any two groups rise, the chances of intermarriage decline (Spickard 1989) and the chances of discrimination against the subordinate population in jobs, housing, and politics tend to rise. At the same time, as competition among groups for such resources increases or decreases, status attributions often change. It is easier to exclude a group from sought-after jobs, housing, or other opportunities if that group is defined as somehow less worthy of those resources or even ineligible for them by virtue of its distinctive identity and the characteristics that identity signifies. When the competition for scarce resources heats up, therefore, some groups may try to assign lower statuses to other groups so as to undermine their claims to those resources or assert higher status for themselves so as to justify their own claims.

Changes in status attributions have consequences for identity constructions. The Chinese in the United States, for example, were long viewed with contempt in the society at large, and for much of the period since immigration peaked in the latter part of the 19th century, they were restricted to Chinatowns, excluded from entire categories of jobs and from entire industries, and made a mockery of in popular American culture. Much of that changed during World War II, when China became an American ally in the war against Japan and the Chinese people were turned into heroes by the American media for their resistance to the Japanese. In 1943, the U.S. Congress repealed the Chinese Exclusion Act of 1882, which had restricted Chinese immigration (a meager yearly immigrant quota of 105 persons replaced it, but the fact that it changed at all was notable). In subsequent years, job opportunities suddenly opened up to Chinese who previously had been denied them, and many residential restrictions were removed (Kwong 1979; Nee and Nee 1973). Although Chinese still faced prejudice and sometimes violent discrimination in many aspects of American life, the distance across the ethnic boundary had diminished measurably as the status of the Chinese rose in common American understandings. The identity gained a new dimension in the dominant culture and, to some degree, among Chinese Americans as well.

Status attributions may encourage groups to adopt or resist certain identities. In their studies of West Indian immigrants in New York City, Philip Kasinitz (1992) and Mary Waters (1994) found that some West Indians—particularly in the migrant generation—resist identification as Blacks because they hope to avoid the negative stereotyping and racism that American society at large directs against African Americans, a sentiment already familiar from our account of the Chinese in Mississippi in Chapter 5. West Indians instead tend to emphasize their West Indian identity or to identify as Jamaicans, Dominicans, Barbadans, and so forth, or even simply as immigrants. For many of their children, however, the classifications of the larger society overwhelm these efforts; many of them, as with the Haitians and Cape Verdeans we have already noted, gradually come to adopt the identities imposed by the society around them.

Many such attributions are captured in popular culture, in the representations of ethnic or racial "others" in entertainment, popular literature, advertising, and art. From Sambo, the carefree, contented slave, to Aunt Jemima, offering her pancakes to White families, such images linked African Americans with a supposedly happy (and therefore surely appropriate) servitude. In the early 1970s, a student of American films pointed out that contemporary movies tended to present American Blacks through five dominant stereotypes: "*toms*—they served their masters well; *coons*—funny men . . .; *mulattos*—tragic because they're not all white; *mammies*—sexless archmothers; *bucks*—bestial superstuds" (Bogle 1973, quoted in Pieterse 1992:152). In mid-19th-century Britain, as a stream of Irish immigrants fled the famines of the 1840s and settled in

England, cartoons and other media images increasingly presented the Irish as apelike anarchists (Pieterse 1992:213-14). The point of these examples is not that Blacks or Irish might internalize the images—although some may have done so—but that the images themselves both emphasize a particular boundary and attach to it a value, and in so doing help to construct a particular kind of identity. Those who are assigned the identity—in these two cases Blacks or Irish—may not concede the value attached to it and may in fact not only reject it but also assert their own very different understandings. That value nevertheless is part of the world they encounter, part of what others say they are, and therefore part of the weight they carry.

Daily Experience

By now, we have crossed into the last of the construction sites examined here, for the images that convey status are often part of daily experience. One of the places where cultural assumptions surface—from categories of ascription to classification schemes to status attributions—is in the day-to-day realities of intergroup relations and interactions. Ethnicity and race are constructed not only in distributions of rights and opportunities, in access to jobs or social institutions or political power, or in the formal specifications made by government. Factors such as these may describe the economic and political position of an ethnic or racial group, or the degree to which it has formal recognition—positive or negative—in the society at large, but it is in daily experience that the boundaries between groups often are most clearly drawn or most subtly reinforced. In day-to-day interactions, people enact their assumptions, conveying messages about which identities are important to them and what those identities mean.

By daily experience, then, we refer not to the ways that concrete sets of opportunities and constraints reinforce identities, as in labor markets or marriage pools or legal provisions, but to the many ways, large and small, that identities are signified, underlined, asserted, and reinforced through the informal interactions that compose so much of the fabric of daily living. These range from suggestive but fundamentally disinterested behavior—the unthinking use of racial or ethnic stereotypes that have become part of common parlance—to overt discrimination. Some of the messages in such interactions are unintended, tentative, or of little significance. Others are sent with stunning force.

In July of 1989, two White men pistol-whipped a Chinese American named Jim Loo in a pool hall in North Carolina, mistaking him for a Vietnamese. Suffering severe head injuries, Loo died 2 days later. The Loo killing was one of a number of such incidents in the 1980s in which Whites violently attacked Asian Americans (Espiritu 1992). The reasons behind individual incidents were diverse, from resentments over the lost Vietnam War to perceived economic threats from Japan to the long legacy of White American prejudice against Asians that has roots in late 19th-century competition over jobs and status and in the racial thinking that has informed much of American history and culture. Although some of these attacks were directed against particular Asian groups, others seemed indiscriminate, blaming Asians generally for an assortment of problems. Aside from the consequences attached to each incident, the accumulation of events had an effect of its own: It sent a bluntly physical message to Asian Americans that said that there was a significant boundary between them—all of them—and Whites, a boundary that was capable of organizing personal interactions in sometimes lethal ways. Such incidents were among the factors that encouraged the emergence, in the 1970s and 1980s, of a politicized Asian American pan-ethnic identity, a sense of shared experience and fate among the many hugely diverse Asian groups whose numbers were increasing rapidly in the United States (Espiritu 1992).

Violence in the Asian case was largely unpredictable and directly experienced by relatively few Asian Americans, although its effects were far-reaching. It played a more systematic role in boundary maintenance in the Black experience in the American South. Throughout much of the period of slavery, Blacks in the South not only could not vote and had no independent legal standing in the courts but also found themselves subject to a regime ready and willing to employ citizen violence as a means to reinforce the steep hierarchy of race and to control discontented Blacks. Many Blacks who challenged or somehow offended the system found themselves facing the fist, the gun barrel, or the lynch mob, a threat that continued to be very real long after slavery had come to an end and that still whispers in the background of contemporary race relations in parts of the United States (Brundage 1993; Genovese 1979). The fact that Whites could act violently toward Blacks and could do so, in many cases, with impunity added another stark dimension to the boundary that already defined African Americans. Their formally institutionalized powerlessness was accompanied and undergirded by a potentially crippling vulnerability in the ordinary processes of daily living. Their place in the social order gave to their identity, however proudly carried or fiercely defended, a corrosive sense of positional weakness.

Although such flagrant acts of identity construction are common enough, much of the process moves forward very differently: through the accumulation of small signals that spotlight boundaries, underline statuses, and thereby reinforce identities. A student of ours captured an example of this in her effort to explain what her ethnicity—she is racially White and ethnically Scottish American—meant: "It means that when I walk into the sheriff's office in El Cajon [California] to have a 'fix-it' ticket signed off for the exact same violation as the middle-aged Mexican man who walked in behind me, the sheriff will take my word for it, but follow the Mexican man out to his car to verify that he has a license plate on it." The sheriff's action in her brief anecdote has the efficiency typical of identity construction. It constructs two identities at once: her Whiteness and the Mexican's Otherness. She was reminded of something about her own identity and its meaning and at the same time learned something as well about the identity of the man who walked in after her, and its meaning. If the Mexican man noticed how she was treated, then he too surely was reminded.

The process can be more subtle still. Michael Arlen (1975:4-6), an American writer of half Armenian descent, tells how, at the age of 9, as a student in an English boarding school, he first realized that he might be different from those around him. Thinking of himself as English—"We were English. We spoke English. We traveled on English passports"—Arlen was assigned a skeptical roommate who noticed something different about Arlen. "Are you French, or what?" asked the boy. "I'm English," Arlen protested. "You *can't* be English!" insisted his roommate, raising for the first time in Arlen's mind some crucial and unsettling questions about his own identity. His roommate eventually heard that Arlen was Armenian. "Har-meenian?" he asked. "I'm English," Arlen said again, and got the same response: "You can't be *English*."

Later, says Arlen, when his father came to visit him at school, "I remember looking at him surreptitiously, sneaking glances at his face—looking for what? I don't know. I wanted him to tell me that we were really English, but I didn't know how to ask" (Arlen 1975:4-6).

The message that Arlen heard in his interactions with his roommate—you are not what you thought you were, you are something else—had two sides to it. On one hand was the message regarding what you are not (English); on the other was the question of what you are. Although Arlen's experience was solitary, what he was learning was not. He was learning through interaction where the boundaries lay among persons. To be excluded from one group is to be classified with some other; after all, his roommate's questions assumed that Arlen belonged in some category. He just could not be English.

The connection between individual experience and collective category was underlined for Arlen later, when he had moved on to a school in America:

> I remember, as an older boy at school in New Hampshire, watching terrified from a fire escape while a gang of sixteen-year-olds taunted and pushed about one of their classmates, a sallow, spidery boy called Gordon, who was supposedly Jewish. What was I so terrified of, I've later wondered—for it is not an enhancing memory. I think probably this: I had gradually become aware that to be Jewish in certain Anglo-Saxon milieus was to be "different"—that is, to be alien and unprotected—and I knew that I, too, was "different," although I was somewhat protected by the camouflage of an accepted Anglo-American manner. But I felt that it was no more than a camouflage and might disappear any day. I know that as I looked down from that fire escape at poor Gordon, I thought: There but for *them* go *we*. (Arlen 1975:7)

The boundary between "them" and "we" may be reinforced by occasional reminders, as in <u>Germany, where in the 1970s many Germans referred to migrant workers from southern Europe as "Zigeuner (gypsy), Lumpenpack (rag-pack), Kameltreiber (camel-rider), Zitronenschuttler (lemon-squeezer), or Schlangenfresser (snake-eater)."</u> They thereby reminded both migrants and themselves that the boundary between them not only was significant but defined a hierarchy of better and worse kinds of people (Berger and Mohr 1982:115). It may be rigidified by pervasive codes of interpersonal behavior. In the American South, long after the end of slavery, a system of racial etiquette prevailed (vestiges of it remain today) by which, among numerous other things, Blacks were expected to be deferential to Whites, and Whites to be patronizing and condescending to Blacks. This system both signified and reinforced in relentless daily experience a racial boundary that had overwhelming consequences in people's lives (Loewen 1988). In the 1990s, many middle-class Black Americans experienced a far less elaborate but still often pervasive boundary-reinforcing process as they encountered the stereotypes and racial assumptions that inform and shape many of their day-to-day interactions with Whites, reminding them in various ways that their Blackness mattered, no matter how bright their achievements might be (Benjamin 1991; Feagin and Sikes 1994).

Interpersonal interactions are not the only aspects of daily experience in which identities are constructed. Particular conceptions of ethnic and racial identities often are sustained in popular culture, advertising, and other consumer-oriented media, providing either a focal point or a backdrop for a great deal of day-to-day life. Many of the earliest situation comedies on American television were built around family life in working-class ethnic communities (Lipsitz 1990, chap. 3). Shows from the 1950s such as *The Goldbergs*, about a working-class Jewish family in the Bronx section of New York; *Mama*, about Norwegian immigrants in San Francisco; and *Life With Luigi*, about Italian immigrants in Chicago, were followed in later decades by shows such as *Chico and the Man*, about Mexican Americans; *Sanford and Son*, about Black Americans in the Watts section of Los Angeles; *All in the Family*, which touched on an assortment of White ethnicities as well as on racial issues; *All-American Girl*, about a young Korean American woman on the West Coast; and many others. Although the focus on working-class families did not last, ethnicity and race remained defining features either of the situations and settings or at least of prominent characters, as in one of the biggest hits of the mid-1990s, *Friends*, with one leading character who is notably Italian American. The versions of ethnic and racial identities presented in these programs were often largely stereotypes or even caricatures, and the shows frequently were attacked on just these grounds by members of the featured groups. In such cases, these shows still made a contribution to identity construction as critics asserted their own identities partly in opposition to television's caricatures. Whatever the content of the specific identities involved, part of the point is that such programs presented both those identities and ethnicity and race more generally as appropriate and meaningful categories of social life and of personal and collective identification, and they did so nightly in living rooms across the country.

Advertising similarly both echoes the categories operative in the society at large and helps to sustain or even create them. Suzanne Oboler (1995:13) points out that the efforts of marketers to exploit perceived opportunities in so-called "ethnic" markets may help to "design," "invent," or "create" the groups involved by treating them, talking about them, and presenting them as a distinct and homogeneous population. A decade earlier, Laura Gomez argued that Coors Beer's "Decade of the Hispanic" billboard advertising campaign in Latino neighborhoods in the early 1980s was one of a number of factors encouraging at least some Mexican Americans in the Southwest to think of themselves as Hispanics, a view supported, in conversation with her, by the then-chair of the Congressional Hispanic Caucus (1986:53). Such popular or mass media representations become part of what we might think of as the sometimes-listened-to, sometimes-only-half-heard background conversation of daily life, offering terms, drawing boundaries, and proposing meanings: in short, constructing identities.

Daily experience thus constitutes a critical site in which identities are delineated, defined, and positioned. From subtle, perhaps unconscious, and supposedly innocent phenomena such as words, names, advertisements, body language, and the revealing question ("Are you French, or what?"), to more confrontational and extreme experiences (Jim Loo beaten to death for being—supposedly—Vietnamese), the encounters of day-to-day life send out messages telling people who and what they are, and who and what they are not.

Summarizing Contextual Factors

At the start of this chapter, we noted that identity construction is a product of the interaction between the situations groups find themselves in under conditions of social change and the resources and attributes they carry with them—that is, between context and, in a sense, characteristics. In discussing what we have called construction sites, we have been focusing on context, on what groups encounter and where they encounter it. Our concern, fundamentally, has been with contextual factors in identity construction.

It may be helpful to provide in table format a summary of these factors, organized by site. Table 6.1 offers a summary account of how various contextual factors, other things equal, affect the salience of ethnic or racial identities. The more salient the identity, the more likely it is to organize collective life and self-concepts. In a sense, and returning to the terminology we put forward in Chapter 4, the more factors are brought into play, the "thicker" the identity is likely to be.

There are some simplifications in the table, and we should note two in particular. For one thing, the table reduces what are inevitably continuous variables to dichotomous ones (according to the table, these factors either do or do not increase the likely salience of ethnic or racial identities, when in fact they are likely, in their many variations, to increase or decrease it not at all, a little, quite a bit, or a lot). For another, the table makes a set of "other things equal" predictions, suggesting that, for each factor, *if other things were equal*—that is, if no other factor were having an effect—this factor would increase or decrease the salience of the identity. The implication is that you can look at a single factor and leave the others

TABLE 6.1

"Other Things Equal" Effects of Contextual Factors on Salience of Ethnic and Racial Identities

Contextual Factors Likely to Increase *Salience of Ethnic or Racial Identities*	*Contextual Factors Likely to* Decrease *Salience of Ethnic or Racial Identities*
Formal distribution of political power coincides with ethnic or racial boundaries	Formal distribution of political power cuts across ethnic or racial boundaries
Government policy treats ethnic or racial groups differently	Government policy treats ethnic or racial groups similarly
Ethnic or racial population is occupationally concentrated	Ethnic or racial population is occupationally dispersed
Ethnic or racial population is residentially concentrated	Ethnic or racial population is residentially dispersed
Ethnic or racial group has differential access to social institutions	Ethnic or racial group has equal access to social institutions
Normative or legal prohibitions exist against marriage across ethnic or racial boundaries	No normative or legal prohibitions exist against marriage across ethnic or racial boundaries
Ethnicity and race are common categories of ascription in the society at large	Ethnicity and race are uncommon categories of ascription in the society at large
Dominant culture assigns group a distinct ethnic or racial classification	Dominant culture assigns group no particular ethnic or racial classification
Dominant culture asserts large status differential between dominant group and ethnic or racial group	Dominant culture asserts little or no status differential between dominant group and ethnic or racial group
Ethnic or racial distinctions play a prominent role in daily experience	Ethnic or racial distinctions play little role in daily experience

SOURCE: Adapted, with somewhat different categories, from Yinger (1986:31).

out of the picture. In the real world, however, other things are seldom, if ever, equal, and the picture typically is full of other factors that are having effects and, therefore, have to be taken into account. Furthermore, some of these factors are likely to covary. Status attributions and access to social institutions, for example, are unlikely to operate independently of each other. The point of the table is not to convey the complexity of real-world situations but to identify the potential impact of individual factors.

The table aside, several other things should be kept in mind in general reference to construction sites. First, not all sites have to be involved for a particular identity to take shape and be sustained as a primary feature of people's lives. Some cases of identity construction involve all these sites; others may involve only one or two. For American Blacks, for example, the process of identity formation and reproduction has been emphatically multidimensional. Throughout much of American history, the boundary that separates them from the rest of American society, that sets them apart, has been drawn through every one of these sites. It has been at one and the same time a political, economic, spatial, institutional, cultural, and interactional boundary. The Civil Rights Movement of the 1960s led to the dismantling of much of the formal structure of boundary maintenance in some of these sites, in particular the political, economic, and institutional ones. On the other hand, informal constraints sometimes have survived in these same arenas, severely restricting opportunities for people of color, and there has been far less change in the cultural arena, where race still wields uncommon power as a category of organization and action. Consequently, the Black-White boundary remains a central, defining feature of the Black experience and of American life.

For German Americans, on the other hand, the boundary between them and other European-descent groups was never as comprehensively organized and has become, in time, virtually invisible. It lingers on in the classifications of the society at large and finds resonance occasionally in daily experience, but it is dependent far more on what German Americans do than on what they encounter in these various arenas.

Second, as we suggested at the start of this chapter, these sites frequently have implications for one another. We have noted that the labor market had a powerful impact on Irish residential concentrations in Liverpool: Irish immigrants needed to find housing close to scarce waterfront jobs so as to take advantage of unpredictable and fleeting hiring opportunities. The resultant combination of labor and residential concentrations gave substantial circumstantial support to an Irish identity. Residential concentrations in turn often affect marital patterns. In her study of ethnic groups in New Haven, Connecticut, Ceri Peach (1980) found a positive relationship between ethnic residential desegregation and out-marriage—as group members dispersed, they were more likely to marry nonmembers—a relationship found in studies of Japanese Americans as well (Fugita and O'Brien 1991; Spickard 1989). Limited access to social institutions such as schools may make it more difficult for economically disadvantaged populations to acquire the skills necessary to take advantage of higher-status occupational opportunities, perpetuating labor market concentrations in low-status and low-income occupations, while low-income occupations make it more difficult to move up in the housing market. And so forth.

The links between sites are perhaps most readily apparent in the case of culture, where those links are both substantial and bidirectional: Patterns of concrete relationships encourage particular perceptions of where "natural" or appropriate boundaries lie, and the assumptions we make about what is "natural" or appropriate in turn have an impact on the ways we organize our lives, shape social policy, distribute rewards, and treat one another. A culture that assumes that ethnic identities are substantively meaningful tends to encourage the organization of social life in ways that lend support to such identities, whereas those identities, once rooted in concrete material conditions, tend to encourage the assumption that they are indeed important.

Third, although the construction processes in these various sites obviously are interrelated, there is an "other things equal" aspect to each site as well, captured in Table 6.1 but worth noting here. For example, in the absence of other identity-constructing processes (either those that promote particular identities or those that transform or discourage them), we would expect occupational concentrations to increase the salience of an ethnic or racial identity and occupational dispersion to decrease it. As we pointed out above, however, other things may not be equal: Other processes typically are not absent. Given a residentially dispersed population with multiethnic marital opportunities and ready access to other social institutions, occupational concentrations may have little effect on identity because there is so little in the way of other support for it. By the same token, broad and diverse occupational opportunities may do little to undermine an ethnic or racial identity that is rooted in political relationships or access to social institutions, or where ethnicity or race remains a primary feature of the established ways that dominant populations conceptualize their own experience, imagine other persons, and conceptually organize the world around them, or in which daily experience repeatedly reinforces an ethnic or racial boundary. In other words, what happens in one site may have countering effects on what happens in another, or may support it. To look only at one or two sites and read from them a particular pattern of identity construction is inherently risky.

Fourth, in our emphasis on the ways that identities are built, maintained, and transformed in these various sites, we do not mean to suggest that the sites themselves and the things going on in them need no explanation. It should be obvious that what happens in these sites, which describe the opportunities and constraints groups encounter under conditions of social change, is to some degree at least a product of other forces that often operate at a substantial remove from the ethnic or racial populations on whom they have so profound an effect. The failure of the potato harvest drove the first, large groups of Irish to Liverpool and New York; both the crop failure and the economic opportunities they encountered in those cities and elsewhere were products of forces largely indifferent to them, yet they still felt the distinctive effects of those forces.

Another way of putting this is to emphasize that these sites have histories. Timing matters. When southern and eastern European groups migrated to the United States in the latter part of the 19th century, they came to a labor-hungry society in which manufacturing jobs were concentrated in growing industrial cities. Nearly a century later, as new waves of immigrants flowed in from Asia, the Caribbean, and Latin America, they encountered a very different economy, characterized by more constrained opportunities, a dispersed manufacturing base, a greater proportion of service sector jobs relative to manufacturing jobs, and a higher likelihood of finding only low-status, low-wage jobs of a sort American workers by then were reluctant to take (e.g., Marshall 1987; Waldinger 1986). During the intervening century, an economic transformation had occurred that had implications for those new immigrants and, among many other things, set their experience apart from that of those who had preceded them.

Similarly, a culture of ethnicity or race is not the creation of a moment nor a passing phase in the cultural life of a society. It is a product of specific relationships, evolving over time; of specific events, their interpretations and justifications; and of particular constituencies who, in pursuit of their own long-term agendas, find ethnicity and race convenient to their purposes. Its staying power comes in part from the depth and breadth of its foundations (see, for example, Omi and Winant 1994). Asian or Mexican immigrants to the United States who arrive in the 1990s or, surely, beyond the turn of the century encounter a situation in which race, ethnicity, and even immigration are *historical* concepts, by which we mean that they have histories of their own. They constitute collections of concepts, understandings, and rhetorics that have evolved over time through extended interactions among societies and peoples. To be defined as a race, to be defined as an immigrant, to claim an ethnic identity—all of these are actions bringing particular histories into play. The groups at issue have to deal not only with an immediate set of circumstances but also with the histories that give those circumstances force and staying power. For any particular case, a review of the sites we have listed here describes a set of proximate conditions under which identity construction occurs, but such a review captures only a moment in an ongoing history. These sites are not static. Even as we examine them for evidence of identity construction, the conditions they describe may be changing, for each contains not only a set of immediate conditions but also a history that gives shape to those conditions and that captures, better than the conditions themselves, the potential for change.

Conclusion

Construction sites are arenas in which the processes of identity construction occur. In those arenas, various groups—some with power, some without—try to cope with the situations they encounter, pursue their objectives, make sense of the world around them, and identify themselves and others. The role of dominant groups in these processes has been apparent in this discussion: They control much of what goes on in these sites, shaping opportunities and constraints for themselves and others.

What about those others, those who enter these sites with limited capacities? Are they merely passive participants in identity construction, accepting the opportunities and constraints they encounter and adopting the identities those opportunity sets, including the classifications of dominant groups, promote? This is hardly the case. Identities are constructed as human populations, carrying their own characteristics, ideas, and agendas, engage the ideas, opportunities, and actors involved in these various sites. It is to those populations and their assets that we now turn.

NOTE

1. We draw this phrase from Yelvington's (1993:9) discussion of ethnicity in Trinidad. His use of the term differs somewhat from ours. He in turn draws on Alexander's (1977) reference to "the culture of race" in Kingston, Jamaica.

7

What They Bring: Group Factors in the Making of Identities

Identity construction is most apparent during periods of social change. In the sites we have just reviewed, construction is energized when groups of human beings encounter new forces or altered circumstances that encourage them to rethink their ideas of themselves, to see themselves and the world around them in new ways. As we noted in Chapter 4, the reverse is also true: As people see themselves in new ways and act accordingly, they may themselves become forces for social change. The key point for now is that what animates the construction process is change in the situations in which human groups find themselves.

Social change, however, is not like a potter, whimsically reshaping compliant clay on a potter's wheel. The human populations that encounter new situations typically have characteristics of their own that also contribute to the construction process, variously limiting, resisting, directing, or promoting it. They do not enter construction sites empty-handed or empty-headed. On the contrary, they bring a great deal with them: established identities, existing internal and external relationships, resources, practices, and characteristics of various kinds. To repeat a point we have already made, the construction of identities takes place in an interaction between, on one hand, the opportunities and constraints groups encounter in construction sites and, on the other, what they bring to that encounter. To understand the process, then, we have to consider not only these sites and the forces operative within them but also the populations involved: the people whose identities are being created, reproduced, or transformed.

This chapter is about what those people contribute—sometimes consciously, often unconsciously—to the making of their own identities. Some of what they contribute is relatively obvious. Because both ethnicity and race are, among other things, matters of contrast—ways of distinguishing among human groups—anything that facilitates such contrast is a potential contribution. Thus, both physical and cultural characteristics, if sufficiently distinctive, may promote identity construction, offering material for the drawing of a group boundary by either insiders or outsiders. Common physical distinctions such as skin color or common cultural distinctions such as shared language, religious practice, or even behavior, facilitate social categorization, offering readily available hooks on which to hang the claim that "they" are not "us" or that "we" are superior to "them." As we noted in Chapter 2, such differences are not sufficient for the construction of ethnic or racial identities, for they have no social significance in and of themselves. It is only when a society or some group within it decides to give one or more of these differences a major role in the organization of social life—only when they decide to make it socially meaningful—that those differences play a part in identity construction. Ethnicity and race are constructed not out of physical and cultural distinctions but out of the significance or role that people give to those distinctions.

Although the ways that such differences are put to work in identity construction are complex, their potential contribution seems to us straightforward. In this chapter, we consider six other group assets or characteristics that have implications for identity construction and whose potential contributions are less obvious: preexisting identities, population size, internal differentiation, social capital, human capital, and symbolic repertoires.

Preexisting Identities

"No man is an island," wrote 17th-century English poet John Donne. He did not say so explicitly, but no woman is an island either. Human beings are connected to one another, necessarily so at times, other times by choice, and often by circumstance.

This observation is important for the understanding of identity construction. It underlines the point that the making of a collective identity is not, generally speaking, a process through which unconnected, isolated individuals come together and gain a consciousness of themselves as constituting a group. Few such isolated individuals exist. Virtually all human beings are not only connected to other human beings in various ways but also see themselves as members of groups, as occupiers of categories, as variously similar to and different from other people. In a fundamental sense, that is where they start from: a situation of connectedness and a self-definition that is partly categorical. Their sense of who they are is partly a matter of the categories they occupy: for example, a woman, a Puerto Rican, a daughter, an attorney, a New Yorker, and so on. Consequently, the construction of any particular collective identity is a process through which that identity joins other consciously held identities, or replaces, overshadows, disrupts, or otherwise alters them.

This is certainly the case for ethnicity and race. The development of an ethnic or racial identity never occurs in a vacuum. New ethnic or racial identities variously modify, succeed, add to, combine, accompany, or fragment already existing identities. As a result of gradual or sudden social change, already existing groups of people, defined in various ways and engaged in diverse interactions with each other, encounter new situations or find themselves in new or changing relationships, and consequently either rethink who they are in ethnic or racial terms, or are rethought, so to speak, by others.

Preexisting Identities and Assignment

In Chapter 6, we noted that one of the things ethnic groups encounter in the arena of culture is the view outsiders have of them, including the classifications that outsiders make. Thus, for example, traders, British colonialists, and others over time came to identify various groups in what is now Malaysia as Malays, a label that was not used by many of the groups to whom it was applied but that is now generally accepted. Neapolitans and Calabrians came to the United States, were received as Italians, and eventually adopted the label themselves. Comanche Indians on the southern plains, who had seen themselves primarily as Yamparikas or Quehadas or members of other bands, over time gave increasing prominence to their shared Comanche identity, the one almost invariably employed by outsiders. They and numerous other groups eventually came to see themselves also as American Indians or Native Americans.

As these examples suggest, however, outsider classifications are not the only ones that group members might adopt. They might well maintain or give more prominence to the collective identities they already carry, which may be very different from those that outsiders use or try to impose.

West Indian migrants to the United States, for example, may ultimately become, in their own minds, Black Americans, taking on the racial identity that the surrounding society assigns to them, but they begin as immigrants and as West Indians of diverse national origins—Jamaicans, Trinidadians, Dominicans, Barbadans, and so on. The transitions in identity that occur among them do not happen easily. In varying degrees, individuals and groups resist the classifications others make. They do so, in this case, in part because the migrants and their children are reluctant to be handicapped by the stereotypes the larger society attaches to Black Americans; in part because sometimes it makes political, social, or economic sense to organize and act on the basis of national identities; and in part because, for the immigrant generation at least, these national identities have significant resonances of their own, referring to the societies in which the immigrant generation grew up and to which it typically retains some familial, cultural, or emotional connection. By the second generation, however, as Mary Waters (1994) shows in her study of West Indian high school students in New York City, group identities have become more complex, reflecting the multiple ties and tensions that play roles in these students' lives and in the immigrant community they come from. They are the children of West Indian immigrants of diverse national origins, going to school in a racially divided society; juggling the classifications that their parents, their peers in ethnically diverse schools, Americans in general, American Blacks, and other persons make; and developing out of that juggling act a diverse array of self-concepts, from West Indian immigrant to Black American to American. Those self-concepts constitute understandings regarding which group boundaries are important and where the self stands—or wishes to stand—among those boundaries, and they reflect an interaction between experience and the possible ways of interpreting that experience. Some of the second generation adopt one way, some another. The identities they adopt are not necessarily permanent. Ethnic identities, like other collective identities, are not static; on the contrary, they are always in the process of being created or reproduced or transformed. That does not mean they have no impact. Once established, they become factors in subsequent processes of identity construction.

How much of a factor, however, varies. Not all ethnic or racial identities are the same. For some persons, ethnic identities are little more than labels—"I'm Jamaican" or "I'm Irish" or "I'm Filipino"—a way of classifying the self. For them, the identity carries few behavioral implications and is largely a residue, something learned from parents or others, a part of their self-definition that in fact organizes very little of daily life and commands little in the way of emotional attachment. For others, the same identities—Jamaican, for example, or Irish, or Filipino—may include elaborate behavioral prescriptions or expectations, organize much of daily living, and carry a powerful emotional charge (see Cornell 1996). In the late 1970s, Herbert Gans argued that for many third- and fourth-generation European-descent Americans, ethnicity had become largely symbolic. It was important to them, and was celebrated in eating habits and familial stories and in certain holidays such as Columbus Day for Italian Americans and St. Patrick's Day for Irish Americans, but it was no longer attached to vibrant ethnic communities or to elaborately distinct ethnic cultures. It was characterized, wrote Gans (1979:9), by "a love for and a pride in tradition that can be felt without having to be incorporated in everyday behavior" (see also Alba 1990; Waters 1990). Such identities engage people's imaginations but little else, and the role they play in people's lives—and in subsequent processes of identity construction—is limited.

Generations and Preexisting Identities

As these American examples suggest, the generational composition of a group has an effect here, particularly in the case of immigrant populations. Immigrants carry with them, in many cases (not all—we will have more to say about this later in this chapter), a powerful conception of who they are, rooted in their experience in their home country or region and sometimes magnified by the often wrenching or at least disconcerting transition they are making to an unfamiliar place and situation. That conception may differ from the perceptions of receiving societies—whose classification schemes, as we saw in Chapter 6, may follow a different logic—and may even make little sense of the experiences migrants have in those societies; but it is part of the cognitive cargo that migrants bring with them. Therefore, it has power. On the other hand, the children of those migrants may have a far more modest version of that conception, more modest because it is much less a product of their own experience and much more at odds with the social relationships that organize major portions of their lives. They learn the conception from their parents, but the world around them may send a very different message. Their parents' identity thus becomes a present but much reduced factor in the shaping of their own sense of who they are.

The point is simply that, once established, identities become part of the ways that people look at the world and part of how they see themselves within it. The more embedded in social relationships and in the organization of daily experience an identity is—the thicker it is—the more prominent a part it is likely to play in how people think about themselves and the world around them. Thus, there is a self-perpetuating quality to ethnic and racial identities: The more established and socially embedded they are, the more likely they are to endure. Certainly, as the social relationships supporting ethnic or racial boundaries change, the identities they help to sustain are likely to change as well, but not necessarily easily or immediately. People learn to see themselves in particular ways. Those ways may survive, for a time, changes in the circumstances that first produced them. To the extent that a particular collective identity captures and embraces a sense of self, it gains in staying power, affecting responses to changing conditions.

Population Size

As we noted in Chapter 5, one of the largest groups of immigrants to enter the United States during the 19th century was Germans. Walter Kamphoefner (1987) has studied one group of migrants who came to the United States from the German region of Westfalia in the decades preceding the Civil War, settling eventually in two rural counties in the state of Missouri. There they flourished, particularly in agriculture, and their ethnic identity seems to have flourished with them. As late as the 1930s, farm children in the area were still speaking German in everyday conversation, and what one observer had earlier called "the German spirit," while fading, had yet to disappear (p. 177).

Kamphoefner points to a number of factors that helped to sustain German ethnicity in the supposed melting pot of the United States. In addition to the preservationist efforts that we noted in Chapter 5, some of them are demographic. He asks how large a migrant group must be if it is to retain a significant degree of ethnic solidarity, and responds, based on the German experience in Missouri, "First of all, it must be large enough to make widespread outmarriage unnecessary. Secondly, since a church parish usually formed the nucleus of an ethnic community, the group must be able to support a viable congregation" (p. 189).

The Significance of Numbers

In short, numbers matter. The larger the population, the greater the chances that relationships of various kinds, from marriage to cooperative business ventures to the provision of community services to day-to-day interactions, can occur within the boundary of the group. The smaller the numbers, the greater the chances that such activities will reach across that boundary. Among European-descent ethnic populations in the United States, for example, there is a substantial correlation between group size and in-group marriage: With some exceptions, the larger the group, the more likely women are to marry within it (Lieberson and Waters 1988:207-208). The populations of some American Indian nations are so small that group members would have difficulty marrying within the group without violating one or another incest taboo; for a significant number of other Indian nations, the pool of eligible potential mates who share the specific ethnic identity, although not so severely limited, remains very small. The result in many cases is a high rate of outmarriage—often to other Native Americans, sometimes to non-Indians. Although the effect of this on ethnic identity varies, as we noted in the previous chapter, the tendency, other things equal, is to undermine it.

In addition, the larger the population, the more likely, other things equal, that outsiders will have frequent contacts with this population. It is difficult to generalize about the result of this, but in societies in which certain racial or ethnic boundaries have major significance, as with minorities of color in the United States, increased contact can lead to increased antipathy on the part of outsiders who see in large numbers a threat to their own position of power or control or to specific resources—jobs, for example, or housing or education—of importance to them. The result is a sharper drawing of the group boundary.

Population size obviously matters in other ways as well, not least in the competition among groups for scarce resources. Other things equal, for example, large numbers increase political clout. The U.S. local and national elections of 1996 provide an illustration. Growing numbers of Latinos—largely Mexican Americans—in Orange County, California, voted for Democratic candidates, abruptly altering the political profile of that historically conservative county and unseating a longtime Republican congressman. In the 19th century, it was partly the sheer numbers of German Americans in U.S. cities that persuaded some public schools to offer instruction in German. In the country of Mauritius, an island nation in the southwestern part of the Indian Ocean, there is a substantial Indian population, descendants of laborers brought to the island from India when it was a French and later a British colony. By the 1870s, Indians had become more than half the population of Mauritius; today, at 65% of the population, they dominate its politics (Eriksen 1992:124).

Although size may lead to political clout, the effect of political clout on identity is not easy to predict. Much depends on group objectives. Those who struggle politically to gain access to the institutions of the larger society, if their efforts are successful, may in time facilitate a decline in the salience of the identity. The German Americans in Chapter 5 are a case in point. In addition, size and cohesion may at times be at odds with each other. Some of the multiple divisions apparent in India have been reproduced in Mauritius, where political clout has not necessarily meant political solidarity. The Indo-Mauritian population is split along caste, political, regional, and other lines, and some of its subgroups, such as the Tamils, even define themselves as non-Indians (Eriksen 1992:127).

Population Size and Social Context

The advantages of large size may have an influence as well on the identity the group chooses to emphasize. Sociologist Michael Hannan (1979) has argued that in modern societies, ethnic groups have to deal with large-scale organizations such as states. In such dealings, small size is a disadvantage. Ethnic groups who find themselves in such situations tend to organize along the most comprehensive boundaries possible. In Nigeria, members of the Onitsha and Owerri groups organize along a more comprehensive Igbo boundary in part because it offers the advantages of scale (Horowitz 1985). In the United States, Puerto Ricans and Mexicans organize as Latinos in part for the same reason (Padilla 1985). In a number of countries in Asia, the Middle East, and the Americas, Indians and Pakistanis of diverse origins, religions, and language groups organize along national or regional boundaries—as Indians, Pakistanis, or South Asians—in part because of the classifications made by nongroup members in the society at large, but also because of the political and other advantages that larger population size brings (Clarke, Peach, and Vertovec 1990).

As Hannan points out, however, larger-scale organization requires that larger-scale identities be available: Groups have to be able to see themselves as properly occupying the broader category. What this means is that small population size may encourage a group to subordinate one identity in favor of another, more comprehensive one, but only if a more comprehensive identity is available.

The significance of population size also is highly contextual. The small numbers that Kamphoefner discusses in his study of German Americans in Missouri were sufficient for the building of ethnic community in a rural area of low population density and low ethnic diversity. The same numbers in a more diverse and densely populated urban area might be insufficient to accomplish the same things. In 1860, there were more than 15,000 Germans in Milwaukee, more than a third of the city's population (Conzen 1976:20). This was a larger and geographically more concentrated German population than the one studied by Kamphoefner in Missouri in 1860, but it faced a more complex task of identity maintenance, thanks to the greater density of interethnic relations, the increased probabilities of occupational and residential mobility, and the greater opportunities for intermarriage across the ethnic boundary. Finally, as with all of the factors examined here, the effect of population size on identity construction depends a great deal on other aspects of the population: the nature of internal relations, the hopes and objectives of the group, the other resources it has at its disposal, and the nature of the situation it encounters.

Internal Differentiation

The process of categorization—which is at the heart of identity construction—involves the organization of differences and similarities. In categorizing other people—identifying them as an ethnic or racial group, for example—we emphasize what we see as the similarities among them and their differences from us. We tend to do more as well. There is a good deal of evidence, for example, that people tend to assume more homogeneity in out-groups (groups of which they are not members) than in in-groups (those of which they are members), stereotyping the "other" while remaining attuned to the subtle differences among themselves (Oakes, Haslam, and Turner 1994:54-55). "They" are both different from "us" and very much like each other; "we" are different from "them" in important ways but also different from each other in less important but still significant ways. However, all groups obviously contain differences among their members, sometimes profound ones. Certain dimensions of that internal differentiation have important consequences for identity construction, among them sex ratios, generational differences, and class.

Sex

Although numbers often matter in identity construction, sex ratios matter nearly as much. Unfortunately, it is even more difficult to generalize about their impact.

Migratory populations that are composed largely of a single sex often include significant numbers of married persons who have left their families in the sending society, planning either to return to them or to bring them later, they also often include single men or women. Unless they are planning to return to the sending society or anticipate some change in the migrant population, these persons have to cross the ethnic or racial boundary to marry, which typically undermines that boundary. On the other hand, as we noted in our discussion of the marriage pools in the preceding chapter, law or custom may forbid intermarriage or attach to it high costs, in which case the sex ratio reinforces the ethnic or racial boundary. Single immigrants must remain single, according to the receiving society, because they are African American, or Chinese, or something else: They are different.

Males were dominant among the German migrants that Kamphoefner studied: The 1850 census found 132 men for every 100 women among the German population of the two Missouri counties he examined. This was a more lopsided ratio than the much smaller French population of the area but a good deal more balanced than either the tiny British or Irish populations, which were very heavily male. Furthermore, a greater proportion—87%—of German women in the two counties were married than of any other ethnic group (1987:113), leading to a high overall marriage rate in the German population and very little outmarriage.

Chinese migrants to the United States had a radically different experience. Significant Chinese migration began in response to the demand for labor before the Civil War. By 1870, there were nearly 50,000 Chinese in California, about a twelfth of the state's population. Only 1 in 13 were women (Saxton 1971:7). Most of the men hoped eventually either to return to China or to bring wives and families to the United States. Restrictions on Chinese immigration, however, tightened by the Chinese Exclusion Act of 1882 and the Immigration Act of 1924, made it virtually impossible to bring wives or families into the country, and the latter piece of legislation ended Chinese immigration altogether. Some Chinese men returned to China periodically to marry and have children, but during much of the late 19th and early 20th centuries, it was impossible to find adequate work in China, and these men typically lived the bulk of their working lives as sojourners in the United States. For the vast majority of those who either lacked the means to return to China or chose not to, the marriage pool was nonexistent, because marriage with Whites was prohibited. The result was a "bachelor society" (Nee and Nee 1973:11). An imbalanced sex ratio among migrants combined with the receiving society's racial restrictions on marriage to emphasize, in ways that had enormous practical consequences for the human beings involved, the significance of Chinese identity.

Sex ratios also had effects—in some ways similar and in some ways different—on the ethnicity of male migrants to California's Imperial Valley from the Punjab region of India in the early part of the 20th century. Many of these migrants entered the cotton business, first as pickers and soon afterward as growers. Immigration laws prevented them from bringing wives and families from India, and there was considerable local hostility to Punjabi associations with White women. The constraints on

Punjabi men, in other words, were quite similar to those on Chinese, but the outcome was very different. The Imperial Valley included a large and growing Mexican population, made up in part of families displaced by the Mexican Revolution who were entering the United States in search of work. Many of them headed for the cotton fields of Texas and southern California. There, Punjabis and Mexicans met. There was less hostility to associations with Mexican than with White women (although opposition from Mexican men was at first substantial). In time, significant numbers of Punjabis married Mexican women. The result was a set of Punjabi-Mexican families who eventually came to form a new community of their own. Years later, the descendants of these families would continue to celebrate the ancestries that produced them and would choose to emphasize various ones of those ancestries at different points in their lives, favoring the Mexican or the Punjabi side but ultimately seeing themselves, increasingly, as Americans. When, following the relaxation of immigration quotas in 1965, a new influx of migrants from India arrived, their presence reminded the descendants of the Punjabi-Mexican marriages, in some cases against their wishes, of the significant social and cultural distances that now lay between themselves, products of more than a generation in America, and the newcomers, who carried so much of the homeland with them (Leonard 1992). The sex ratio of those original immigrants, the situation they encountered in the United States, and their response to it had combined to set in motion a trajectory of group processes that eventually led, via a circuitous route, toward the American mainstream.

As these cases suggest, many immigrant populations tend to be disproportionately male. This is usually a consequence of one or more of three factors: the demand for workers in labor markets that favor men, the supply of workers from cultural backgrounds that in some cases discourage women from working outside the home, and governmental policies that restrict the immigration of families or women. A classic pattern, both past and present, is for men to go abroad and either to send money home to support families who have remained there or to bring their families with them once established in the receiving society. In either case, the pattern tends to produce larger numbers of male than of female migrants. A study of Latino populations in the United States, for example, found that women outnumbered men among Mexican and Cuban populations who were U.S. citizens, populations with large proportions of the descendants of migrants. Among noncitizen populations of Mexicans and Cubans in the United States, however—groups composed largely of migrants themselves—men significantly outnumber women (de la Garza, DeSipio, Garcia, Garcia, and Falcon 1992:48, 146).

Males do not always predominate. Groups fleeing political or religious persecution, for example, often are composed largely of families or even entire communities, as in the case of many of the refugees who fled Vietnam for Canada, France, China, the United States, and other countries in the aftermath of the Vietnam War (Kitano and Daniels 1995). Even when migrations are predominantly economic in motivation, women may outnumber men, as they did, for example, among Irish immigrants to the United States during portions of the 19th century, many of whom worked as domestic laborers in New York (Steinberg 1981:161-62), as they have among recent immigrants to the United States from the Dominican Republic, heavily concentrated in New York's garment industry (Pessar 1987). Where women outnumber men, similar marriage pool issues arise: It becomes more difficult to marry within the group.

What all this material suggests is that contextual factors have a significant effect on the impact of sex ratios on identity. Where barriers—formal or informal—to interethnic or interracial sexual relations or marriage are high, lopsided sex ratios sustain the group boundary and thus the salience of the identity. Where such barriers are low, lopsided sex ratios promote boundary crossing, reducing the salience of the identity.

Generation

Many ethnic and racial groups are products of migration. People who may or may not have constituted a self-conscious group in one society move to another and learn a new identity there. By "generation" we refer not to the age composition of an ethnic or racial group—the number of older or younger persons in the population—but to the generational distance from the act of migration. Conventionally, the so-called "first generation" of a migrant or migrant-descent population is made up of migrants themselves, those who were born elsewhere but migrated, thus becoming the first generation to appear in the receiving society. The second generation is composed of their offspring, born in the receiving society. The third generation is composed of *their* offspring, and so on.[1] Generational composition, thus defined—and in particular the presence of first-generation migrants—has consequences for identity construction.

Migrations vary in duration. Some migrations, even substantial ones, are brief. In the summer of 1974, the Ethiopian military overthrew the government of Emperor Haile Selassie of Ethiopia, initiating more than a decade and a half of political upheaval and brutal dictatorship in that country. Faced with deteriorating economic, social, and political conditions in Ethiopia, between 1977 and 1992 virtually the entire Jewish population of Ethiopia—some 30,000 people—left for an originally resistant but ultimately welcoming Israel. Nearly half of them made their move toward the very end of this period in a massive Israeli airlift in May of 1991, following extended and difficult negotiations among the governments of Israel, Ethiopia, and eventually the United States. By 1992, few Jews remained in Ethiopia, and the migration had come to an end (Wagaw 1993). As those who made the migration to Israel grow older, a few more may join them, but not many—very few remain behind. Those who already have made the journey are likely to be virtually the last of Israel's first-generation Ethiopian Jews. When they are gone, the firsthand experience of Jewry in Ethiopia will be reduced to the media record.

Other migrant streams are cut off. World War I halted European migration to the United States for a time, and the Immigration Acts of 1921 and 1924 formally ended immigration from both Europe and Asia. The Chinese Exclusion Act of 1882 had already shut down most Chinese immigration. In the previous chapter, we noted contemporary governmental efforts to control Chinese immigration to Malaysia.

Such cutoffs are important for a variety of reasons, not least for what they reveal about the attitudes of receiving societies. One reason they are important is their impact on the generational composition of the already existing immigrant population. What a continuing migrant stream does is to maintain a first-generation presence in the receiving society, a continuing presence of persons born and probably raised in the sending society, even as the numbers of the second, third, and subsequent generations continue to grow. The first generation is important because that is the generation most likely to speak the language the group spoke in the sending society, maintain distinctive cultural practices, and maintain a conception of groupness clearly founded on specific origins. As the numbers of first-generation immigrants diminish over time, much of that cultural material inevitably is lost. Also lost is the firsthand memory of the experience of migration itself. Often physically rigorous, risky, or even life-threatening, and almost always filled with uncertainty, this experience can have a binding force of its own among migrants, becoming part of the distinctive history that they consciously share. It may still play a major role in collective memory once those who shared it directly are gone, but it does so as story, not experience. It is powerful, perhaps, but distant. Cultural practices may survive in the second and later generations, depending on the situation—after all, the German Americans Kamphoefner studied in Missouri continued to speak German long after the migrant stream had peaked and eventually dried up, thanks in part to the fact that this was a rural community—but continuity becomes more problematic without the refreshment or replenishing effect that a continuing influx of new migrants—for whom those practices are second nature—typically provides.

On the other hand, although continuing migrant streams may help to sustain certain identities, they can be simultaneously problematic for new, emergent ones. Sociologist Yen Espiritu (1992:95) argues that, in the decades following the end of the immigration quota system in 1965, new streams of Asian immigrants to the United States exacerbated tensions among Asian groups. The newcomers often challenged the existing leadership of the pan-ethnic Asian American community that emerged in the 1970s and 1980s. Not only were new groups arriving whose numbers previously had been small, such as Vietnamese and Cambodians, but there was an influx as well of new members of the more established populations—Chinese, Filipino, and Japanese. Both sets of migrants brought with them experiences and cultural practices very different from those of either the immigrants of generations past or the currently established Asian American communities. These differences complicated the working out of a more unified Asian American political agenda, making an Asian American identity trickier to articulate and sustain.

In general, however, even without restrictions on immigration and barring some sudden massive influx, the proportion of first-generation migrants obviously declines over time as they have children, grandchildren, and so on. As the proportion of second, third, and subsequent generations increases, so does the average distance from the society of origin and all that is associated with it. Language use tends to decline with generational distance from the immigrant generation, and intermarriage tends to increase, although the latter is much less the case when racial boundaries are involved. These developments are hardly fatal to ethnic and racial identities, but they tend, other things equal (an important caveat), to reduce the salience of the ethnic and racial identities of the migrant group.

This is apparent, for example, in data on European-descent ethnic groups in the United States. For a number of reasons, the probability that members of these groups will identify themselves in ethnic terms drops with each generation (Alba 1990:54-55). In other words, as the distance from the immigrant experience grows, the salience of ethnicity declines. It is important to note that this is happening to a population that encounters relatively few contextual factors that support those identities: In general, American society no longer discriminates against European-descent persons on the basis of their ethnicity. It is not at all clear that the descendants of Mexican migrants to the United States, for example—given a similarly steep decline in the proportion of first-generation migrants—would experience the same generational decline in ethnic identification, because the situation they encounter is radically different.

Class

Class differences within populations have significant implications for identity construction. Filipino Americans offer an illustrative case.

Filipinos are one of the largest and fastest growing Asian groups in the United States. Significant numbers of Filipinos have been migrating across the Pacific since the first decade of the 20th century, soon after the United States seized the Philippines from Spain and made it a U.S. colony in the Spanish-American War of 1898. Yen Espiritu (1996), one of the leading students of Asian American ethnicities, has studied three different groups of Filipino immigrants. The first is the wave of Filipinos who, in the early decades of this century, immigrated to Hawaii, where they became farm laborers in the sugar industry. This group, she points out, was largely homogeneous along class as well as regional lines. Two thirds of them came from a rural region known as Ilocano, and most came from similar, relatively poor socioeconomic backgrounds. The second group is the Filipinos who joined the United States Navy, beginning before World War I and continuing until the present time. Most of these enlistees came from the Tagalog-speaking provinces of the Philippines, where some major U.S. naval installations were located. They also tended to share class and educational backgrounds.

The third group Espiritu discusses is quite different. Following the 1965 Immigration and Naturalization Act, which ended the national-origins quota system and led to significant increases in the numbers of Asian immigrants to the United States, Filipino immigration skyrocketed. It was of two very different kinds. The Immigration and Naturalization Act had replaced the old quota system with a system in which visas were awarded either to reunite families by bringing in relatives of persons who had come to the United States prior to 1965, or to bring in persons with skills currently in demand in the U.S. labor market. Consequently, two very different migrant streams emerged. This third wave of immigrants was composed of two very different populations. Family reunification immigrants tended to come from the largely rural provinces that had dominated previous migrations, whereas those entering under the occupational provisions of the legislation came predominantly from the urban centers of the Philippines, in particular from the capital, Manila, and its environs. Regional differences here parallel important class differences. The family reunification immigrants tended to share the socioeconomic backgrounds of the family members—earlier migrants—whom they came to join, which means most were less educated and either unskilled or semiskilled. The occupational immigrants, on the other hand—and the family members who accompanied or followed them—were almost entirely educated professionals, including large numbers of doctors, nurses, and other health-related workers.

This changing composition of the immigrant stream has had an impact on identity construction, although, as Espiritu points out, the effect of this bifurcated third immigrant population and of the 1965 legislation that produced it has been mixed. "On the one hand, by allowing the 'old-timers' to bring in their relatives, the family reunification provisions rejuvenated the old, established Filipino communities" in the United States. At the same time, some of the post-1965 immigrants, particularly those admitted on occupational or skill grounds, "have formed essentially new Filipino communities dominated by professionals . . . who have minimal physical and social ties with the pre-1965 population" (Espiritu 1996:42). In Hawaii at least, and perhaps elsewhere, these two populations have negative stereotypes of each other, and bridging the gap between them is difficult. It remains to be seen whether these divisions will endure. It may be that the racial and ethnic classifications of U.S. society—which assigns all Filipinos a single identity—will alter Filipino self-concepts over time and forge out of this diversity a solid group, much as has happened in the past with Italian Americans, Chinese Americans, and others. In the meantime, the class differences within the population have significantly complicated the construction of a single, solidary, Filipino American identity.

The Filipino case is not an isolated one. The 1965 Immigration and Naturalization Act had similar effects on a number of immigrant populations in the United States, stimulating new migrant streams of educated professionals and leading to class divisions of one kind or another—and of varying prominence—within those groups (see, for example, Bhardwaj and Rao 1990).

A further point of the Filipino example is that the boundaries that seem obvious to one group in the society may not be obvious to another. Filipinos see significant differences among themselves, regional as well as class. These differences may not be readily apparent to the outside observer whose own classificatory terms make other assumptions, or to the committed advocate whose fiercely defended ethnic or racial ways of viewing the world leave little room for such distinctions. Those boundaries, however, are important. Each constitutes an alternative basis of action. Some Filipinos may believe that the appropriate boundary on which to organize action is *not* the one that identifies all Filipinos as part of a single category. They may see their own experiences as better accounted for by other identities, or they may see their own interests as better pursued using other boundaries as bases of organization. However they see themselves, the outcome will be determined to a significant degree by the situation they encounter: the opportunities and constraints in the various arenas or sites they occupy. Examples like the Filipino one underline the interaction between group characteristics, on one hand, and context, on the other.

Class differences can affect identity construction in other ways as well. Recent Taiwanese immigration to the United States, like Filipino immigration, has included large numbers of well-educated, skilled, middle-class or upper-middle-class migrants. In Los Angeles, which has the largest Taiwanese population in the United States, many of these migrants have tended not to settle with other lower-class Taiwanese but instead have used their own financial resources to move directly into middle- and upper-middle-class, predominantly White, neighborhoods, and to start businesses that serve non-Asian clienteles (Tseng 1995). This constitutes a break from past patterns among the Taiwanese, in which newcomers tended to settle with coethnics. One effect is to break down the residential concentrations that, in previous migrations, helped to sustain the ethnic community and, through it, the ethnic boundary. That boundary hardly seems to be disappearing, and there are numerous factors, including racial discrimination directly against Asians generally in U.S. society, that work to sustain it. The point is that more recent immigration has altered the nature of the Taiwanese population and has led to certain behavioral choices—where to settle and whom to target as a market for business—that tend to increase interactions and relationships across the ethnic boundary, and thereby to reduce the salience of that boundary.

This pattern of middle-class dispersion and lower-class concentration, found among many immigrant groups, is not the only possible pattern, and it may reflect, among other things, the social geography of the contemporary city, in which movement away from the center is often movement up in both economic and status hierarchies. A century ago, in Prague, then part of Bohemia and now the capital of the Czech Republic, a reverse pattern prevailed. Ethnic Germans in Prague also were split along class lines. The majority were concentrated in the middle and upper classes and in the more prosperous inner-city sections of Prague, where they maintained close links with each other and relatively more distant links with Czechs. Poorer Germans, on the other hand—petty employees, laborers, retailers, and shop foremen—were more dispersed through the city's industrial areas, living among Czechs, engaged in numerous daily interactions with them, and speaking both Czech and German on a daily basis. As Czech nationalism grew in the 1880s and 1890s, the more prosperous Germans responded with an increased emphasis on German identity and community, whereas the poorer Germans in Prague were more likely to respond to Czech pressure by shifting their allegiances and, ultimately, their identity, to the Czechs (Cohen 1992). This not only underlines the relevance of spatial or residential concentration for the maintenance of robust ethnic identities—a topic we treated in detail in the previous chapter—but also supports the idea that class differences within an ethnic population may lead to divergent identity processes.

Class and regional differences increasingly complicate identity construction in the case of American Blacks, although to what ultimate effect is by no means clear. The rigid racial classification system adhered to by U.S. society at large and manifest in continuing discrimination against African Americans assumes—as categorization typically does—that intergroup differences are more important than intragroup ones. Furthermore, in its stubborn adherence to the concept of race, it assumes that racial differences are most important of all. Differences within the African American population, however, are growing. The development in recent decades of a substantial Black middle class and the continuing immigration of West Indian and other non-American Blacks have led to significant divergences in certain kinds of experience, in some aspects of culture, in self-concepts, and even in political agendas (Collins 1983; Waters 1994; Wilson 1978, 1987). Some Black groups organize along subracial ethnic boundaries—identifying as Jamaicans or Haitians or more generally as West Indians, for example. Others—or perhaps the same ones at different times—organize along the more comprehensive racial boundary, depending on what it is they hope to accomplish and the situation in which they have to operate (Kasinitz 1992). To date, these divergences within the Black population have been overwhelmed, for the most part, by the power of the racial categories that profoundly shape so much of American life, and, in particular, of Black American life. They nevertheless make the future of these ethnic and racial boundaries—the ones on which Black Americans themselves variously organize and act—unpredictable.

Sex, generation, and class are three dimensions of internal differentiation that have potentially large effects on identity construction. As should be clear from the examples we have put forward, their potential effects are not always easy to predict. Contextual factors are likely in most cases to play a large role in determining the impact of these differences, and there are other dimensions that also may have significant impacts on occasion. In both the Filipino and the Black cases outlined above, differences in the region of origin—rural versus urban origins in the Philippines, American versus West Indian origins among Blacks—clearly have had important implications for identity. All ethnic and racial populations have within their ranks or in their experience the bases of subdivision, and subdivisions in turn offer potential bases for fragmentation, leading either to new ethnicities, to alliances across the ethnic boundary, or to new, non-ethnic identities altogether.

Social Capital

Social capital refers to relationships among persons. It includes such things as interpersonal networks, sets of obligations, shared norms, or mutual trust: the sorts of things that bind or link group members to one another. It is called capital because it is fungible: The relationships that constitute social capital can be turned into other things, such as cooperation in solving individual or community problems or collective action in pursuit of common interests. Groups that have high social capital—that are characterized by substantial or dense interpersonal relationships of trust or obligation—are capable of doing things that groups with low social capital have difficulty doing. In other words, social capital is a resource, something individuals and groups can use in trying to accomplish their objectives (Coleman 1988, 1990, chap. 12; Putnam 1993:167-71).

Its status as a resource is what makes social capital important in identity construction. Those who can solve life problems by recourse to existing relationships within their own ethnic or racial group have less reason to cross the boundary between groups in search of solutions. Those who cannot solve such problems within the boundaries of the group, on the other hand, must turn elsewhere to deal with those problems. Working within group boundaries tends to reinforce group identity.

An Illustration: Western Samoans in New Zealand

The country of Western Samoa embraces the westernmost islands of the Samoan chain in the South Pacific. In 1946, at the end of World War II, the United Nations made Western Samoa, which had been a New Zealand colony, a trusteeship of New Zealand. Sixteen years later, in 1962, Western Samoa became an independent nation. Both during that trusteeship and following independence, significant numbers of Samoans migrated to New Zealand. Some were pursuing economic opportunity, some sought education for their children, and some may simply have wanted the prestige that, among Samoans, attaches to those who venture abroad. By the late 1960s, when social scientists in New Zealand first began to pay much attention to these migrants, some 10,000 Samoans were living in New Zealand. The three quarters of them living in Auckland, New Zealand's largest city, had joined with numerous other Pacific Islanders and the indigenous Maori people to make Auckland, by the 1970s, the largest Polynesian city in the world (Pitt and Macpherson 1974).

In migrating to New Zealand, these migrants, like migrants everywhere, had to find solutions to a common set of life problems: finding work and money, finding shelter for their families, raising and educating their children, maintaining a sense of self and a sense of confidence in meeting the challenges of daily living, and so forth. In the Samoan case, they were well equipped to meet these challenges because of the social capital they brought with them: relationships and institutions on which they could depend. Chief among these was the extended family.

Many of the migrants of the immediate postwar period were single males who brought their families to New Zealand as soon as they were able to do so; in later migrations, entire families often moved together. Samoans with relatives in New Zealand often left Western Samoa to join them. Those in New Zealand worked to bring their kin. The result in many cases was a set of dense kin networks in the New Zealand migrant community made up of extended families that were modeled on—essentially replicas of—the extended family that is the foundation of social life in Western Samoa. One such family, 15 years after its first two members had come to New Zealand from Samoa, had grown to include 169 migrants and their children, all related, living in 23 separate households, and in frequent interaction with one another (Pitt and Macpherson 1974). Such extended families provided a number of things to their members, among them the sense of security and confidence that comes with a set of ready-made social relations, financial capital when needed, accommodation for newly migrated relatives, information and assistance to new migrants in finding jobs, and emotional and financial support during major life transitions such as marriage, birth, and death.

Institutional Completeness

What the Samoan migrants had in the extended family was a high degree of "institutional completeness." The term comes from Raymond Breton

(1964:194), who defined it as the capacity of the community to satisfy the needs of its members, "such as education, work, food and clothing, medical care, or social assistance." When institutional completeness is high, the community has a set of organizational mechanisms capable of solving life problems; when institutional completeness is low, members of the community have to look elsewhere for solutions to life problems. Some classic cases of such mechanisms, in addition to the Samoan extended family example, include systems of fictive kin, as in the extraordinary efforts African American slave communities made to provide families for those children who had lost parents to the market mechanisms of slavery (Gutman 1976), the rotating credit associations that many migrant communities develop as ways of assembling the capital necessary for housing or business development (e.g., Velez-Ibañez 1983), barter systems as ways of dealing with economic needs in low-income communities (e.g., Sherman 1988), the provision of traditional healing practices in communities that lack access to mainstream health care or do not trust it (e.g., Spicer 1977), and the establishment of political organizations to represent the ethnic community in interactions with dominant-society authorities or organizations (e.g., Kwong 1984).

In some cases, such mechanisms develop as a response to needs encountered in new situations. This is obviously so in the case of the fictive kin mechanisms developed by African Americans, which built on African traditions but were reinvented to cope with the nearly impossible conditions of slavery. Necessity often is involved in less extreme situations as well, in which the institutions of the larger society, although accessible, are either poorly equipped to deal with group members' needs or disinclined to do so. In regard to the Samoans in New Zealand in the early 1970s, for example, Pitt and Macpherson point out that "the institutions of European society are of little account to the migrant. They appear at best as vague, ineffective, and paternalist; at worst as intolerant" (1974:48). The institutional completeness of the ethnic community, in other words, may be encouraged or discouraged by the accessibility of the institutions of the larger society. Thus, aspects of situations and aspects of groups once again interact.

Samoans would have brought their institutions with them to New Zealand anyway, for they were built into the familial pattern of migration. Something similar is apparent among Mexican and Cuban migrants to the United States, many of whom typically do not arrive with only their personal, individual resources. Both frequently join family and friends in the United States, and they frequently enter established communities that have resources of their own on which new migrants can draw as they try to deal with the problems of living and working in a new and often unfamiliar situation (Portes and Bach 1985; also Sanchez 1993, chap. 6).

European immigrants to the United States likewise benefited from the presence of institutional resources within the group. We saw in Chapter 5 that the size of the second wave of German immigrants facilitated their success in the United States. This was the case not only nationally but also locally, where size and diversity made many things possible. In Milwaukee, for example, the German American population "was sufficiently diverse to include both employers and employees, skilled and unskilled, cultured and unlettered; it could therefore supply its own leaders, provide for most of the needs of its members—economic, social, cultural—within its own bounds, and contain the upwardly mobile" (Conzen 1976:225). Germans and non-Germans shared the city of Milwaukee but lived, in an institutional sense, apart, helping to sustain the ethnic boundary as an organizational feature of both practical living and individual and group self-concept.

Institutional completeness essentially is a matter of social capital. Social capital is what Samoans bring with them to New Zealand; it is what migrants from the highlands of Papua New Guinea, inexperienced in urban living and with few readily salable skills, seek to establish when they arrive in Port Moresby and other towns, searching out friends and kin who have preceded them and can assist them in adjusting to a radically different environment (Levine and Levine 1979). Social capital is what Haitian migrants to New York bring in the form of kin and friendship networks that can provide subsequent immigrants with housing, money, and employment assistance (Stafford 1987); it is what some Korean migrants to Los Angeles rely on when they turn to informal but enduring associations of trusted friends and family—the associations are known among Koreans as *kye*—for the start-up capital that goes into the small businesses that have been the key to their economic success (Light and Bonacich 1988, chap. 10).

Social Capital and Forms of Migration

The examples in the last two sections all involve migration. Some involve international migration, and some involve rural-to-urban migration. Not all ethnic or racial groups, of course, are migrant groups, nor do the processes of identity construction depend on migration. Migration, however, is a common element in such processes, and migration frequently sets such processes in motion, putting previously unacquainted groups in contact with one another, precipitating competition among individuals and groups as they struggle to obtain the resources and rewards that attracted them to a new location in the first place, and upsetting old arrangements and old understandings of who people are and what their place is in the social order. In some societies, migration is a key element in the whole structure of intergroup relations. All the inhabitants of the Americas, for example, save Native Americans, are relative newcomers, immigrants in the last five centuries from some other part of the world. At the transition from 20th to 21st century, great numbers of persons are in motion not only within countries but across the globe as well, and migration has become an ever more prominent aspect of the human experience.

Migrations vary. Some are voluntary, and some are forced. Some societies welcome immigrants, and some resist them. Most societies pick and choose, welcoming certain immigrants and refusing others. One of the dominant public issues of the 1990s in France, the United Kingdom, the Netherlands, Australia, New Zealand, the United States, and elsewhere in the developed world has been how many of which kinds of immigrants are enough. We will have occasion to return to this topic, but from the point of view of social capital, the critical distinction to be made here is between individualistic migrations and chain migrations.

Individualistic migrations are composed largely of individuals who share little in the way of common social relations; they are connected to one another by little more than a shared society of origin. Chain migrations, on the other hand, are composed largely of persons who are linked to one another by kinship ties or other forms of social relations. The terms themselves—individualistic and chain—describe tendencies. Not every migration is entirely one or the other.

Walter Kamphoefner (1987:189-91) has captured the major distinctions between the two. Although it would be easy to overstate the case, individualistic migrants in general tend to be opportunistic, responding to the *pull* of economic or social opportunity in the receiving society rather than the *push* of economic disaster or political persecution in the sending society. Decisions to migrate are individual decisions, and the act of migration is an individual act. Historically, males have tended to predominate in individualistic migrations. Many of them have been single, relatively young, and willing and able to break away from the established social order and try something new. Such migrations often include a higher proportion of those with education, skills, and some financial resources. As one might deduce from the names of the two migrations, migrants in individualistic migrations tend to be less connected to one another and are less likely to form networks or communities of fellow migrants in the receiving society.

In contrast, chain migrations tend to involve communities or linked sets of persons. The decision to migrate is often a family or group decision, and migrants are more likely to move together. A few pioneers may go first, but their objective is then to bring friends and relatives along, initiating a migrant stream based on preexisting social relationships. It is this chain of linkages among successive migrants that gives chain migration its name, although sometimes whole communities may move at more or less the same time. Chain migrants are more often (although by no means always) responding to push factors such as the failure of crops, religious or political persecution, or the declining economic fortunes of the community. Families predominate in chain migrations, which typically include more balanced sex ratios and broader age distributions, and often include larger proportions of migrants with fewer skills and less education. Chain migrants are more likely than individualistic ones to form communities in the receiving society, in essence transferring significant aspects of their own community life from one setting to the next. Some chain migrations surely began as individualistic ones: Someone grabbed the opportunity to move to a new country and succeeded there, then news of that success persuaded friends or family to move as well. Soon a chain of migrants follows.

Other things equal, preexisting identities are more readily maintained in chain migrations than in individualistic ones. One reason is the difference in available social capital. Migrants in individualistic migrations are less likely to try or to be able to sustain links with fellow migrants; after all, they have relatively few links to begin with. Lacking communities of their own, they are more likely to look to the resources and opportunities of the receiving society to solve life problems, readily crossing the ethnic or racial boundary—if the receiving society will let them. Chain migrants, on the other hand, typically move as members of communities, even if they move alone, and carry at least some social capital with them: institutions, networks, and norms. Community members have the option of turning to fellow migrants and to the community itself for assistance and support. The German migrants to Missouri whom Kamphoefner studied were chain migrants, for the most part, who were able to rebuild much of the social fabric of their former life in the changed conditions of the rural Midwest, not only facilitating the realization of their individual and collective purposes but also maintaining an ethnic identity in the process. To be sure, individualistic migrants may remain strongly attached to an ethnic identity, but that identity is less likely to be rooted in ongoing relationships and day-to-day interactions with fellow ethnics, and therefore may be more vulnerable to changing sets of interests and more readily displaced by alternative forms of identity. Most important, the lack of social capital that is typical of individualistic migrants means that, although they may maintain a strong sense of ethnic identity, it will organize less of their daily life and behavior. Other things equal, it will be a thinner identity than that carried by the chain migrant.

This last point underlines the more general significance of social capital for identity construction. When social capital within the group is high, groups are more likely to be able—should they wish to do so—to solve problems and advance interests through *intra*group cooperation and interaction, by relying on one another and building institutional mechanisms of their own. This in turn is likely to reinforce the ethnic or racial boundary and give additional salience to the ethnic or racial identity. When social capital within the group is low, on the other hand, group members are more likely to have to establish relations across the ethnic or racial boundary as they struggle to pursue their interests and to solve the problems they face.

Human Capital

Like social capital, human capital refers to certain kinds of assets or resources available to groups and individuals. In contrast to social capital, however, human capital refers not to sets of relationships but to the knowledge and abilities people acquire through formal and informal education, training, and experience. Those with high human capital have particularly valuable skills or knowledge; those with low human capital have less valuable skills and knowledge. Like social capital, human capital is fungible. A person may be able to translate a good education or a set of relatively rare skills into a better job, higher income, more authority, or a more satisfying set of activities.

The human capital of a group is simply the aggregation of the human capital of its members. Such aggregations vary across groups and do so in several ways. One group, for example, might include a high proportion of professionals, whereas another has a high proportion of persons with experience in some kind of agriculture or in particular craft industries. Second, a group may vary in the diversity of its human capital. Groups might, for example, include significant numbers of both professionals and farmers. Third, a group may vary in general skill or education levels, as in highly skilled versus less skilled populations or well-educated versus poorly educated members.

It should be obvious that human capital has significant implications for where individuals end up in the stratification system. In industrial societies, for example, higher levels of education generally yield greater employment opportunities, assuming that there are no barriers—such as racial discrimination—directed specifically against group members. Where group members end up in the stratification system—whether they are in the lower middle class, the upper class, and so forth—has only limited implications for identity, for class categories are broad. Groups that find themselves in a common class position typically are not alone: Classes, particularly the middle and lower classes, tend to be ethnically and racially diverse. This means that class position in and of itself plays a limited role in identity construction. More important is occupational concentration, which we discussed at some length in Chapter 6. Human capital often has significant implications for occupational concentrations and, through such concentrations, for identity construction. The effect of human capital on occupational concentrations, however, varies.

In the previous chapter, we briefly mentioned the Urhobo people in Nigeria, whose poor education but substantial experience in working with oil palms enabled them to carve out a niche for themselves in the oil palm industry instead of competing for urban jobs in which their lack of education would be a handicap. Their human capital endowment was meaningless outside the context of the particular opportunities and constraints presented to them by the larger society of which they were a part. Their distinctive set of skills combined with a particular set of opportunities to concentrate them in a single industry, a fact that in turn helped to sustain the ethnic boundary. A different set of skills or opportunities might have led to dispersion into the larger economy or to concentration in an economic activity shared more widely with non-Urhobo. In either case, occupational concentration would have played a lesser role in the maintenance of Urhobo identity.

Business skills often lead to occupational concentrations that become the foundation of lasting ethnic communities, particularly when a migration stream includes an entrepreneurial class (Portes and Bach 1985:203). Such entrepreneurs often find among fellow immigrants—assuming large enough numbers—both ready customers and ready workers, and many build their businesses at first by serving the ethnic community of which they are a part. The result is an ethnic enclave economy as found, for example, among Cubans in Miami (Portes and Bach 1985). By providing the ethnic community with needed services from among its own ranks, such entrepreneurs help to sustain it. In effect, human capital leads to social capital. This is by no means the only—or even the most common—pattern among ethnic entrepreneurs, many of whom target markets outside their own communities. Many Koreans in Los Angeles, for example, have come to form a "middleman minority," starting businesses that serve not coethnics but members of other ethnic groups, in particular African Americans and Latinos (Light and Bonacich 1988).

On the other hand, higher skill or education levels may operate on occasion to undermine ethnic boundaries and identities. Better-educated or more highly skilled groups often enjoy a wider set of employment opportunities, leading to broader dispersal both geographically and through the occupational system. Since 1965, growing numbers of Asian immigrants to the United States have come with professional training and substantial education. Given generally greater and more dispersed employment opportunities—for example, for health professionals in rural areas and in public hospitals in major cities—they have been less likely to join or form ethnic communities (Portes and Rumbaut 1990:18-20). As already noted, the Taiwanese immigrants studied by Tseng (1995) used the financial resources that had come with their more highly skilled occupations and business success in Taiwan to settle in predominantly White, middle-class neighborhoods in Los Angeles, and to open businesses targeted not at their fellow Taiwanese but at the larger public, ignoring the opportunity to settle in areas of high Taiwanese concentration. Their high human capital made their choices easier: to cross the ethnic boundary in both residential and occupational arenas.

Symbolic Repertoires

The construction of ethnic and racial identities involves, among other things, the construction of a particular way of looking at the world in which two things typically happen. First, a particular identity becomes important. It helps to make sense of things, as, for example, when a group of persons realizes that they are mistreated on the basis of a shared identity, or that a particular identity is the appropriate basis on which to organize and act. In either case, the point is the recognition that this identity has power in their lives. Second, the identity in question gains a distinctive meaning. The identity not only becomes important in its ability to make sense of things but also comes to signify something distinctive about the group. It captures some value, positive or negative, and attaches that to the group and its members, asserting it as in some sense essential.

Symbolic repertoires refer to the array of collective representations—the symbolic resources—that groups have at their disposal through which they can communicate such meanings. When such resources are substantial and numerous, the symbolic repertoire is large. The Afrikaner case in Chapter 5 provides an example. Afrikaner political and intellectual elites either created or had already at their disposal interpretive schemes, ritual events, and other symbolic resources through which they communicated to their people both that Afrikaner identity was central to a complete understanding of events and that Afrikaner identity was imbued with special and exclusive meanings and significance. In doing so, they contributed directly to the creation and maintenance of Afrikaner identity as the basis of individual and collective organization and action. They succeeded in arousing in group members a sense of commonality, exalted significance, and collective power.

The case of Yugoslavia discussed in the same chapter likewise offers examples of the creation or enhancement of symbolic resources as material for the construction of identities. In the Serb version of the battle of Kosovo in 1389, for example, we see a framing of history that is designed to support a particular interpretation of events and a particular conception of "us" and "them" (Sells 1996). The new interpretation of the battle becomes a resource.

Stories

Symbolic resources are ways of representing the group to itself—and, at times, to others—so as to establish or reinforce the sense among group members of sharing something special—a history, a way of being, a particular set of beliefs—that captures the essence of their peoplehood. Symbolic repertoires include many different kinds of such resources. One, as the Afrikaner and Serb cases suggest, is stories. At the start of Chapter 3, we gave an account of the genocidal conflict that engulfed the central African country of Rwanda in the mid-1990s and earlier. Adjacent to Rwanda lies the country of Burundi. It, too, has a violent history of conflict between Hutu and Tutsi peoples, who, as in Rwanda, make up much the greater part of its population. In the early 1970s, during one of the eruptions of violence, large numbers of Hutu fled Burundi for neighboring Tanzania, where many of them ended up living for years in refugee camps. Anthropologist Liisa Malkki spent a good deal of time with these refugees and found many of them preoccupied with their own history as Hutus. When she asked many of them to talk about their lives, she found that "the refugees regularly slipped from the domain of personal life history into the wider field of the collective history of the group." They seemed to be "intensively and continually engaged in a kind of historical ordering and reordering of their past" (Malkki 1990:37), from the colonial history of Burundi through the interethnic violence that had driven them from their homes to the current period of exile in another land. The result of this effort to reinterpret the past was what Malkki calls a "mythico-history," a kind of collective narrative, complete with pivotal episodes and recurrent themes, "which heroizes them as a distinct people with a historical trajectory setting them apart from other peoples" (1990:34). By constructing such a narrative, the Hutus came to a common understanding of who they were and what it was that they distinctively shared. They made a statement about what it meant to be Hutu. That statement became part of the symbolic repertoire through which they construct themselves as a people.

Stories play a similar role among the Saramakas, a Maroon community in the interior forests of the Republic of Suriname on the northeast coast of South America. The Saramakas are descendants of Africans who were brought to Suriname as slaves by the Dutch in the late 17th and early 18th centuries. Over the years, significant numbers of these slaves escaped, making their way deep into the rain forest, where they formed their own fugitive communities and fought an extended war against Dutch efforts to recapture them. Today, this period of escape and resistance is captured by Saramakas in stories about "First-Time," the time when Saramakas fought for and eventually won their freedom. First-Time is a critical element in Saramaka identity. Writes Richard Price (1983:11-12),

> Saramaka collective identity is predicated on a single opposition: freedom versus slavery. The central role of First-Time in Saramaka life is ideological; preservation of its knowledge is their way of saying "Never again". . . . For Saramakas today, talk about First-Time is very far from being mere rhetoric, preserved for reasons of nostalgic pride. Rather, First-Time ideology lives in the minds of twentieth-century Saramaka men because it is relevant to their own life experience—it helps them make sense, on a daily basis, of the wider world in which they live.

First-Time, says Price, "is the fountainhead of collective identity; it contains the true root of what it means to be Saramaka" (1983:6).

These Hutu and Saramaka narratives are examples of collective representations of the group that capture something of its supposed essence.
They are much more than stories. By being told and retold, they remind
group members of their own peoplehood, of what sets them apart, be it
history or beliefs or sheer determination or something else. In the process, symbolic resources are transformed into such things as solidarity,
emotional attachment, pride, commitment, and mobilization. They teach
the importance of particular identities and maintain an awareness of
what those identities mean or should mean. Thus, they accomplish something of what categorical ascriptions, classifications, and status attributions do in the culture site described in Chapter 6, but they do so very
differently. They use not the terms chosen by the larger society but the
group's own terms. They use its own classifications, assert its own sense
of its status, and put its own spin on the discourse of ethnicity or race.

Ritual and Celebration

Symbolic repertoires may include resources other than the kinds of stories the Hutus or Saramakas tell. A common resource, as the Afrikaner
case suggests, is ritual events. Some such events may last only hours or
perhaps a day. Others, such as the Afrikaners' reenactment of their historical trek into the interior of what is now South Africa, may last for
months. The Huichol Indians of north-central Mexico carry out an annual
ritual that lasts, on occasion, as long as 40 days. Huichol religious ceremonies make extensive use of the hallucinogenic plant peyote. Every
year, the Huichol make a pilgrimage, much of it on foot, to the sacred
land of Wirikuta, a place several hundred miles from the mountains
where the Huichols live and a place where their ancient ancestors, according to Huichol belief, lived long ago. In Wirikuta, led by shaman-
priests and in ritual fashion, they gather the peyote they use in their ceremonies. This pilgrimage—the peyote hunt—is a ritual event of central
importance not only in Huichol religion but also in the affirmation of
Huichol community and identity, for the pilgrims gather not only peyote
in Wirikuta. Through this ritual "the pilgrims retrieve their spiritual and
historical beginnings" (Myerhoff 1974:50). The ritual transcends social
barriers and differences among the Huichol. It transcends as well the history that separates them from this spiritual homeland: It unifies and re-
stores them (Myerhoff 1974, chap. 6). It is a symbolic resource of remarkable power.

Celebration and festivity have at least some of the same effects, although not at the deep level of the Huichol peyote hunt. Since 1970, the

multiethnic Latino community of Washington, D.C., has held an annual festival, known as the Hispano American Festival or the Latino Festival, in the Adams Morgan neighborhood, an ethnically diverse part of the city. This festival has grown rapidly over the years. By the 1980s, this festival, which includes foods, crafts, music, parades, and assorted other activities, had become the largest community festival in Washington, attracting crowds of more than 150,000 annually. The festival accomplishes a number of things. It provides entertainment, color, new experiences, and an air of gaiety to those who attend, and it celebrates the cultural diversity of the neighborhood, which includes immigrants and their descendants from the Caribbean, Central and South America, Africa, and elsewhere. It also plays a role in the development of a Latino ethnic identity among the diverse groups who constitute the growing Latino population of the city. "Although traditional animosities exist between several Latino groups," writes Olivia Cadaval (1991),

> the festival offers a solution of diversity rather than division, with the result that there is pan-Latino support for the alleged purpose of the event— the celebration of a common heritage. What goes on behind the scenes in terms of conflict over how to organize and whom to represent gives way in the festival to solidarity, to *communitas*. (p. 205)

The festival and its various component parts—distinctive foods, bright colors and symbols from the various nations represented, music, the parade floats, and so on—symbolize commonality and diversity at once, both recognizing the boundary between Latinos and others and celebrating particular aspects of Latino identity and population, putting cultural richness and diversity forward as distinguishing characteristics, and making the festival a key event in the ethnicization of the Latino population in Washington: the making of a (pan)ethnic group.

Native American powwows serve some similar purposes. Common in Indian communities throughout the United States, powwows typically involve from 1 to 4 or 5 days of dancing, feasting, and celebration, often lasting far into the night. Although most powwows are locally sponsored events, hosted by individual tribes, they draw Indians from throughout the region and often throughout the country. Although distinctively tribal elements are often apparent, most of the dances and foods and much of the activity at powwows typically speak to a more generally Indian set of symbols and ideas. They are events at which Native Americans from diverse cultures and communities connect with one another, celebrate their common heritage, and both share and revitalize the symbols of that heritage. These symbols include not only distinctive dancing,

dress, and foods, but also less tangible things. Many powwows also celebrate and manifest certain ideas: "circularity, time as an outgrowth of
event (rather than vice versa), models of reciprocation, competition
within culturally acceptable and meaningful contexts . . ., the importance
of the family as a unit . . ." (Toelken 1991:154). These ideas are seen by
many Indians as boundary markers of a sort: They capture something
distinctive about Native American cultures, and the celebration and en-
actment of that distinctiveness reinforces a sense of solidarity within the
group (see also Whitehorse 1988).

Nineteenth-century German Americans in cities such as Milwaukee
and New York transformed American holidays such as the Fourth of July
into festive German American events, and in the process they celebrated
their own ethnicity. Particularly in large urban areas, that ethnicity sometimes rested on only modest foundations. German Americans, writes
Kathleen Conzen (1989:48), "lacked a common religion, common regional
or class origins, a common political ideology, a common immigrant pre-
dicament, in short, most of the generally accepted bases for the crystal-
lization of ethnic sentiment." They clearly formed, nevertheless, an ethnic group. They both saw themselves and were perceived as such, and
they often acted in common. Celebratory events played a significant role
in the development and maintenance of that ethnicity. "Everything from
Sunday afternoons to national anniversaries was enveloped in a web of
group celebration and marked with consciously crafted rites whose symbolism stamped them unmistakably as German-American" (Conzen
1989:45). Such events and a shared enthusiasm for them drew German
Americans together and forged ethnic links across religious, class, and
other divisions. This "festive culture" (Conzen 1989) was one key to the
maintenance of their ethnicity.

Cultural Practices

What distinguishes symbolic resources from day-to-day cultural practices such as religion and language is that they constitute not so much a
shared practice as a set of symbols. Symbolic resources are not the taken-
for-granted activities of daily life that survive through some combination
of utility, inertia, and embeddedness in social relationships. Instead, they
are consciously employed in a process of signification. Stories, celebrations, and the iconic forms of dress or food or ritual are used to signify an
identity, to mark it, and in some sense to "tell" it, to condense and capture
part of what that identity means to those who carry it, or what they want

it to mean. There is an intentionality to symbolic resources that language and religion, in their typical daily manifestations, do not carry.

This is not to say that language and religion may not serve as symbolic resources. They often do. In the case of language, it may happen in bits and pieces, as in particular words or phrases that take on a consciously signifying role. This is perhaps most clearly the case in the names groups claim for themselves, as in the shift among American Blacks from Negro to Black to African American to Black again, or in the various terms—Chicano, Hispanic, Latino—that different groups of Latinos use for themselves, or in the effort of Asian-descent groups in the United States to eliminate the term Oriental, long common among Whites, and replace it with Asian American.

On occasion, the use of language as a complete system of communication becomes a symbolic resource, even a rallying point for ethnic assertions. At the end of the 19th century, for example, when Ireland was still under English rule, a movement emerged to revive the Gaelic language—Ireland's own language, in declining use since at least the early part of the century. The movement emerged as part of an effort to reduce the English influence in Ireland, and the revival of Gaelic became central to the assertion of Irish pride and identity, a symbol of Irish nationalism and peoplehood (Edwards 1984).

The power of language in such situations comes in part from its exclusivity. For example, in a conversational setting in which everyone speaks English but not everyone speaks French—a common situation in parts of Canada, where English and French are both official languages— if one of the conversationalists suddenly switches to French, there is a good chance that some persons will feel a suddenly heightened commonality with the speaker—who has just spotlighted a shared and exclusive attribute—whereas others will feel a sudden distance. The speech act invokes the boundary between the two groups and evokes the sentiment of commonality, a key component of identity (Lincoln 1989:10).

The Use and Growth of Symbolic Repertoires

Symbolic repertoires have little impact on identity construction unless those repertoires can be put to use. One of the ways that the Soviet Union, particularly during the Stalinist period that began in the 1930s, attempted to suppress ethnic identities among the many peoples under its control was by prohibiting flags, anthems, traditional celebrations, and other icons emblematic of those identities and of the communities that carried them. It rewrote the histories of those communities, reinventing their pasts in ways that glorified Russia and promoted the Soviet state's own socialist goals. In effect, it attempted to deny to those peoples their own symbolic resources, their ability to define and sustain their own identities in their own ways.

The effort ultimately failed. Among the most striking phenomena to surface in the wake of the Soviet Union's 1989 collapse were a host of still vibrant national and ethnic identities, previously hidden under the lid of Soviet oppression. These reemergent identities gave the lie to the Soviet claim that the process of building a new, communist society would lead to the disappearance of particularistic national and ethnic identities. How had those identities survived? Some clearly survived as a result of Soviet policies themselves that—sometimes inadvertently, sometimes not—helped to sustain them in administrative and other structures (Khazanov 1995; Slezkine 1994). Symbolic resources also were at work. Stephen Jones (1994) points to "the informal channels of resistance," mobilized against official myths, that kept many of these identities very much alive, if often subdued and carefully protected. Building on his own studies of ethnicity and memory in Georgia, formerly part of the Soviet Union and now a separate state, Jones argues that "public imagery, commemorative days, songs, and customs" are among the ways that identities are preserved (p. 154). Georgians preserved and signified their own identities in, among other things, poetry, song, and folktales, drawn from the Georgian past, memorized and repeated orally because the state controlled so much of what was written. They celebrated their own past in feasts organized for birthdays and saints' days, when family and friends would gather and toast one another with elaborate tracings of genealogies and histories. They read historical novels that celebrated ancient Georgian heroes and myths, and they decorated the walls of their homes with images of Georgian churches and ruins. Through such verbal and graphic images, Georgians sustained a sense of their own distinctiveness, a sense rooted in a Georgian version of Georgian history, defying the official Soviet account (Jones 1994). In essence, they represented themselves to themselves, using an array of symbolic resources to remind one another of who they were, and in so doing continued to nurture an identity that official policy claimed was little more than a shadow.

Groups can create symbolic resources, expanding their repertoires, and many do. Some, such as the Hutu refugees in Tanzania, do it more or less inadvertently as they try to come to terms with calamitous events and to construct an identity that can make sense of both past and present. Others, such as the Latinos who organize the Latino festival in Washington, do so more purposefully, searching for ways to bridge their differences and signify their commonalities. In her discussion of Asian American panethnicity, Yen Espiritu highlights the emergence of Asian American Studies programs on college campuses in the late 1960s and 1970s, arguing that they "built, and continue to build, an Asian American heritage" (1992:36). She underlines the importance of Asian American scholars and their effort "to reinterpret Asian history in the United States to bring out what is common to all Asian Americans" (p. 37). Reinterpretations and elaborations of the African American past have appeared in novels, biographies, plays, films, and television—the novels of Toni Morrison, for example, or Alex Haley's (1976) book *Roots* that explored his own past and became a major television special—and in the burgeoning historiography on slavery and the Black experience that emerged in the 1970s and afterward (Novick 1988). This scholarly work vastly enlarged the inventory of images, insights, and knowledge on which African Americans could draw as they reframed their own sense of themselves.

All of these efforts manage to alter the meanings attached to both past and present, to offer new representations of the group or the materials necessary to build such representations. Each contributes to "the solidarity resources of the community" (Young 1976:46), its ability, in this case through the use of symbolic repertoires, to sustain itself as a conscious community and to command the allegiance of its members. They attach distinctive meanings to particular identities, and in so doing help to create, reproduce, and transform them.

Groups, Contexts, and Agendas

Table 7.1 presents an "other things equal" version of the effects of these group factors on the salience of ethnic and racial identities. As with Table 6.1, there is an unavoidable simplification involved, and the caveats we noted at the end of the last chapter are equally applicable here. Like Table 6.1, this table also reduces continuous variables to dichotomous ones and pays no attention to the interactions among the listed factors—to the possibility, for example, that the impact of a large population will be much reduced by internal differentiation, or that internal differentiation might be overcome by a powerful repertoire of symbolic resources.

There is a more important omission in Table 7.1. Just as the table in Chapter 6 is missing the characteristics and assets of groups, so this table is missing context. It makes no note of the degree to which contextual factors mediate the impact of group factors. The impact of population

TABLE 7.1

"Other Things Equal" Effects of Group Factors
on Salience of Ethnic and Racial Identities

Group Factors Likely to Increase *Salience of Ethnic or Racial Identities*	*Group Factors Likely to* Decrease *Salience of Ethnic or Racial Identities*
Preexisting ethnic or racial identity is embedded in social relations	No preexisting ethnic or racial identity is embedded in social relations
Group is numerically large relative to dominant population	Group is numerically small relative to dominant population
Group includes approximately equal numbers of men and women	Group includes unequal numbers of men and women
Group includes a high proportion of first-generation migrants	Group includes a low proportion of first-generation migrants
Group members are largely similar in class background	Group members are diverse in class background
Group has high social capital	Group has low social capital
Group was established largely via chain migration	Group was established largely via individualistic migration
Cultural practice (e.g., language, religion) differs from that of society at large	Cultural practice (e.g., language, religion) is similar to that of society at large
Group has a large symbolic repertoire	Group has a small symbolic repertoire

SOURCE: Adapted, with somewhat different categories, from Yinger (1986:31).

size, for example, is a matter of context and concentration: Dispersed numbers are less likely to lead to more salient ethnic boundaries than are concentrated ones, which means that to understand the likely impact of numbers we have to know something about the situation in which those numbers occur, such as the extent of occupational and residential concentration. Similarly, a disproportionately male or female sex ratio has unpredictable effects on ethnic boundaries unless we know what sorts of restrictions there are on intermarriage. The predominance of males among Chinese immigrants to the United States in the late 19th and early 20th centuries did not lead to increased marriage across the ethnic boundary and therefore to a decline in the salience of Chinese identity. The prohibitions against interracial marriage meant that Chinese immigrants were condemned to bachelorhood or to a return to China to marry. From the point of view of ethnicity, context determined the impact of the sex ratio.

In short, generalizing about the effects of group factors on identity construction is riskier than generalizing about the effects of contextual factors. Context is more likely to overwhelm groups than the reverse— although certainly the reverse can happen. It is invariably the case that the projected effect of any particular group factor must take context into account.

Finally, Table 7.1 simplifies by virtue of what it leaves out. Part of what it leaves out is intent. What is it that the groups in question want to achieve? What are their agendas, and what is the agenda of the dominant elements in the society of which they are a part?

These surely vary, and in their variation they affect the significance of some of the factors involved. For example, a group that is pursuing integration or assimilation needs symbolic resources that emphasize commonalities across ethnic or racial boundaries, not the boundaries themselves. Internal differentiation may cripple a political struggle for autonomy that depends on group solidarity if it is to succeed but be of little significance in an effort simply to be recognized in a pluralist society. Symbolic repertoires may be of little importance to those who see their migration as temporary and still identify with the society from which they came and to which they hope one day to return.

Conclusion

Identities are not inevitable outcomes of particular arrays of factors, of the characteristics of populations or of the ways various sites are organized. Indeed, there is nothing inevitable about them. Instead, they are products of people's efforts to understand and respond to the situations in which they find themselves, using such resources as they command. Identities are human creations, existing only in the ways that we come to think about ourselves and others. Ultimately, the construction of an identity occurs as an ongoing act of interpretation, shaped by the factors we have reviewed in this chapter and Chapter 6, but never simply their offspring. Those factors may describe a particular set of conditions that renders some identities more likely, possible, or compelling than others, but human beings still have to make their own sense of those conditions and, in the process, make themselves.

N O T E

1. Michael Piore argues that the critical distinction between the first and second generations should refer not to where one is born but to where one grew up and, in particular, to where one spends his or her adolescence. Speaking of migrants from nonindustrial to industrial societies, Piore writes, "People who come to the industrial region in their late teens and early twenties seem to retain an affinity with their place of origin. . . . Children who migrate before adolescence, on the other hand, seem to adopt the culture of the destination" (1979:66). Piore's argument fits a common perception in some parts of the United States. We are reminded of the person who commented once to one of the authors that "no matter how long you've lived in Somerville [Massachusetts], you're not *from* Somerville unless you went to Somerville High." The convention in studies of migration, nevertheless, is to distinguish between first and second generations by birthplace.

8

Making Sense and Making Selves in a Changing World

We began this book by pointing out that ethnicity and race have played a prominent and often sensational role in human affairs in the 20th century. This fact, obvious in virtually every part of the world, is part of the perplexing puzzle that ethnicity and race present. As we noted in Chapter 1, it was not what many of those who gave thought to the matter in the first half of the century expected. On the contrary, the general expectation was that the great integrative and universalizing forces of modernity would sweep such attachments away. They might be replaced by other group bonds such as the consciousness of shared class positions and interests, or they might be replaced by an either enlightened or alienated individualism that shunned group identities altogether. But the bonds of ethnicity and race were believed to be residues of the past, their power likely to diminish in a rapidly changing world.

Instead, they proved both resilient and resurgent. As we make the transition from the 20th to the 21st century, it seems likely that ethnicity and race will continue to both shape and reflect the world in which we live. How will they do that and in what forms? What will sustain them as bases of collective identity, and what role are they likely to play in the future?

The Impact of Modernity

The very processes that were expected to undermine ethnicity and race seem instead to have occasioned their resurgence, transforming them into objects of conflict, negotiation, assertion, and visible construction. The explanation of this unanticipated outcome has to do in part with the paradoxical character of modernity itself and, in particular, with the complexity of two of its most prominent aspects: globalization and rationalization.

Modernity embraces a set of processes that are "inherently globalising" (Giddens 1990:63). Among these are the following:

- The enormous growth and global reach of the capitalist economy, which increasingly binds diverse and distant peoples and places into massive, interconnected markets and production systems;

- The global expansion of state power and, in particular, military power, beginning in the modern period with the British Empire, continuing during the U.S.-Soviet superpower rivalry of the Cold War, and now proceeding under relatively uncontested American hegemony;

- The development of mass media and communications systems that are increasingly global in their reach, through which not only information and ideas but also cultural practices, images, and symbols move across the world with unprecedented speed and penetration.

These processes mean that "local" events are almost never local anymore; what happens in one place is inevitably linked to phenomena happening in another place, or more likely in many other places, some of them half a world away. Some of these links among events are economic or political; some are composed of cultural influences, either dramatic or subtle; some are what we might call "exemplar" effects, in which one group of people interpret their situations or act in particular ways partly because some other group of people, somewhere, have done the same, and the ideas or actions of those others resonate with their own lives. These innumerable, multiplying, global interconnections make ever more obsolete an older and never entirely accurate way of thinking and talking about societies as if they were discrete, clearly bounded entities. Human beings can imagine their worlds in many different ways, organizing them conceptually into discrete units, but the discreteness is more and more an illusion. Increasingly, it is the connections that matter (Giddens 1990; Hall, Held, and McGrew 1992).

These globalizing processes tend to operate in a particular direction: The flows of influence have been heavily outward from a predominantly although not exclusively western core—the United States, Europe, the Soviet Union in its own imperial heyday, and more recently and to a lesser degree, Japan—toward the rest of the world. The result is ever more dense networks of economic, political, and cultural power linking parts of the world to each other in ways that tend to be dominated by the West.

It is easy to overstate this domination. Although globalization has linked the various parts of the world together, it has not simply subordinated one half to the other. Peoples of the nonwestern world have tended "to organize what is afflicting them in their own cultural terms" (Sahlins 1994:413). They have struggled to make their own histories, identities, and ways of life out of materials both indigenous and foreign, fitting external influences and externally driven events into their own evolving interpretive schemes (see, for compelling historical examples, Bradley 1987 and Sahlins 1985 and 1994). Nonetheless, their efforts have been occasioned by a globalizing process that has been driven by largely western actions and has carried western influences far and wide.

One result of these globalizing processes—and a further dimension of globalization itself—has been increased migration. Although economic, political, and cultural influences to a large degree have been moving outward from a predominantly western core, people have been going the other way. In the aftermath of decolonization and in response to these multiplying and increasingly dense connections, growing numbers of people from Asia, Africa, the Caribbean, the Pacific, and Latin America have been migrating toward the core, feeding the burgeoning immigrant populations of the United States, Canada, Europe, Australia, and New Zealand. Migration has been a constant characteristic of the world, but its dimensions have changed radically. The numbers have become enormous; the distances have become global.

Intimately bound up in these globalizing developments has been another aspect of modernity: rationalization. As Max Weber argued a century ago (see Chapter 1), rationality has become increasingly the principle on which modern organizations, relationships, and actions are built—or at least the principle on which they are defended.

The thrust of these developments has been profoundly unsettling for much of the world. Changing economies and social systems increased uncertainty and competition among groups. Decolonization opened up centers of political power to new contestants and to the formerly disfranchised, many of whom shared little more than their previously colonized status. As populations moved, they did not necessarily melt together. Instead, they often were thrown into competition with each other as immigration challenged long-established advantages and prevailing assumptions. The rising expectations and demands of some groups triggered the resistance of others. The growing complexity of a more mobile and diverse social life encouraged a search for simplifying categories. Rationalization left some people feeling alienated from the large and impersonal institutions that increasingly dominated their lives. It left others searching for ideological means to rationalize and maintain their own power and privilege.

Collective attachments and affiliations have been among the things most unsettled in these situations. Although the effects of globalization have been in some ways integrative and homogenizing, in other ways they have had the opposite effect. They variously resuscitated old identities and inspired new ones, differentiating people from each other in new or altered ways or, at the very least, introducing new conceptions of difference. Changing interests and the demands of new situations challenged established understandings of "us" and "them," precipitating a flurry of identity construction and reconstruction as groups and persons struggled to adjust their conceptions of themselves and others.

In these circumstances, ethnicity and race turned out to have a great deal to offer: readily identifiable boundaries, in most cases, on which to stake one's claims; usable bases for collective organization and action; a sense of continuity and permanence in the midst of change; a means of intimate connection and communion—even if only imagined—in a world in which most connections are impersonal and communion is in short supply. They were both simplifying and, often, powerful: available and appealing vessels that could be filled with meanings in the face of competition or threat, alienation or uncertainty, dislocation or change.

Thus, the forces of modernity, instead of doing away with ethnicity and race as bases of identity, invigorated them.

What now? Will the 21st century offer us more of the same? The forces of modernity are unlikely to abate. Given that, it seems unlikely also that ethnicity and race will lose their power and appeal. But just as their role in the century past has been driven both by their distinctive characteristics as bases of identity and by the forces of social change, so those characteristics and forces will play a major role in determining how those identities are used and how they manifest themselves in the years ahead.

At century's end, two very different trends are apparent. One is the emergence of more complex and individualized forms of ethnic and racial identity; the other is the continuing separation and consolidation of ethnic and racial groups and categories. Part of what makes the future of ethnicity and race in this new century so very difficult to predict is the apparent divergence between these two trends. In the following two sections, we examine each in turn.

Mixing and Multiplicity

In an article on Pacific Islander Americans, Paul Spickard and Rowena Fong (1995) tell a story about an argument between two players in a schoolyard basketball game in Kaneohe, Hawaii.

> As basketball players will, they started talking about each other's families. One, who prided himself on his pure Samoan ancestry, said, "You got a Hawaiian grandmother, a Pake [Chinese] grandfather. You other grandfather's Portegee [Portuguese], and you mom's Filipino. You got Haole [White] brother-in-law and Korean cousins. Who da heck are you?" The person with the bouquet of ethnic possibilities smiled (his team was winning) and said, simply, "I all da kine [I'm all of those things.] Le's play." (p. 1365).

By drawing attention to the diversity of his opponent's ethnic background, the basketball player in Hawaii was pointing to a well-established aspect not only of Hawaiian life but of many other parts of the Pacific. Most Pacific Islanders have long recognized and embraced both the idea of being multiethnic and the existence of a community composed of typically multiethnic persons. Multiethnicity was common in much of the Pacific long before Europeans appeared. Various of the peoples of the vast Pacific had developed their own technologies for finding one another on tiny islands in a blue ocean. Some encoded their knowledge of stars and ocean currents in oral chants that were passed on from generation to generation. Chanting, they piloted their canoes across thousands of miles of open water to trade and visit with one another (see, for example, Brower 1983). In time, the scope of Pacific mixing grew. European explorers appeared, followed by European settlers. Colonial administrations brought in workers from India and elsewhere. Eventually, there were Chinese, Japanese, more Europeans, and an assortment of others.

Hawaii was a gathering spot for many of these peoples. Spickard and Fong note a Hawaiian woman whose five names represent the four ethnicities in her ancestry—Japanese, Maori, Hawaiian, and Samoan—plus a first name that is a family invention. They tell the story of a Hawaiian political activist and lawyer named William Kauaiwiulaokalani Wallace who begins his public speaking appearances by chanting his genealogy. His ethnic ancestries include Hawaiian, Samoan, Tongan, Tahitian, German, Scottish, and Chinese. He married a Maori woman from New Zealand. It takes time to get through all the details, and he accompanies his own chant by playing his nose flute and drum (Spickard and Fong 1995:1368-69). Many other people of the Pacific, particularly in Hawaii, could describe similar ancestries. Few of them think of themselves as Pacific Islanders, a term used by the U.S. Census and government administrators. What supposedly links them in that category is the dominance of Polynesian ancestries, but it is someone else's category, not their own. Although many share multiple ancestries, they tend to focus on only one or two, and they are more likely to describe themselves "as Tongans (or Tongan-Americans), Samoans, Fijians, and so on" (Spickard and Fong 1995:1368).

Multiethnicity—mixed ancestry—is an ancient phenomenon. Its history surely is as old as the history of interaction among distinct human peoples. At the same time, the basketball player was pointing to something quite new, at least in the grand sweep of human history. Multiethnicity is a product of human movement and mixing, and although the mixing of human peoples is very old indeed, the magnitude of movement among human populations has grown enormously in recent centuries. The revolution in transportation technologies has made movement possible on an unprecedented scale, and economic, political, and ecological changes have variously encouraged or forced human populations to take full advantage of those possibilities. Slavery, colonialism, political upheaval, famine, the search for jobs and security, and other forces have moved people from countryside to city, country to country, and continent to continent in extraordinary numbers—a massive redistribution of the world's population in the relatively short span of a few centuries. The result has been a degree and complexity of mixing unseen before in human history.

Although it may be more complex than most, the Hawaiian schoolyard player's mixed ancestry is a common feature of modernity. The specifics in his case are embedded in the history of the Hawaiian Islands, which have been both destination and crossroads for a remarkable collection of the world's peoples. Mixed ancestry, however, is by no means a local affair. It is increasingly a global phenomenon.

Multiethnicity is different from multiculturalism, another common term in the discussion of ethnicity and race. Most discussions of multiculturalism are about the presence and proper place of different identities and groups in a single society. They have to do with the issues that the presence of different racial and ethnic groups in one society often raises—issues of recognition, tolerance, and equality. In contrast, multiethnicity refers to the mixing of ethnic and racial identities and ancestries in single persons, the offspring of interethnic and interracial unions.

Multiplicity in the United States

Pacific Islanders may celebrate their multiple ancestries, but that has not always and everywhere been the case. Multiethnicity and multiracialism have seldom been acknowledged in some parts of the world, much less celebrated. In Europe and the United States, mixed parentage was long viewed as a handicap. Social science in the early 20th century viewed persons of mixed parentage as psychologically disturbed and socially disruptive, and popular films and literature often portrayed interracial offspring as tortured souls (Spickard 1989:329, 1992:20). The refusal to readily accept such persons on their own terms may have given some truth to these views, producing in individuals the very behavior and discontent for which it blamed them.

More recently, psychology has been less at issue than identity and classification. In the United States, for example, the assumption generally has been that whatever the nature of their ethnic inheritance, individuals identify with and carry only a single ethnicity. Both institutions and informal public dialogues have tended to encourage and even require as much. University applications routinely ask for a single ethnic or racial identifier, and census forms implicitly encourage identification with a single ancestry group. Most people have acquiesced, accepting ethnic and racial boxes as adequate indicators—for official purposes, at least—of who they are.

That, recently, has changed. A growing number of Americans who carry more than one ethnic or racial ancestry have become reluctant to choose among them. They insist, instead, on their own composite identities, presenting themselves in multiethnic or multiracial terms. Rather than subordinating one ancestry to another, many multiethnic individuals not only recognize and accept multiple ethnic ancestries; they also either actively assert their multiplicity or construct a single and unique identity that recognizes the mixing that constitutes their perceived heritage. In Chapter 3, we quoted a student whose mother was half Irish and half German, whose father was Chinese by way of Indonesia, but who had been raised as a "regular" American kid and thus saw ethnicity as "a very muddy topic." He refused to fill in only one box. "No can do."

Rising rates of interracial and interethnic marriage in the United States—the number of interracial married couples more than tripled between 1970 and 1995—are part of the reason for this trend. The trend also represents a resistance on the part of the children of such marriages to the implicit denial of one or another part of their heritage that is required by the classifications used and expected both in official records and in daily interactions. The impact of this resistance is only beginning to be felt, and its implications are difficult to predict. For example, there has been a tendency in the United States for couples marrying across ethnic boundaries to simplify their ethnic ancestries so as to "match up" with each other (Lieberson and Waters 1993). Will this begin to change? Persons of mixed ancestry have founded a number of organizations in recent years representing multiracial and multiethnic individuals and families. Among other things, these organizations hope to persuade the federal government to add a category on all official forms, surveys, and statistical compilations for those who claim multiple ancestries, allowing them not only to claim their multiplicity but also to note separately as many of their ancestries as they wish (Fernandez 1996). How long will the federal government's preferred five-part racial classification scheme—Euro-American (or White), Asian American, African American (or Black), Hispanic (or Latino), and Native American (see Fernandez 1996)—last as growing numbers of people assert identities that do not fit its categories? How long can the American conviction that race represents something fixed or natural or biologically meaningful survive if growing numbers of people keep crossing racial and ethnic boundaries to reproduce, having children with ancestries as complex as those of the American children who appeared in a recent article in *The New York Times Magazine*: Pakistani/African American; Colombian/Scottish/Irish; Filipino/Italian/Russian; Finnish/African American; Dutch/Jamaican/Irish/African American/Russian-Jewish; Hungarian/Japanese; Irish/Scottish/Indian (Crouch 1996)? What does this imply for the future of ethnic and racial groups themselves?

This last question has to do not with the disappearance of groups but with the certainty of classification. Over the last few decades, the United States has passed legislation to remedy past and current discrimination against certain racial and ethnic groups. The implementation of this legislation requires counting individuals by those racial and ethnic categories. As long as the rules of classification were clear, this was not a problem. At one time, the federal government did the classifying. Since the 1960s, it has relied largely on self-identification, although it has offered a limited set of categories from which to choose and in many cases has discouraged multiple choices. As growing numbers of individuals claim multiracial or multiethnic identities and resist the categories offered by the government, counting by race and ethnicity becomes increasingly difficult (Waters 1995).

Intermarriage raises problems for such classifications even without this resistance. If an African American man marries a Euro-American woman and they have children, what race are their children? In the past,

American society imposed the rule of hypodescent in such cases: The children were Black. It was less consistent in determining the race of children of White/American Indian or White/Asian marriages (Spickard 1989; Waters 1995), although the common practice was to classify such children in the non-white race. As the numbers of such marriages of all kinds grow and as the ancestries of the participants become more complex, classification becomes increasingly arbitrary.

Sociologist and Harvard University professor Mary Waters tells a story that underlines the point, drawing on the experience of one of her students. One day, this student—a member of Harvard's entering undergraduate class—came to see Waters, seeking help with an identity-related issue. The student was from a rural area in the southern United States. Her mother had told her that she was an American Indian but that her Indian ancestry was mixed with Black ancestry. She also knew that she was part Irish and part Scottish. When she applied for admission to various colleges, she checked all the ethnicity and race boxes that applied in her case. Soon after she arrived at Harvard, she began to receive mail from the Black Students Association. She also began to feel pressure from Black students about spending more time with Blacks on campus. She concluded from this that Harvard had classified her as Black.

This student, however, had not come to the university alone. Also at Harvard was her identical twin sister. She, too, had checked all the ethnicity and race boxes that applied, but *she* was receiving mail from the Native American Students Association on campus and was being pressured to attend their meetings. Evidently Harvard had classified *her* as Indian.

Says Waters,

> My student wanted two things from me. One, she wanted my aid in navigating the university's bureaucracy to find out what identity the university thought she was, and how they decided that. Secondly, she wanted to know what sociological principle could justify what she perceived as an absurd situation—she and her identical twin sister having different racial identities. (Waters 1995:2)

As Waters points out, this story beautifully captures the socially constructed nature of race and ethnicity. "Here were two genetically identical twins attending the same university and yet assigned to different races, and already feeling some social consequences (in the form of peer pressure and political lobbying by student organizations) because of that classification" (Waters 1995:3).

As movement and mixing increase and as the logic of racial classification consequently becomes fuzzier, the argument that race has something to do with biology becomes increasingly difficult for anyone to defend. The disconnection between mixed people and stubbornly unmixed categories—between the realities of the modern world, on one hand, and the ways that some societies, institutions, and people are determined to interpret them, on the other—becomes more and more obvious.

Situationality and Simplification

The various components of most multiethnic or multiracial identities are not equally prominent or important at all times. Identity among multiethnic Pacific Islanders in Hawaii, for example, is largely situational. Individuals act on the basis of different identities according to the situations they encounter. "If I'm with my grandmother," says one young woman, "I'm Portuguese. If I'm with some of my aunts on my dad's side I'm Filipino. If I'm hanging around, I'm just local. If I'm on the mainland I'm Hawaiian" (quoted in Spickard and Fong 1995:1370).

This situationality of identity is not peculiar to those with mixed ancestries or parentage. There are other kinds of multiple identities. Some are concentric. They can be thought of as a set of circles, each larger than the last, that move outward from the individual, capturing ever greater numbers of people and describing different encompassing identities. American Indians offer an example. Many Native Americans see themselves both as members of distinct Indian nations—for example, Yakima, Navajo, Oglala Sioux, Cherokee—and at the same time as Indians or Native Americans. The rise of a supratribal, American Indian identity, chronicled in Chapter 5, did not correspond to any decline in the prominence of tribal identities. Some individuals may no longer identify with any particular Indian nation, but for most, "supratribalism represents not a replacement but an enlargement of their identity system, a circle beyond tribe in which, also, they think, move, and act" (Cornell 1988:144).

In the Indian case, too, identities are activated—made the basis of relationships and actions—situationally. For example, in interactions with one another, most Indians pay a great deal of attention to tribal identities. When Osage and Navajo meet, they meet not only as Indians but as Osage and Navajo, and those identities are likely to organize some of their interaction. When they interact with non-Indians, Indian or Native American identities are much more likely to enter the foreground of both thinking and action. Still others of their identities may arise in other situations: subtribal ones, perhaps, or identity as Americans, activated particularly in other countries or in wartime, or an identity as indigenous peoples linked to other such peoples—Maoris in New Zealand, Australian Aborigines, the Ainu people of Japan, Canada's First Nations, the Inuit of the Arctic, and others. All of these might be carried by a single person, each one representing relationships and statuses of importance to that person, each one with a separate set of meanings attached to it.

The activation of one identity or another may be driven by a number of considerations. One, as in the case of the woman from Hawaii who sees herself as Portuguese in one setting and Filipino in another, is simply whom you are with. Another consideration may be the utility of an identity in various situations. In Malaysia, situational selection of ethnic identity occurs variously as a way of establishing a particular status, as a way of indicating or controlling the social distance between persons, or as the basis of a claim to resources. For example, because the government of Malaysia reserves certain resources for Malays—a term that includes a number of indigenous groups but excludes Chinese and some others—those who usually identify as members of an indigenous group may act in terms of their specific indigenous identity most of the time but assert their Malay identity when those particular resources are at stake (Nagata 1974). In this case, Malay identity is somewhat like Native American identity. It is another of the situationally activated circles of identity that surround the person.

Although different identities may be activated in different situations, there is also a tendency in the case of multiple ethnicities to simplify. Many of the middle-class White Americans that Mary Waters (1990) studied in San Jose and Philadelphia were of mixed ethnic ancestries, but most tended to favor one or another of them, and many engaged in a kind of "selective forgetting." Waters asked one, whose ancestry was mixed English, French, and Polish but who described himself as of English and French ancestry, why he did not include the Polish part. "I don't know," he said. "I guess I just never think about the Polish." Others chose which of their ancestries to emphasize based on what they knew or had been told about them. Said one, "I was very strongly Italian, because the Irish . . . whenever I was in a bad mood, that was the Irish in me. So I always related the Irish with the bad things and the Italian with all of the good things" (quoted in Waters 1990:23-24).

Pacific Islanders tended to simplify their ethnicities as well, emphasizing one while holding onto the others (Spickard and Fong 1995). One important difference between them and the middle-class Whites that Waters studied is that the Pacific Islanders in Hawaii tend to be deeply involved in communities where ethnicity remains thick. Their ethnic identities are more than ancestral references. As a consequence of either choice or circumstance, those identities still organize significant portions of their lives.

Boundaries and Centers

These dual processes of movement and mixing raise issues about the nature and meaning of ethnic boundaries. Boundaries, supposedly, are the things that separate ethnic and racial groups. Boundaries are more clear in some cases than in others. The one-drop rule, for example—one drop of Black ancestry means you are Black—is in retreat in the United States, legally if not yet culturally. Some boundaries between groups are largely cultural—they are marked in part by cultural practices or shared understandings—and therefore are often difficult to pin down. Among some Native Americans, actions and ideas reveal ethnicity. For some Oglala Sioux, for example, you are truly Oglala only if you engage in certain behaviors or observe certain obligations and share certain understandings of the world. Those things constitute the meaning of being Oglala for those people. It is difficult to know, under those circumstances, just where the boundary between "real" Oglalas and not so "real" Oglalas lies. The two categories are easy to identify in the abstract and at the extremes, but as one approaches the boundary, the difference between categories gets fuzzy. Those on either side may disagree on just where to draw the line.

In a society characterized by increasing rates of movement, mixing, and intermarriage, and by growing numbers of persons who assert their multiplicity, boundaries become less obvious, less potent, and far more difficult to maintain. "The boundaries surrounding Pacific Islanders are not very important at all. Pacific Islander Americans have inclusive, not exclusive, ethnic identities. What is important for Pacific Islander American ethnicity is not boundaries but centers: ancestry, family, practice, place" (Spickard and Fong 1995:1378). In other words, what matters is the things people share rather than the lines that divide them from one another. "If one qualifies for acceptance at the centers of ethnicity, then one is of that ethnic group, no matter to what other ethnic groups one may also belong" (Spickard and Fong 1995:1378).

This does not mean that Hawaii is an ethnic paradise. Even among Pacific Islanders, it has its share of ethnic categories, hostilities, and conflicts (Spickard and Fong 1995). It suggests, however, that as populations become more multiethnic there is at least the possibility that ethnic and racial identities will become less exclusive, less matters of imposed distinctions and more matters of chosen affiliation, less oriented toward past injuries or abuses and more toward present and future connection and community. In short, perhaps they will be less about boundaries and more about centers.

They also may become less important. Sociologist Georg Simmel, in his essay "The Web of Group-Affiliations" (1922/1955), argued that one of the characteristics of modernity is the multiplicity of group affiliations that meet in each individual. He was not referring to ethnicity, at least not explicitly. He had in mind the rapid multiplication of occupations, associations, groups, and activities with which individuals are affiliated in the modern world. No two individuals share the same set of affiliations. Part of what distinguishes each individual is the particular set of affiliations that come together in her or him.

In a predominantly multiethnic society—which, in the long run, is where human societies seem to be headed—ethnic and racial groups may become insignificant as distinct communities. There may be few ethnic groups but many multiethnic individuals distinguished by the complex combinations of ancestries that meet, uniquely, in each one. Brothers and sisters may share those combinations, but each combination will last only a generation before some other set of ancestries joins in to produce offspring whose ethnic lineages are more complicated still. Boundaries will disappear. In time, even centers may lose their meaning. That, at least, is one scenario.

Separation and Consolidation

There is another scenario, rooted in a different set of developments, that leads in a very different direction. In 1976, a Black American named Alex Haley published a book titled *Roots* in which he told the story of his own family, tracing his roots back through his mother, through generations in America, through slavery, and finally to Africa, ending up at a beginning, of sorts, in Gambia. A decade later, another Black American named Ishmael Reed pointed out that Blacks in the United States "have a multiethnic heritage." He was not referring to the mix of African peoples who were brought to North America. He was commenting on Haley's book. Reed pointed out that "if Alex Haley had traced his father's bloodline, he would have traveled twelve generations back to, not Gambia, but *Ireland*" (Reed 1989:227).

Historian David Hollinger points out that tracing his father's bloodline instead of his mother's was never really an option for Haley, for American social conventions classified Haley as Black, ignoring or calling inconsequential his White ethnic heritage. Hollinger calls this "Haley's Choice" and views it as hardly a choice at all. Haley could choose either the African part of his heritage or the Irish part. If he were to choose the latter, he would be crossing a racial divide, siding with those who had been responsible historically for the oppression of his people and who still refused to recognize the European part of his heritage as truly his. He would be turning his back, in effect, on "the people who most shared his social destiny" (Hollinger 1995:20).

Multiplicity may be one wave of the future. Another is this continuing and in some cases resurgent power of race and ethnicity in a host of human societies and the separation, conflict, and consolidation it so often produces.

The Limits on Multiplicity and Choice

The middle-class Whites that Mary Waters studied have genuine identity choices. They can engage in selective forgetting or choose to be Italian instead of Irish. As Waters (1990, chap. 7) and Hollinger both point out, however, many Americans lack that choice in any meaningful way. Being Asian, Latino, Native American or, most obviously, Black in America is a very different experience from being Italian, Polish, or English. It offers fewer options. The only identity choice most non-White Americans face, regardless of their heritage, is a Haley's Choice, for on issues of race in America, assignment generally prevails.

A student of ours brought the point home in an essay on her own identity. She is the daughter of an African American father and a German mother who met while her father was serving in the U.S. military in Europe. Her parents raised her to value both of the identities she carries and the very different backgrounds that come together in her. In fact, she claims these identities proudly, seeing herself as both African American and German American. She is the first to admit that those identities are very different. One is largely symbolic, a matter of food and music, the occasional trip back to Europe and the stories her mother tells. The other, in stark contrast, looms large in her life. It does so because the meanings attached to it are elaborate, contentious, and weighted in American society. It does so because that identity carries significant consequences for her own life chances and because it is an identity she cannot easily shed or escape, even if she wanted to. She looks Black, and that effectively organizes much of her life. She asserts both identities, but only one is commonly assigned to her.

In her case, even assignment has become complex. The society at large is not the only source of the message that she is really Black. To some of her African American friends, her insistence on being not only African

American but also German American challenges their vision of what being African American means. For them, she writes, being Black requires a wholehearted, unwavering, and unmitigated commitment, and they urge her to turn her back on the rest. Thus, there are two sources of the assignment she faces, one on each side of the racial divide. One holds her Blackness against her; the other sees it as all she has to offer. For both of them, in the tensions of American society, her Germanness has disappeared. She feels the loss.

The United States is not the only country where identity choices may be limited. We have touched on several others in earlier chapters. Centuries of occasional ethnic mixing in Yugoslavia had little effect once the boundary-builders went to work, constructing identities with a vengeance—in more ways than one. The invisibility of boundaries in Rwanda did not stop the killing. A rumor that someone had Tutsi blood or that someone else had been seen among Hutus was cause enough to take a life. The 20th century may be a century of movement and intermingling, but it is also the century that produced the examples of ethnic and racial violence and conflict with which we began this book.

The fact is that potential boundaries are numerous and ubiquitous. What matters is the decision to establish a boundary in the first place, to find a way of distinguishing "us" from "them," and the power to make that boundary meaningful in the lives of individuals and societies. Given a decision, a boundary, and power, virtually anything can happen.

The lesson here is that the impact of mixing and multiplicity is mediated by the stability of human categories, and they, in turn, respond to the logic of identity construction and to the assertions and assignments that groups make. As we suggested in Chapter 4, that logic is variable. Group interests or situational inertia may sustain categories; they may be defended because they provide meanings that matter to one group or another. In such cases, human beings tend to use ethnic and racial categories to defy the complexities of genealogy, imposing boundaries and simplicity on others' identities and on their own.

The Unmixing of Peoples

The Yugoslav case we reviewed in Chapter 5 captures well this second trend, which is amply evident as we make the transition between centuries. It is a trend toward dissimilation, the separation of peoples, and the consolidation of ethnic and racial identities. It is apparent not only in the collapse of Yugoslavia but also in the post-Soviet migration of ethnic Russians from former Soviet Republics back to Russia (Brubaker 1995). It is apparent in the effort by the government of French-speaking Quebec to separate from Canada and in the threat by aboriginal peoples to separate from Quebec (Salée 1995). We can see it in the Tamil-Sinhalese conflict in Sri Lanka, in the quest for autonomy and an end to immigration among the indigenous peoples of Assam in India, and in the relentless slaughter in Rwanda and Burundi. It is apparent in the anti-immigrant and white supremacy movements in Europe and the United States and in the argument by the U.S. National Association of Black Social Workers that transracial adoption is genocide.

The task for those who promote this "unmixing of peoples" (Brubaker 1995) is to root out ambiguity and multiplicity and to preserve and protect above all else the integrity, rights, and independence of the group. Their rhetoric is the essentialist rhetoric of primordialism, finding ultimate links among persons if not in blood then in a cultural endowment too deep and fundamental to be ignored or in a historical experience too indelible to ever disappear. The unmixing of peoples involves perpetuating or establishing those links—real or imagined—as the bases of human organization, identity, and action.

One of the most interesting aspects of this trend is that much of it is driven by the very peoples who once hoped to throw off ethnic and racial labels in favor of more cosmopolitan citizenship or other forms of group identity. Ethnicity and, in particular, race once were largely the work of the powerful who used them as ways to identify and subordinate peoples and keep them apart. Today, they have become as well the fierce possessions of the offended, the poor, the disconnected, and the powerless. They, too, use ethnicity and race to establish identity and distance but also as bases of a struggle for recognition and against subordination. Their wholehearted endorsement of those identities and their effort to claim them as their own suggest that the roots of this trend lie in the continuing disparities in wealth, power, and status among groups and nations, in the insecurities and uncertainties of modernity, and in the simplifying power of ethnic and racial categories. Those categories continue to serve as both refuge and resource in the contemporary world.

Making Sense, Making Selves

It is difficult to say which of these trends—mixing and multiplicity, separation and consolidation—will prevail in the 21st century. They are not mutually exclusive. In American society, for example, there has been massive mixing among European groups and some others and more moderate mixing across some racial boundaries. There also is a persistent separation along other boundaries, in particular along the divide that separates Black from White. In some societies, one pattern appears to be ascendant; in some societies, the other. In some parts of the world, as in the United States, both are apparent. There also are societies where ethnicity and race play little role in social life or in individual or collective identities. Which is the more powerful trend? In 20 years, or in 50 years, which pattern will best describe a changing world?

We pose these questions but cannot fully answer them. It seems unlikely that ethnicity and race will disappear. The factors that promote them as bases of identity and action will continue to have an impact in human affairs. On the other hand, the intermingling of human peoples has become a global phenomenon. It seems equally likely to continue and perhaps to accelerate. The relative fortunes of multiplicity and consolidation will be determined in part by the specific situations in which human beings—mixed and unmixed—find themselves. Perhaps the most reliable prediction is that both trends will prevail in the century ahead, but in different places.

These trends are a study in contrasts. One emphasizes individuals and commonalities; the other emphasizes groups and differences. One downplays boundaries; the other is obsessed with them. One celebrates the complexity of identities; the other relentlessly simplifies them.

Despite these and other differences between them, these trends have much in common. Both have roots in the global processes that are transforming the world. Both reflect the diverse efforts of human beings to make sense of their lives and the changing world around them, to pursue their interests, or to find or fashion meanings for themselves.

It is possible also that the two will combine, albeit in a distinctive way. It might be argued that the world is moving toward a simplifying kind of separatism: the emergence of a relatively small number of collective identities that cut across the political boundaries of states, building a mosaic of global ethnicities. Like multiethnicity, this scenario involves mixing; like separation, it involves difference. Where it departs from both is in scope and scale. Its defining feature is diasporas: globally dispersed populations whose origins lie in a single homeland or set of linked homelands. Perhaps the best-known diasporic population is Jewry, but the extent and diversity of contemporary international migration have given diasporas new prominence. Thus, Black populations in the United States, Canada, Britain, the Caribbean, and Latin America can see themselves as carrying, to some degree, a common identity. They share African roots. They share the historical experiences of slavery or other systematic forms of exploitation or discrimination. They share, historically at least, the experience of migration and adjustment to countries and cultures in no way their own. Increasingly, thanks to the globalizing effects of mass media and the facilitations of communication and transportation technologies, they can share as well a language of identity and a set of symbols and practices that make Blackness—the construction by Black peoples of a common ethnicity—not only a local but a global phenomenon. "Black Britain," for example,

> defines itself crucially as part of a diaspora. Its unique cultures draw inspiration from those developed by black populations elsewhere. In particular, the culture and politics of black America and the Caribbean have become raw materials for creative processes which redefine what it means to be black, adapting it to distinctively British experience and meanings. (Gilroy 1987:154)

Diasporas have become a common feature of the modern world. Not all will lead to diasporic identities, but some surely will. One of the effects of the growing salience of such identities in some people's lives is to reduce the sense of affiliation to the states in which those diasporic populations reside. Those states become the settings of identities "whose center is elsewhere" (Taylor 1994:63), an elsewhere that may not be geographical at all but consists of an imagined core of understandings and experience, a narrative of diaspora itself.

Just how powerful such diasporic identities are likely to become in the future is difficult to say. Constructed through global connections, a common rhetoric, and long-distance cultural exchange, they tend to be thinner than ethnicities that are locally made and are typically adjuncts to thicker and more localized conceptions of the group. As the quote on Britain's Blacks suggests, the materials used in constructing identities may draw from far and wide, but their use and interpretation is mediated through local conditions and understandings. Comparing the descendants of Indian immigrants to the island states of Mauritius and Trinidad, anthropologist Thomas Eriksen (1992:122) points out that "Indians in a poly-ethnic society outside of India cannot adequately be viewed simply as Indians. They are Indians in a particular historical and socio-cultural context, and this is an inextricable part of their life—even those aspects of their life which pertain to their very Indianness."

Globalization has precipitated identity construction on an unprecedented scale, altered the conditions under which it occurs, and vastly expanded the repertoires of symbols and ideas available to ethnic and racial groups around the world, but the thickest identities—those that most completely organize daily experiences and agendas—tend to be locally constructed. They are the outcomes of local conditions, needs, interests, experiences, and understandings—that is, of the situations groups and persons deal with every day.

Conclusion

The process of identity construction is at times purposeful, at times disinterested, unintentional, or wholly circumstantial. Collective identity may emerge as part of how groups meet their perceived needs, or it may be part of a gradually assembled view or explanation of the group and the surrounding world. To construct an identity is to construct an account of who "we"—or "they"—are. Behind the ethnic or racial label, behind the name, there lies a sometimes explicit, sometimes implicit story: "We are the people who . . . ," or alternatively, "They are the people who . . . ." What follows is a narrative—a selection and arrangement of events and interpretations—that indicates what separates "us" from "them," that gives significance to that separation, and that attaches a meaning or a value to the resulting category (Cornell 1999). "The problem of identity is the problem of arriving at a life story that makes sense" (McAdams 1985:18). From William Kauaiwiulaokalani Wallace chanting his genealogy to the Afrikaners' celebration of their peoplehood; from the Hutus' search for a history they could call their own to Black Americans' reclaiming of theirs—in these and myriad other cases, human beings variously search out, re-create, discover, and invent life stories that make sense. They do so not only as individuals but as groups, imagining themselves and others, turning those imaginings into identities. Out of real or imagined events—migration, colonization, struggle, triumph, defeat, survival—they create stories that in turn fashion people and relationships. They build narratives that variously assert or justify claims, mobilize compatriots, establish worth or meaning, defend interpretations, resolve dilemmas, undermine or reinforce relations of dominance or subordination. Some do so under conditions of relative freedom; they have the power not only to create narratives about themselves or others but to distribute them to a wider public and to establish them as something more than stories: as fact, wisdom, truth. Others struggle to resist the stories told about them or to make their own stories heard at all.

Ethnicity and race are among the idioms through which people compose such tales. People often tell their stories or the stories they fashion about other groups in ethnic and racial ways, focusing on ethnic or racial aspects of the narrative or using those categories to describe the stories' subjects and explain the constituent events. In so doing, they both assert that ethnicity or race is important and make claims about what kinds of groups "we" or "they" are.

The idioms of ethnicity and race are unusually powerful. In their implied references to physicality, blood, biology, or descent, they suggest something deeper and more compelling than convenience or utility or a search for meaning. But even their implied primordiality is a construction; it is not part of the world out there but part of the story we tell about it.

These stories have consequences. Some become justifications for the ways groups treat one another. They are used to explain—or to explain away—discrimination, exclusion, violence, genocide. Others become foundations of collective resistance, articulating claims and justifying action. Some are stories of inclusion that reach across boundaries and distances, celebrating and linking together not one past but many. Others focus on boundaries, specifying distance and difference. Some are told first in passionate assertion or defense of group boundaries and consolidation but eventually come to matter—and to be told—less and less as the years go by. Others last only a short time before the interests that motivate them change and the identities they helped create fade away to little more than a memory.

The consequences matter far more than the idioms do. There is little inherently good or bad about ethnicity or race. They are categories invented—like other categories—by human beings, and in this they are of little distinctive importance. What makes them significant is what human beings do with them: the ways those categories have been and continue to be used. The critical issue for the 21st century is not whether ethnicity and race will continue to serve as categories of collective identity but what kinds of ethnic and racial stories groups tell and how those stories are put to use.

References

Aguirre, Adalberto, Jr., and Jonathan H. Turner. 1995. *American Ethnicity: The Dynamics and Consequences of Discrimination*. New York: McGraw-Hill.

Alba, Richard D. 1985. *Italian Americans: Into the Twilight of Ethnicity*. Englewood Cliffs, NJ: Prentice Hall.

————. 1990. *Ethnic Identity: The Transformation of White America*. New Haven, CT: Yale University Press.

Alba, Richard D. and Mitchell B. Chamlin. 1983. "A Preliminary Examination of Ethnic Identification Among Whites." *American Sociological Review* 48:240-47.

Albers, Patricia C. and William R. James. 1986. "On the Dialectics of Ethnicity: To Be or Not to Be Santee (Sioux)." *Journal of Ethnic Studies* 14:1-27.

Alexander, Jack. 1977. "The Culture of Race in Middle-Class Kingston, Jamaica." *American Ethnologist* 4:413-35.

Alexander, Jeffrey. 1988. "Core Solidarity, Ethnic Outgroup and Social Differentiation." Pp. 78-106 in *Action and Its Environments*. New York: Columbia University Press.

Almaguer, Tomás. 1994. *Racial Fault Lines: The Historical Origins of White Supremacy in California*. Berkeley: University of California Press.

Altschuler, Glenn C. 1982. *Race, Ethnicity and Class in American Social Thought, 1865-1919*. Arlington Heights, IL: Harlan Davidson.

Anderson, Benedict. 1983. *Imagined Communities: Reflections on the Origin and Spread of Nationalism*. New York: Verso.

Appadurai, Arjun. 1990. "Disjuncture and Difference in the Global Cultural Economy." *Public Culture* 2:1-24.

Arlen, Michael. 1975. *Passage to Ararat*. New York: Farrar, Straus, and Giroux.

Bakalian, Anny. 1993. *Armenian-Americans: From Being to Feeling Armenian*. New Brunswick, NJ: Transaction.

Banac, Ivo. 1984. *The National Question in Yugoslavia: Origins, History, Politics*. Ithaca, NY: Cornell University Press.

Banton, Michael. 1977. *The Idea of Race*. London: Tavistock.

————. 1983. *Racial and Ethnic Competition*. Cambridge, UK: Cambridge University Press.

Barney, Robert Knight. 1994. "Forty-Eighters and the Rise of the Turnverein Movement in America." Pp. 19-42 in *Ethnicity and Sport in North America*, edited by George Eisen and David K. Wiggens. Westport, CT: Greenwood Press.

Barrera, Mario. 1979. *Race and Class in the Southwest*. Notre Dame, IN: University of Notre Dame Press.

Barth, Fredrik. 1969. "Introduction." Pp. 9-38 in *Ethnic Groups and Boundaries: The Social Organization of Culture Difference*, edited by Fredrik Barth. Boston: Little, Brown.

Bell, Derrick. 1992. *Faces at the Bottom of the Well: The Permanence of Racism*. New York: Basic Books.

Beloff, Nora. 1985. *Tito's Flawed Legacy: Yugoslavia and the West, 1939-1984*. London: Gollancz.

Benjamin, Lois. 1991. *The Black Elite: Facing the Color Line in the Twilight of the Twentieth Century*. Chicago: Nelson-Hall.

Bentley, G. Carter. 1987. "Ethnicity and Practice." *Comparative Studies in Society and History* 29:24-55.

Berger, John and Jean Mohr. 1982. *A Seventh Man*. London: Writers and Readers.

Berry, Brewton. 1965. *Race and Ethnic Relations*. 3d ed. Boston: Houghton Mifflin.

Bhardwaj, Surinder M. and N. Madhusudana Rao. 1990. "Asian Indians in the United States: A Geographic Appraisal." Pp. 197-217 in *South Asians Overseas: Migration and Ethnicity*, edited by Colin Clarke, Ceri Peach, and Steven Vertovec. Cambridge, UK: Cambridge University Press.

Black, C. E. 1966. *The Dynamics of Modernization: A Study in Comparative History*. New York: Harper and Row.

Blauner, Robert. 1969. "Internal Colonialism and Ghetto Revolt." *Social Problems* 16:393-408.

Blu, Karen I. 1980. *The Lumbee Problem: The Making of an American Indian People*. Cambridge, UK: Cambridge University Press.

Bogle, Donald. 1973. *Toms, Coons, Mulattoes, Mammies, and Bucks: An Interpretive History of Blacks in American Films*. New York: Viking.

Bonacich, Edna. 1973. "A Theory of Middleman Minorities." *American Sociological Review* 38:583-94.

———. 1976. "Advanced Capitalism and Black/White Race Relations in the United States: A Split Labor Market Interpretation." *American Sociological Review* 41:34-51.

Bonacich, Edna and John Modell. 1980. *The Economic Basis of Ethnic Solidarity: Small Business in the Japanese American Community*. Berkeley: University of California Press.

Bradley, James W. 1987. *Evolution of the Onondaga Iroquois: Accommodating Change, 1500-1655*. Syracuse, NY: Syracuse University Press.

Brass, Paul R. 1991. *Ethnicity and Nationalism: Theory and Comparison.* Newbury Park, CA: Sage.

Brereton, Bridget. 1993. "Social Organisation and Class, Racial and Cultural Conflict in 19th Century Trinidad." Pp. 33-55 in *Trinidad Ethnicity*, edited by Kevin A. Yelvington. Knoxville: University of Tennessee Press.

Breton, Raymond. 1964. "Institutional Completeness of Ethnic Communities and the Personal Relations of Immigrants." *American Journal of Sociology* 70:193-205.

Brower, Kenneth. 1983. *A Song for Satawal.* New York: Harper and Row.

Brubaker, Rogers. 1995. "Aftermaths of Empire and the Unmixing of Peoples: Historical and Comparative Perspectives." *Ethnic and Racial Studies* 18: 189-218.

Brundage, W. Fitzhugh. 1993. *Lynching in the New South: Georgia and Virginia, 1880-1930.* Urbana: University of Illinois Press.

Buckley, Stephen. 1996. "Wounds That Won't Heal." *Washington Post National Weekly Edition*, June 17-23, p. 16.

Burgess, M. Elaine. 1978. "The Resurgence of Ethnicity: Myth or Reality?" *Ethnic and Racial Studies* 1:265-85.

Butler, Jeffrey, Robert I. Rotberg, and John Adams. 1977. *The Black Homelands of South Africa.* Berkeley: University of California Press.

Cadaval, Olivia. 1991. "Making a Place Home: The Latino Festival." Pp. 204-22 in *Creative Ethnicity: Symbols and Strategies of Contemporary Ethnic Life*, edited by Stephen Stern and John Allan Cicala. Logan: Utah State University Press.

Calhoun, Craig. 1993. "Nationalism and Ethnicity." *Annual Review of Sociology* 19:211-39.

Carmichael, Stokely and Charles Hamilton. 1967. *Black Power.* New York: Vintage.

Carter, Bob, Marci Green, and Rick Halpern. 1996. "Immigration Policy and the Racialization of Migrant Labor: The Construction of National Identities in the USA and Britain." *Ethnic and Racial Studies* 19:135-57.

Castles, Stephen. 1984. *Here for Good: Western Europe's New Ethnic Minorities.* London: Pluto Press.

Castles, Stephen and Godula Kosack. 1973. *Immigrant Workers and Class Structure in Western Europe.* London: Oxford University Press.

Clarke, Colin, Ceri Peach, and Steven Vertovec. 1990. "Introduction." Pp. 1-29 in *South Asians Overseas: Migration and Ethnicity*, edited by Colin Clarke, Ceri Peach, and Steven Vertovec. Cambridge, UK: Cambridge University Press.

Clines, Francis X. 1995. "Ethnic Clichés Put Anger in Irish Eyes." *The New York Times*, March 12, p. 18.

Cohen, Abner. 1969. *Custom and Politics in Urban Africa.* Berkeley: University of California Press.

————. 1974. *Two-Dimensional Man: An Essay on the Anthropology of Power and Symbolism in Complex Society.* Berkeley: University of California Press.

Cohen, Gary B. 1981. *The Politics of Ethnic Survival: Germans in Prague, 1861-1914.* Princeton, NJ: Princeton University Press.

————. 1992. "The German Minority of Prague, 1850-1918." Pp. 267-93 in *Ethnic Identity in Urban Europe*, edited by Max Engman. New York: New York University Press.

Cohen, Roger. 1995. "History Finds Bosnia Somewhere Between Ethnic Harmony, Hatred." *San Diego Union-Tribune*, December 15, p. A-27.

Colburn, David R. and George E. Pozzetta. 1994. "Race, Ethnicity and the Evolution of Political Legitimacy." Pp. 119-48 in *The Sixties: From Memory to History*, edited by David Farber. Chapel Hill: North Carolina University Press.

Coleman, James S. 1988. "Social Capital in the Creation of Human Capital." *American Journal of Sociology* 94:S95-S120.

————. 1990. *Foundations of Social Theory.* Cambridge, MA: Harvard University Press.

Collins, Sharon M. 1983. "The Making of the Black Middle Class." *Social Problems* 30: 369-82.

Comaroff, John. 1991. "Humanity, Ethnicity and Nationality: Conceptual and Comparative Perspectives on the USSR." *Theory and Society* 20:661-87.

Connor, Walker. 1978. "A Nation Is a Nation, Is a State, Is an Ethnic Group, Is a. . . ." *Ethnic and Racial Studies* 1:377-400.

————. 1990. "When Is a Nation?" *Ethnic and Racial Studies* 13:92-103.

————. 1993. "Beyond Reason: The Nature of the Ethnonational Bond." *Ethnic and Racial Studies* 16:373-89.

Conzen, Kathleen Neils. 1976. *Immigrant Milwaukee 1836-1860.* Cambridge, MA: Harvard University Press.

————. 1985. "German-Americans and the Invention of Ethnicity." Pp. 131-147 in *America and the Germans: An Assessment of a Three-Hundred-Year History.* Vol. 1, *Immigration, Language, Ethnicity*, edited by Frank Trommler and Joseph McVeigh. Philadelphia: University of Pennsylvania Press.

————. 1989. "Ethnicity as Festive Culture: Nineteenth-Century German America on Parade." Pp. 44-76 in *The Invention of Ethnicity*, edited by Werner Sollors. New York: Oxford University Press.

Conzen, Kathleen N., David A. Gerber, Eva Morawska, George E. Pozzetta, and Rudolph J. Vecoli. 1992. "The Invention of Ethnicity: A Perspective From the USA." *Journal of American Ethnic History* 12:3-41.

Cornell, Stephen. 1988. *The Return of the Native: American Indian Political Resurgence.* New York: Oxford University Press.

————. 1990. "Land, Labour, and Group Formation: Blacks and Indians in the United States." *Ethnic and Racial Studies* 13:368-88.

————. 1996. "The Variable Ties That Bind: Content and Circumstance in Ethnic Processes." *Ethnic and Racial Studies* 19:265-89.

————. 1999. "That's the Story of Our Life: Ethnicity and Narrative, Rupture and Power." In *We Are a People: Narrative and Multiplicity in the Construction of Ethnic Identities*, edited by Paul R. Spickard and Jeffrey Burroughs. Philadelphia: Temple University Press.

Crouch, Stanley. 1996. "Race Is Over: Black, White, Red, Yellow—Same Difference." *The New York Times Magazine*, September 29, pp. 170-71.

Dahya, Badr. 1974. "The Nature of Pakistani Ethnicity in Industrial Cities in Britain." Pp. 77-118 in *Urban Ethnicity*, edited by Abner Cohen. London: Tavistock.

Davidson, Basil. 1992. *The Black Man's Burden: Africa and the Curse of the Nation-State*. New York: Times Books.

Davis, F. James. 1991. *Who Is Black? One Nation's Definition*. University Park: Pennsylvania State University Press.

Davis, G. Scott, ed. 1996. *Religion and Justice in the War Over Bosnia*. New York: Routledge.

de la Garza, Rodolfo O., Louis DeSipio, F. Chris Garcia, John Garcia, and Angelo Falcon. 1992. *Latino Voices: Mexican, Puerto Rican, and Cuban Perspectives on American Politics*. Boulder, CO: Westview Press.

Despres, Leo A. 1975. "Ethnicity and Resource Competition in Guyanese Society." Pp. 87-117 in *Ethnicity and Resource Competition in Plural Societies*, edited by Leo A. Despres. The Hague: Mouton.

Destexhe, Alain. 1995. *Rwanda and Genocide in the Twentieth Century*. New York: New York University Press.

Deutsch, Karl. 1961. "Social Mobilization and Political Development." *American Political Science Review* 55:493-514.

□□□. 1966. *Nationalism and Social Communication*. Cambridge: MIT Press.

De Vos, George A. and William O. Wetherall. 1974. *Japan's Minorities: Burakumin, Koreans and Ainu*. London: Minority Rights Group.

Djilas, Aleksa. 1991. "Yugoslavia's Trap of Ethnic Confrontation." *The New York Times*, July 7, p. E3.

Dollard, John. [1937] 1957. *Caste and Class in a Southern Town*. Reprint, New York: Doubleday.

Dominguez, Virginia R. 1986. *White by Definition: Social Classification in Creole Louisiana*. New Brunswick, NJ: Rutgers University Press.

Dragadze, Tamara. 1996. "Self-Determination and the Politics of Exclusion." *Ethnic and Racial Studies* 19:341-51.

D'Souza, Dinesh. 1995. *The End of Racism*. New York: Free Press.

Eberle, Scott. 1987. "Neighbors: The People of Erie County." Pp. 73-101 in *Second Looks: A Pictorial History of Buffalo and Erie County*, edited by Scott Eberle and Joseph A. Grinde. Norfolk: The Donning Company.

Edwards, John. 1984. "Language, Diversity and Identity." Pp. 276-310 in *Linguistic Minorities, Policies and Pluralism*, edited by John Edwards. London: Academic Press.

Eisenstadt, Shmuel N. and Stein Rokkan, eds. 1973. *Building States and Nations*. Beverly Hills, CA: Sage.

Eller, Jack David and Reed M. Coughlan. 1993. "The Poverty of Primordialism: The Demystification of Ethnic Attachments." *Ethnic and Racial Studies* 16:183-202.

Elshtain, Jean Bethke. 1996. "Nationalism and Self-Determination: The Bosnian Tragedy." Pp. 45-62 in *Religion and Justice in the War Over Bosnia*, edited by G. Scott Davis. New York: Routledge.

Enloe, Cynthia H. 1980. *Ethnic Soldiers: State Security in Divided Societies*. Athens: University of Georgia Press.

Epstein, A. L. 1978. *Ethos and Identity: Three Studies in Ethnicity*. London: Tavistock.

Eriksen, Thomas Hylland. 1992. *Us and Them in Modern Societies: Ethnicity and Nationalism in Mauritius, Trinidad and Beyond*. Oslo: Scandinavian University Press.

Eschbach, Karl. 1995. "The Enduring and Vanishing American Indian: American Indian Population Growth and Intermarriage in 1990." *Ethnic and Racial Studies* 18:89-108.

Esman, Marjorie R. 1983. "Internal Conflict and Ethnic Activism: The Louisiana Cajuns." *Human Organization* 42:57-59.

Espiritu, Yen Le. 1992. *Asian American Panethnicity: Bridging Institutions and Identities*. Philadelphia: Temple University Press.

———. 1996. "Colonial Oppression, Labour Importation, and Group Formation: Filipinos in the United States." *Ethnic and Racial Studies* 19:29-48.

Farley, John E. 1995. *Majority-Minority Relations*. 3d. ed. Englewood Cliffs, NJ: Prentice Hall.

Farnsworth, Clyde H. 1995. "Quebec, by Razor-Thin Margin, Votes 'No' on Leaving Canada." *The New York Times*, October 31, pp. A1, A12.

Feagin, Joe R. and Clairece Booth Feagin. 1996. *Racial and Ethnic Relations*. 5th ed. Upper Saddle River, NJ: Prentice Hall.

Feagin, Joe R. and Melvin P. Sikes. 1994. *Living With Racism: The Black Middle-Class Experience*. Boston: Beacon.

Fernandez, Carlos A. 1996. "Government Classification of Multiracial/Multiethnic People." Pp. 15-36 in *The Multiracial Experience: Racial Borders as the New Frontier*, edited by Maria P. P. Root. Thousand Oaks, CA: Sage.

Finnegan, William. 1995. "The Victor in Bosnia: Not Serbs, Muslims, or Croats, but Tribalism Itself." *The New Yorker*, October 9, pp. 5-6.

Frankenberg, Ruth. 1993. *White Women, Race Matters: The Social Construction of Whiteness*. Minneapolis: University of Minnesota Press.

Fugita, Stephen S. and David J. O'Brien. 1991. *Japanese American Ethnicity: The Persistence of Community*. Seattle: University of Washington Press.

Gans, Herbert J. 1979. "Symbolic Ethnicity: The Future of Ethnic Groups and Cultures in America." *Ethnic and Racial Studies* 2:1-20.

Geertz, Clifford. 1963. "The Integrative Revolution: Primordial Sentiments and Civil Politics in the New States." Pp. 105-57 in *Old Societies and New States: The Quest for Modernity in Asia and Africa*, edited by Clifford Geertz. New York: Free Press.

Genovese, Eugene D. 1976. *Roll, Jordan, Roll: The World the Slaves Made*. New York: Vintage.

———. 1979. *From Rebellion to Revolution: Afro-American Slave Revolts in the Making of the Modern World*. Baton Rouge: Louisiana State University Press.

Gerhart, Gail M. 1978. *Black Power in South Africa: The Evolution of an Ideology*. Berkeley: University of California Press.

Giddens, Anthony. 1990. *The Consequences of Modernity*. Stanford, CA: Stanford University Press.

Gilberg, Trond. 1980. "State Policy, Ethnic Persistence and Nationality Formation in Eastern Europe." Pp. 185-235 in *Ethnic Diversity and Conflict in Eastern Europe*, edited by Peter F. Sugar. Santa Barbara, CA: ABC-Clio.

Giliomee, Hermann. 1979. "The Growth of Afrikaner Identity." Pp. 83-127 in *Ethnic Power Mobilized: Can South Africa Change?*, edited by Heribert Adam and Hermann Giliomee. New Haven, CT: Yale University Press.

Gilroy, Paul. 1987. *There Ain't No Black in the Union Jack: The Cultural Politics of Race and Nation*. Chicago: University of Chicago Press.

Gladwell, Malcolm. 1996. "Black Like Them." *The New Yorker*, April 29 and May 6, pp. 74-81.

Glazer, Nathan and Daniel P. Moynihan. 1963. *Beyond the Melting Pot: The Negroes, Puerto Ricans, Jews, Italians, and Irish of New York City*. Cambridge: MIT Press.

———. 1970. *Beyond the Melting Pot: The Negroes, Puerto Ricans, Jews, Italians, and Irish of New York City*. 2d ed. Cambridge: MIT Press.

———. 1975. "Introduction." Pp. 1-26 in *Ethnicity: Theory and Experience*, edited by Nathan Glazer and Daniel P. Moynihan. Cambridge, MA: Harvard University Press.

Glick, Clarence. 1938. "Transition From Familism to Nationalism Among Chinese in Hawaii." *American Journal of Sociology* 43:734-43.

Gomez, Laura. 1986. "What's in a Name? The Politics of Hispanic Identity." B.A. Honors Thesis, Harvard College, Cambridge, MA.

Gordon, David M., Richard Edwards, and Michael Reich. 1982. *Segmented Work, Divided Workers: The Historical Transformation of Labor in the United States*. New York: Cambridge University Press.

Gordon, Milton. 1964. *Assimilation in American Life: The Role of Race, Religion, and National Origins*. New York: Oxford University Press.

———. 1978. *Human Nature, Class, and Ethnicity*. New York: Oxford University Press.

Gossett, Thomas F. 1963. *Race: The History of an Idea in America*. New York: Schocken.

Gould, Stephen Jay. 1981. *The Mismeasure of Man*. New York: W. W. Norton.

———. 1994. "The Geometer of Race." *Discover* 15 (November):64-69.

Gourevitch, Philip. 1995. "Letter From Rwanda: After the Genocide." *The New Yorker*, December 18, pp. 78-95.

Griswold, Wendy. 1994. *Cultures and Societies in a Changing World*. Thousand Oaks, CA: Pine Forge Press.

Gutman, Herbert G. 1976. *The Black Family in Slavery and Freedom, 1750-1925*. New York: Random House.

Hagan, William T. 1976. *United States-Comanche Relations: The Reservation Years*. New Haven, CT: Yale University Press.

Haley, Alex. 1976. *Roots*. Garden City, NJ: Doubleday.

Hall, Stuart. 1992. "New Ethnicities." Pp. 252-59 in *"Race," Culture and Difference*, edited by James Donald and Ali Rattansi. London: Sage.

Hall, Stuart, David Held, and Tony McGrew, eds. 1992. *Modernity and Its Futures*. Cambridge, UK: Polity Press.

Handlin, Oscar. 1973. *The Uprooted*. 2d ed. Boston: Little, Brown.

Hannan, Michael T. 1979. "The Dynamics of Ethnic Boundaries in Modern States." Pp. 253-75 in *National Development and the World System: Educational, Economic, and Political Change, 1950-1970*, edited by John W. Meyer and Michael T. Hannan. Chicago: University of Chicago Press.

Hanson, Allan. 1989. "The Making of the Maori: Culture Invention and Its Logic." *American Anthropologist* 91:890-902.

———. 1991a. "Reply to Langdon, Levine, and Linnekin." *American Anthropologist* 93:449-50.

———. 1991b. *When the Natives Talk Back: Thinking About Narrative in Anthropology*. Paper presented to the Hall Center Narrative Seminar, University of Kansas, Lawrence.

Hawgood, John A. 1940. *The Tragedy of German-America: The Germans in the United States of America During the Nineteenth Century—and After*. New York: G. P. Putnam.

Hechter, Michael. 1975. *Internal Colonialism: The Celtic Fringe in British National Development, 1536-1966*. Berkeley: University of California Press.

Hedges, Chris. 1995. "Arabs, Too, Play the Ethnic Card." *The New York Times*, March 5, p. E4.

Henry, Ralph M. 1993. "Notes on the Evolution of Inequality in Trinidad and Tobago." Pp. 56-80 in *Trinidad Ethnicity*, edited by Kevin A. Yelvington. Knoxville: University of Tennessee Press.

Henry, William A., III. 1993. "The Politics of Separation." *Time* 142(21):73-75.

Hiltzik, Michael A. 1992. "Ethnic Pride Gets a Test in Africa." *The Los Angeles Times*, February 11, p. A-1.

Hirschman, Charles. 1986. "The Making of Race in Colonial Malaya: Political Economy and Racial Ideology." *Sociological Forum* 1:330-61.

Hollinger, David A. 1995. *Postethnic America: Beyond Multiculturalism.* New York: Basic Books.

Horowitz, Donald L. 1985. *Ethnic Groups in Conflict.* Berkeley: University of California Press.

Huggins, Nathan. 1979. *Black Odyssey: The Afro-American Ordeal in Slavery.* New York: Vintage.

Hutchinson, John and Anthony D. Smith. 1994. "Introduction." Pp. 3-13 in *Nationalism,* edited by John Hutchinson and Anthony D. Smith. New York: Oxford University Press.

Iganski, Paul and Geoff Payne. 1996. "Declining Racial Disadvantage in the British Labour Market." *Ethnic and Racial Studies* 19:113-34.

Ignatiev, Noel. 1995. *How the Irish Became White.* New York: Routledge.

Isaacs, Harold R. 1975. *Idols of the Tribe: Group Identity and Political Change.* Cambridge, MA: Harvard University Press.

Ito-Adler, James. 1980. *The Portuguese in Cambridge and Somerville.* Cambridge, MA: Department of Planning and Development.

Jenkins, Richard. 1994. "Rethinking Ethnicity: Identity, Categorization and Power." *Ethnic and Racial Studies* 17:197-223.

Jesudason, James V. 1990. *Ethnicity and the Economy: The State, Chinese Business, and Multinationals in Malaysia.* Singapore: Oxford University Press.

Jones, Stephen. 1994. "Old Ghosts and New Chains: Ethnicity and Memory in the Georgian Republic." Pp. 149-65 in *Memory, History, and Opposition Under State Socialism,* edited by Rubie S. Watson. Santa Fe, NM: School of American Research Press.

Jordan, Winthrop D. 1968. *White Over Black: American Attitudes Toward the Negro, 1550-1812.* Baltimore: Penguin.

Just, Roger. 1989. "Triumph of the Ethnos." Pp. 71-88 in *History and Ethnicity,* edited by Elizabeth Tonkin, Maryon McDonald, and Malcolm Chapman. London: Routledge.

Kamphoefner, Walter D. 1987. *The Westfalians: From Germany to Missouri.* Princeton, NJ: Princeton University Press.

———. 1996. "German Americans: Paradoxes of a 'Model Minority.' " Pp. 152-60 in *Origins and Destinies: Immigration, Race and Ethnicity in America,* edited by Sylvia Padraza and Ruben Rumbant. New York: Wadsworth.

Kaplan, Robert D. 1993. *Balkan Ghosts: A Journey Through History.* New York: St. Martin's Press.

Karabel, Jerome. 1979. "The Failure of American Socialism Reconsidered." Pp. 204-27 in *The Socialist Register 1979,* edited by Ralph Miliband and John Saville. London: Merlin Press.

Kasinitz, Philip. 1992. *Caribbean New York: Black Immigrants and the Politics of Race.* Ithaca, NY: Cornell University Press.

Katznelson, Ira. 1976. *Black Men, White Cities: Race, Politics, and Migration in the United States, 1900-1930, and Britain, 1948-1968*. Chicago: University of Chicago Press.

———. 1981. *City Trenches: Urban Politics and the Patterning of Class in the United States*. New York: Pantheon.

Keane, Fergal. 1995. *Season of Blood: A Rwandan Journey*. London: Viking.

Khazanov, Anatoly M. 1995. *After the USSR: Ethnicity, Nationalism, and Politics in the Commonwealth of Independent States*. Madison: University of Wisconsin Press.

Kim, Illsoo. 1987. "The Koreans: Small Business in an Urban Frontier." Pp. 219-42 in *New Immigrants in New York*, edited by Nancy Foner. New York: Columbia University Press.

King, James C. 1981. *The Biology of Race*. 2d ed. Berkeley: University of California Press.

Kitano, Harry H. L. and Roger Daniels. 1995. *Asian Americans: Emerging Minorities*. 2d ed. Englewood Cliffs, NJ: Prentice Hall.

Kwong, Julia. 1984. "Ethnic Organizations and Community Transformation: The Chinese in Winnipeg." *Ethnic and Racial Studies* 7:374-86.

Kwong, Peter. 1979. *Chinatown, New York: Labor and Politics, 1930-1950*. New York: Monthly Review Press.

Leonard, Karen Isaksen. 1992. *Making Ethnic Choices: California's Punjabi Mexican Americans*. Philadelphia: Temple University Press.

Levine, Hal B. and Marlene Wolfzahn Levine. 1979. *Urbanization in Papua New Guinea: A Study of Ambivalent Townsmen*. Cambridge, UK: Cambridge University Press.

Lewontin, R. C., Steven Rose, and Leon J. Kamin. 1984. *Not in Our Genes: Biology, Ideology, and Human Nature*. New York: Pantheon.

Lexington. 1996. "A Cheer for Olympo-Americans." *The Economist*, August 3, p. 30.

Lieberson, Stanley and Mary C. Waters. 1988. *From Many Strands: Ethnic and Racial Groups in Contemporary America*. New York: Russell Sage Foundation.

———. 1993. "The Ethnic Responses of Whites: What Causes Their Instability, Simplification, and Inconsistency?" *Social Forces* 72:421-51.

Lifton, Robert Jay. 1967. *Death in Life: Survivors of Hiroshima*. New York: Basic Books.

Light, Ivan and Edna Bonacich. 1988. *Immigrant Entrepreneurs: Koreans in Los Angeles, 1965-1982*. Berkeley: University of California Press.

Lim, Mah Hui. 1985. "Affirmative Action, Ethnicity and Integration: The Case of Malaysia." *Ethnic and Racial Studies* 8:250-76.

Lincoln, Bruce. 1989. *Discourse and the Construction of Society: Comparative Studies of Myth, Ritual, and Classification*. New York: Oxford University Press.

Linnekin, Jocelyn and Lin Poyer. 1990. *Cultural Identity and Ethnicity in the Pacific*. Honolulu: University of Hawaii Press.

Lipsitz, George. 1990. *Time Passages: Collective Memory and American Popular Culture*. Minneapolis: University of Minnesota Press.

———. 1991. "The Freidrich Jahn Statue: The Turnverein Legacy in St. Louis." Pp. 37-40 in *The Sidewalks of St. Louis*. Columbia: University of Missouri Press.

Loewen, James W. 1988. *The Mississippi Chinese: Between Black and White*. 2d ed. Prospect Heights, IL: Waverly Press.

Malkki, Liisa. 1990. "Context and Consciousness: Local Conditions for the Production of Historical and National Thought Among Hutu Refugees in Tanzania." Pp. 32-62 in *Nationalist Ideologies and the Production of National Cultures*, edited by Richard G. Fox. Washington: American Anthropological Association.

Maquet, Jacques J. 1961. *The Premise of Inequality in Ruanda: A Study of Political Relations in a Central African Kingdom*. London: Oxford University Press.

Marshall, Adriana. 1987. "New Immigrants in New York's Economy." Pp. 79-101 in *New Immigrants in New York*, edited by Nancy Foner. New York: Columbia University Press.

Massey, Douglas S. and Nancy A. Denton. 1993. *American Apartheid: Segregation and the Making of the Underclass*. Cambridge, MA: Harvard University Press.

McAdams, Dan P. 1985. *Power, Intimacy, and the Life Story: Personological Inquiries into Identity*. Homewood, IL: Dorsey.

McCall, Daniel F. 1955. "Dynamics of Urbanization in Africa." *Annals of the American Academy of Political and Social Science* 298:151-60.

McDowall, David. 1996. *A Modern History of the Kurds*. London: I. B. Tauris.

McKay, James. 1982. "An Exploratory Synthesis of Primordial and Mobilizationist Approaches to Ethnic Phenomena." *Ethnic and Racial Studies* 5:395-420.

Moodie, T. Dunbar. 1975. *The Rise of Afrikanerdom: Power, Apartheid, and the Afrikaner Civil Religion*. Berkeley: University of California Press.

Mormino, Gary R. and George E. Pozzetta. 1987. *The Immigrant World of Ybor City: Italians and Their Latin Neighbors in Tampa, 1885-1985*. Urbana: University of Illinois Press.

Myerhoff, Barbara G. 1974. *Peyote Hunt: The Sacred Journey of the Huichol Indians*. Ithaca, NY: Cornell University Press.

Nagata, Judith A. 1974. "What Is a Malay? Situational Selection of Ethnic Identity in a Plural Society." *American Ethnologist* 1:331-50.

———. 1981. "In Defense of Ethnic Boundaries: The Changing Myths and Charters of Malay Identity." Pp. 88-116 in *Ethnic Change*, edited by Charles F. Keyes. Seattle: University of Washington Press.

Nagel, Joane. 1986. "The Political Construction of Ethnicity." Pp. 93-112 in *Competitive Ethnic Relations*, edited by Susan Olzak and Joane Nagel. New York: Academic Press.

————. 1994. "Constructing Ethnicity: Creating and Recreating Ethnic Identity and Culture." *Social Problems* 41:152-76.

————. 1995. "Resource Competition Theories." *American Behavioral Scientist* 38:442-48.

————. 1996. *American Indian Ethnic Renewal: Red Power and the Resurgence of Identity and Culture*. New York: Oxford University Press.

Nagel, Joane and Susan Olzak. 1982. "Ethnic Mobilization in New and Old States: An Extension of the Competition Model." *Social Problems* 30:127-43.

Nagel, Joane and C. Matthew Snipp. 1993. "Ethnic Reorganization: American Indian Social, Economic, Political and Cultural Strategies for Survival." *Ethnic and Racial Studies* 16:203-35.

Nairn, Tom. 1977. *The Break-Up of Britain*. London: New Left Books.

Nee, Victor G. and Brett de Bary Nee. 1973. *Longtime Californ': A Documentary Study of an American Chinatown*. New York: Pantheon.

Newbury, Catharine. 1988. *The Cohesion of Oppression: Clientship and Ethnicity in Rwanda, 1860-1960*. New York: Columbia University Press.

Nisbet, Robert A. 1953. *The Quest for Community*. New York: Oxford University Press.

Novick, Peter. 1988. *That Noble Dream: The "Objectivity Question" and the American Historical Profession*. Cambridge, UK: Cambridge University Press.

Oakes, Penelope J., S. Alexander Haslam, and John C. Turner. 1994. *Stereotyping and Social Reality*. Oxford, UK: Blackwell.

Oboler, Suzanne. 1995. *Ethnic Labels, Latino Lives: Identity and the Politics of (Re)presentation in the United States*. Minneapolis: University of Minnesota Press.

O'Brian, Patrick. [1970] 1990. *Master and Commander*. Reprint, New York: W. W. Norton.

Olzak, Susan. 1992. *The Dynamics of Ethnic Competition and Conflict*. Stanford, CA: Stanford University Press.

Olzak, Susan and Joane Nagel, eds. 1986. *Competitive Ethnic Relations*. Orlando, FL: Academic Press.

Omi, Michael and Howard Winant. 1994. *Racial Formation in the United States: From the 1960s to the 1990s*. 2d ed. New York: Routledge.

Otite, Onigu. 1975. "Resource Competition and Inter-Ethnic Relations in Nigeria." Pp. 119-30 in *Ethnicity and Resource Competition in Plural Societies*, edited by Leo A. Despres. The Hague: Mouton.

Oxford University Press. 1993. *The New Shorter Oxford English Dictionary*, edited by Lesley Brown. Oxford, UK: Oxford University Press.

Padilla, Felix M. 1985. *Latino Ethnic Consciousness: The Case of Mexican Americans and Puerto Ricans in Chicago*. Notre Dame, IN: University of Notre Dame Press.

Park, Robert E. 1930. "Assimilation, Social." In *Encyclopedia of the Social Sciences* (vol. 2), edited by R. A. Seligman and Alvin Johnson. New York: Macmillan.

————. 1934. "Race Relations and Certain Frontiers." Pp. 57-85 in *Race and Culture Contacts*, edited by E. B. Reuter. New York: McGraw-Hill.

————. 1939. "The Nature of Race Relations." Pp. 3-45 in *Race Relations and the Race Problem*, edited by Edgar T. Thompson. Durham, NC: Duke University Press.

————. [1926] 1950. "Our Racial Frontier on the Pacific." Pp. 138-51 in *Race and Culture*. Glencoe, IL: The Free Press.

Park, Robert E. and Ernest W. Burgess. 1921. *Introduction to the Science of Sociology*. Chicago: University of Chicago Press.

Parkin, Frank. 1979. *Marxism and Class Theory: A Bourgeois Critique*. New York: Columbia University Press.

Patterson, Orlando. 1975. "Context and Choice in Ethnic Allegiance: A Theoretical Framework and Caribbean Case Study." Pp. 304-49 in *Ethnicity: Theory and Experience*, edited by Nathan Glazer and Daniel P. Moynihan. Cambridge, MA: Harvard University Press.

————. 1977. *Ethnic Chauvinism: The Reactionary Impulse*. New York: Stein and Day.

Peach, Ceri. 1980. "Ethnic Segregation and Intermarriage." *Annals of the Association of American Geographers* 70:371-81.

Pedraza-Bailey, Sylvia. 1985. *Political and Economic Migrants in America: Cubans and Mexicans*. Austin: University of Texas Press.

Peel, J. D. Y. 1989. "The Cultural Work of Yoruba Ethnogenesis." Pp. 198-215 in *History and Ethnicity*, edited by Elizabeth Tonkin, Maryon McDonald, and Malcolm Chapman. London: Routledge.

Pessar, Patricia R. 1987. "The Dominicans: Women in the Household and the Garment Industry." Pp. 103-29 in *New Immigrants in New York*, edited by Nancy Foner. New York: Columbia University Press.

Petersen, William. 1981. "Concepts of Ethnicity." Pp. 234-42 in *The Harvard Encyclopedia of American Ethnic Groups*, edited by Stephan Thernstrom, Anne Orlov, and Oscar Handlin. Cambridge, MA: Harvard University Press.

Peterson, Brent O. 1991. *Popular Narratives and Ethnic Identity: Literature and Community in "Die Abendschule."* Ithaca, NY: Cornell University Press.

Pieterse, Jan Nederveen. 1992. *White on Black: Images of Africa and Blacks in Western Popular Culture*. New Haven, CT: Yale University Press.

Piore, Michael J. 1979. *Birds of Passage: Migrant Labor and Industrial Societies*. Cambridge, UK: Cambridge University Press.

Pitt, David and Cluny Macpherson. 1974. *Emerging Pluralism: The Samoan Community in New Zealand*. Auckland: Longman Paul.

Pooley, Colin G. 1992. "The Irish in Liverpool Circa 1850-1940." Pp. 71-97 in *Ethnic Identity in Urban Europe*, edited by M. Engman. New York: New York University Press.

Portes, Alejandro and Robert L. Bach. 1985. *Latin Journey: Cuban and Mexican Immigrants in the United States.* Berkeley: University of California Press.

Portes, Alejandro and Ruben G. Rumbaut. 1990. *Immigrant America: A Portrait.* Berkeley: University of California Press.

Price, Richard. 1983. *First-Time: The Historical Vision of an Afro-American People.* Baltimore: Johns Hopkins University Press.

Putnam, Robert D. 1993. *Making Democracy Work: Civic Traditions in Modern Italy.* Princeton, NJ: Princeton University Press.

Pye, Lucian W. 1966. *Aspects of Political Development.* Boston: Little, Brown.

Ragin, Charles. 1977. "Class, Status, and 'Reactive Ethnic Cleavages': The Social Bases of Political Regionalism." *American Sociological Review* 42:438-50.

Reed, Adolph, Jr. 1996. "Skin Deep: The Fiction of Race." *The Village Voice*, September 24, p. 22.

Reed, Ishmael. 1989. "America's 'Black Only' Ethnicity." Pp. 226-29 in *The Invention of Ethnicity*, edited by Werner Sollors. New York: Oxford University Press.

Reitz, F. W. 1900. *A Century of Wrong.* London: Review of Reviews.

Reskin, Barbara and Irene Padavic. 1994. *Women and Men at Work.* Thousand Oaks, CA: Pine Forge Press.

Roosens, Eugeen E. 1989. *Creating Ethnicity: The Process of Ethnogenesis.* Newbury Park, CA: Sage.

Sacks, Karen Brodkin. 1994. "How Did Jews Become White Folks?" Pp. 78-102 in *Race*, edited by Steven Gregory and Roger Sanjek. New Brunswick, NJ: Rutgers University Press.

Sahlins, Marshall. 1985. *Islands of History.* Chicago: University of Chicago Press.

———. 1994. "Cosmologies of Capitalism: The Trans-Pacific Sector of 'The World-System.'" Pp. 412-55 in *Culture, Power, History: A Reader in Contemporary Social Theory*, edited by Nicholas B. Dirks, Geoff Eley, and Sherry B. Ortner. Princeton, NJ: Princeton University Press. Pp. 412-55.

Salée, Daniel. 1995. "Identities in Conflict: The Aboriginal Question and the Politics of Recognition in Quebec." *Ethnic and Racial Studies* 18:277-314.

Sanchez, George J. 1993. *Becoming Mexican American: Ethnicity, Culture and Identity in Chicano Los Angeles, 1900-1945.* New York: Oxford University Press.

Sánchez, Rosaura. 1995. *Telling Identities: The Californio "Testimonios."* Minneapolis: University of Minnesota Press.

Sarna, Jonathan D. 1978. "From Immigrants to Ethnics: Toward a New Theory of Ethnicization." *Ethnicity* 5:370-78.

Saxton, Alexander. 1971. *The Indispensable Enemy: Labor and the Anti-Chinese Movement in California.* Berkeley: University of California Press.

Schermerhorn, R. A. 1978. *Comparative Ethnic Relations: A Framework for Theory and Research.* Chicago: University of Chicago Press.

Schutte, Gerhard. 1989. "Afrikaner Historiography and the Decline of Apartheid: Ethnic Self-Construction in Times of Crisis." Pp. 216-31 in *History and*

Ethnicity, edited by Elizabeth Tonkin, Maryon McDonald, and Malcolm Chapman. London: Routledge.

Scott, G. M., Jr. 1990. "A Resynthesis of the Primordial and Circumstantialist Approaches to Ethnic Group Solidarity: Towards an Explanatory Model." *Ethnic and Racial Studies* 13:147-71.

See, Katherine O'Sullivan. 1986. *First World Nationalisms: Class and Ethnic Politics in Northern Ireland and Quebec.* Chicago: University of Chicago Press.

Sells, Michael. 1996. "Religion, History, and Genocide in Bosnia-Herzegovina." Pp. 23-44 in *Religion and Justice in the War Over Bosnia*, edited by G. Scott Davis. New York: Routledge.

Sherman, Richard. 1988. *A Study of Traditional and Informal Sector Micro-Enterprise Activity and Its Impact on the Pine Ridge Indian Reservation Economy.* Unpublished manuscript, Aspen Institute for Humanistic Studies, Washington, DC.

Shibutani, Tamotsu and Kian M. Kwan. 1965. *Ethnic Stratification: A Comparative Approach.* New York: Macmillan.

Shils, Edward. 1957. "Primordial, Personal, Sacred and Civil Ties: Some Particular Observations on the Relationships of Sociological Research and Theory." *British Journal of Sociology* 8:130-45.

Shils, Edward A. and Morris Janowitz. 1948. "Cohesion and Disintegration in the Wehrmacht in World War II." *Public Opinion Quarterly* 12:280-315.

Simmel, Georg. [1922] 1955. *Conflict and the Web of Group-Affiliations.* Translated by Reinhard Bendix. New York: Free Press.

Slezkine, Yuri. 1994. "The USSR as a Communal Apartment, or How a Socialist State Promoted Ethnic Particularism." *Slavic Review* 53:414-52.

Smedley, Audrey. 1993. *Race in North America: Origin and Evolution of a Worldview.* Boulder, CO: Westview.

Smith, Anthony D. 1981. *The Ethnic Revival in the Modern World.* Cambridge, UK: Cambridge University Press.

———. 1986. *The Ethnic Origins of Nations.* New York: Basil Blackwell.

Snipp, C. Matthew. 1989. *American Indians: The First of This Land.* New York: Russell Sage Foundation.

Sollors, Werner, ed. 1989. *The Invention of Ethnicity.* New York: Oxford University Press.

Soyinka, Woye. 1996. *The Open Sore of a Continent: A Personal Narrative of the Nigerian Crisis.* New York: Oxford University Press.

Spicer, Edward H., ed. 1977. *Ethnic Medicine in the Southwest.* Tucson: University of Arizona Press.

Spickard, Paul R. 1989. *Mixed Blood: Intermarriage and Ethnic Identity in Twentieth-Century America.* Madison: University of Wisconsin Press.

———. 1992. "The Illogic of American Racial Categories." Pp. 12-23 in *Racially Mixed People in America*, edited by Maria P. P. Root. Newbury Park, CA: Sage.

————. 1996. *Japanese Americans: The Formation and Transformations of an Ethnic Group*. New York: Twayne.

Spickard, Paul R. and Rowena Fong. 1995. "Pacific Islander Americans and Multiethnicity: A Vision of America's Future?" *Social Forces* 73:1365-83.

Stafford, Susan Buchanan. 1987. "The Haitians: The Cultural Meaning of Race and Ethnicity." Pp. 131-58 in *New Immigrants in New York*, edited by Nancy Foner. New York: Columbia University Press.

Stanton, William. 1960. *The Leopard's Spots: Scientific Attitudes Toward Race in America 1815-59*. Chicago: University of Chicago Press.

Steele, Shelby. 1990. *The Content of Our Character: A New Vision of Race in America*. New York: Harper Perennial.

Stein, Howard F. and Robert F. Hill. 1977. *The Ethnic Imperative: Examining the New White Ethnic Movement*. University Park: Pennsylvania State University Press.

Steinberg, Stephen. 1981. *The Ethnic Myth: Race, Ethnicity, and Class in America*. Boston: Beacon.

Stern, Stephen and John Allen Cicala, eds. 1991. *Creative Ethnicity: Symbols and Strategies of Contemporary Ethnic Life*. Logan: Utah State University Press.

Stocking, George W., Jr. 1968. "The Critique of Racial Formalism." Pp. 161-94 in *Race, Culture and Evolution*. New York: Free Press.

Takaki, Ronald. 1989. *Strangers From a Different Shore*. Boston: Little, Brown.

Tambiah, S. J. 1986. *Sri Lanka: Ethnic Fratricide and the Dismantling of Democracy*. Chicago: University of Chicago Press.

Taylor, Charles. 1993. *Reconciling the Solitudes: Essays on Canadian Federalism and Nationalism*. Edited by Guy Laforest. Montreal: McGill-Queens University Press.

————. 1994. *Multiculturalism: Examining the Politics of Recognition*. Edited by Amy Gutmann. Princeton: Princeton University Press.

Taylor, Ronald L. 1979. "Black Ethnicity and the Persistence of Ethnogenesis." *American Journal of Sociology* 84:1401-23.

Thackeray, Lorna. 1985. "Indians Fight for Voter Districts." *Billings Gazette* [Montana], November 19, p. 5-A.

Thernstrom, Stephan, Anne Orlov, and Oscan Handlin, eds. 1981. *Harvard Encyclopedia of American Ethnic Groups*. Cambridge, MA: Harvard University Press.

Thomas, Robert K. 1968. "Pan-Indianism." Pp. 128-40 in *The American Indian Today*, edited by Stuart Levine and Nancy O. Lurie. Baltimore: Penguin.

Thompson, Leonard. 1985. *The Political Mythology of Apartheid*. New Haven, CT: Yale University Press.

Thompson, Richard. 1989. *Theories of Ethnicity: A Critical Appraisal*. Westport, CT: Greenwood Press.

Toelken, Barre. 1991. "Ethnic Selection and Intensification in the Native American Powwow." Pp. 137-56 in *Creative Ethnicity: Symbols and Strategies of Contemporary Ethnic Life*, edited by Stephen Stern and John Allan Cicala. Logan: Utah State University Press.

Tonkin, Elizabeth, Maryon McDonald, and Malcolm Chapman, eds. 1989. *History and Ethnicity*. London: Routledge.

Tseng, Yen-Fen. 1995. "Beyond 'Little Taipei': The Development of Taiwanese Immigrant Businesses in Los Angeles." *International Migration Review* 29 (Spring):33-58.

Velez-Ibañez, Carlos G. 1983. *Bonds of Mutual Trust: The Cultural Systems of Rotating Credit Associations Among Urban Mexicans and Chicanos*. New Brunswick, NJ: Rutgers University Press.

Verkuyten, M., W. de Jong and C. N. Masson. 1995. "The Construction of Ethnic Categories: Discourses of Ethnicity in the Netherlands." *Ethnic and Racial Studies* 18:251-76.

Vo, Linda Trinh. 1995. "Paths to Empowerment: Panethnic Mobilization in San Diego's Asian American Community." Unpublished Ph.D. dissertation, University of California, San Diego.

Wagaw, Teshome G. 1993. *For Our Soul: Ethiopian Jews in Israel*. Detroit, MI: Wayne State University Press.

Wahrhaftig, Albert L. 1978. "Making Do With the Dark Meat: A Report on the Cherokee Indians in Oklahoma." Pp. 409-510 in *American Indian Economic Development*, edited by Sam Stanley. The Hague: Mouton.

Waldinger, Roger D. 1986. *Through the Eye of the Needle: Immigrants and Enterprise in New York's Garment Trades*. New York: New York University Press.

Waters, Mary C. 1990. *Ethnic Options: Choosing Identities in America*. Berkeley: University of California Press.

———. 1994. "Ethnic and Racial Identities of Second-Generation Black Immigrants in New York City." *International Migration Review* 28:795-820.

———. 1995. *Multiple Ethnicities and Identity Choices: Some Implications for Race and Ethnic Relations in the United States*. Paper presented at the Conference on Ethnicity and Multiethnicity, Brigham Young University, Laie, Hawaii, May 10-13.

Waters, Tony. 1995. "Towards a Theory of Ethnic Identity and Migration: The Formation of Ethnic Enclaves by Migrant Germans in Russia and North America." *International Migration Review* 29:515-44.

Webber, Thomas. 1978. *Deep Like the Rivers: Education in the Slave Quarter Community, 1831-1865*. New York: W. W. Norton.

Weber, Eugen. 1979. *Peasants Into Frenchmen: The Modernization of Rural France, 1870-1914*. London: Chatto and Windus.

Weber, Max. [1905] 1958. *The Protestant Ethic and the Spirit of Capitalism*. Reprint, New York: Charles Scribner's Sons.

———. 1968. *Economy and Society*. Edited by Guenther Roth and Claus Wittich. Berkeley: University of California Press.

Weibel-Orlando, Joan. 1991. *Indian Country, L.A.: Maintaining Ethnic Community in Complex Society*. Urbana: University of Illinois Press.

West, Cornel. 1993. *Race Matters*. Boston: Beacon.

Whitehorse, David. 1988. *Pow-wow: The Contemporary Pan-Indian Celebration.* Publications in American Indian Studies No. 5. San Diego: San Diego State University.

Whitten, Norman E., Jr. 1976. *Sacha Runa: Ethnicity and Adaptation of Ecuadorian Jungle Quichua.* Urbana: University of Illinois Press.

Williams, Carol J. 1993. "A Tragic Portrait of a Civilization Gone Wrong." *The Los Angeles Times,* June 8, p. H-3.

Williams, Tennessee. [1953] 1970. *Camino Real.* Reprint, New York: New Directions.

Wilson, William Julius. 1978. *The Declining Significance of Race: Blacks and Changing American Institutions.* 2d ed. Chicago: University of Chicago Press.

———. 1987. *The Truly Disadvantaged: The Inner City, the Underclass, and Public Policy.* Chicago: University of Chicago Press.

Wittke, Carl F. 1952. *Refugees of Revolution.* Philadelphia: University of Pennsylvania Press.

Woldemikael, Tekle Mariam. 1989. *Becoming Black American: Haitians and American Institutions in Evanston, Illinois.* New York: AMS.

Wolff, Alexander. 1996. "Prisoners of War." *Sports Illustrated,* June 3, pp. 80-90.

Wood, Wilbur. 1986. "Second Battle of Big Horn: Indian Voting Rights Suit." *The Nation,* October 25, p. 406.

Woodward, Susan L. 1995. *Balkan Tragedy: Chaos and Dissolution After the Cold War.* Washington, DC: Brookings Institution.

Yancey, William L., Eugene P. Ericksen, and Richard N. Juliani. 1976. "Emergent Ethnicity: A Review and Reformulation." *American Sociological Review* 41:391-403.

Yelvington, Kevin A. 1991. "Ethnicity as Practice? A Comment on Bentley." *Comparative Studies in Society and History* 33:158-68.

———. 1993. "Introduction: Trinidad Ethnicity." Pp. 1-32 in *Trinidad Ethnicity,* edited by Kevin A. Yelvington. Knoxville: University of Tennessee Press.

Yinger, J. Milton. 1986. "Intersecting Strands in the Theorisation of Race and Ethnic Relations." Pp. 20-41 in *Theories of Race and Ethnic Relations,* edited by John Rex and David Mason. Cambridge, UK: Cambridge University Press.

Young, Crawford. 1976. *The Politics of Cultural Pluralism.* Madison: University of Wisconsin Press.

———. 1985. "Ethnicity and the Colonial and Post-Colonial State in Africa." Pp. 59-93 in *Ethnic Groups and the State,* edited by Paul Brass. Totowa, NJ: Barnes and Noble.

Index